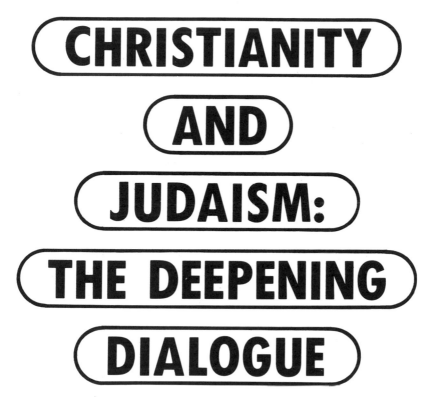

CHRISTIANITY
AND
JUDAISM:
THE DEEPENING
DIALOGUE

EDITED BY

RICHARD W. ROUSSEAU S.J.

RIDGE ROW PRESS

Ridge Row Press: ISBN 0-940866-02-1

Editorial Office: University of Scranton, Scranton, PA 18510

Business Office: 10 South Main Street, Montrose, PA 18801

Printed in the United States of America

Library of Congress Card Catalog Number: 83-60183

University of Scranton Press
Chicago Distribution Center
11030 S. Langley
Chicago IL 60628

CONTENTS

INTRODUCTION

There are two major conveniences to a collection of essays such as this. The first, the obvious one, is the convenience of having in one book a wide variety of essays on a single, major topic, in this case the Jewish-Christian dialogue, many of which have been drawn from journals not at the easy disposal of everyone. The second, less obvious but equally important, is the convenience of an introduction which synthesizes the major points of the essays and an index which pinpoints them.

This introduction then will attempt both a summary synthesis, outlining briefly each of the chapters, and a theoretical synthesis, organizing the ideas themselves in a systematic way. One of the major results of such a process for all concerned should be a greater awareness both of the state of the question and of the unfinished agenda that need to be pursued if the dialogue is to be carried on intelligently, creatively and fruitfully.

PART ONE: *Summary Synthesis*

CHAPTER ONE: ECKARDT

In this first essay, A. Roy Eckardt is dealing with the topic of "Faith under the Judgment of History, as a counterfoil to a second lecture in the Hugh Th. Miller Lecture Series dealing with "History under the Judgment of Faith." Since this second lecture is not included in this collection, it is helpful to keep the rhetorical dialectic in mind while reading this essay.

Eckardt sees a conviction about God acting through happenings in time and place as characterizing both Christianity and Judaism as historical religions.

Though there are both Christian and Jewish thinkers who see Christianity and Judaism as wholly transcendent "realities," moving in "spiritual" ways above the flux of history, the far larger consensus finds decisive theological meaning in historical happenings, including the contemporary. The Jewish-Christian dialectic then, is wrongly identified if seen in terms of transcendentalism versus historicism.

The relevance of the Holocaust of the Jews for Christians lies in the fact admitted by many Christian leaders and scholars that there is something in

1

Christian teaching and in the behavior of Christians that helped to bring it about. Insofar as this latent anti-Semitism is involved, then, the Holocaust poses a challenge for the Christian theological enterprise.

Five themes of that theological enterprise, therefore, need attention. First: the theme of the Jewish people and the person and claim of Jesus. Instead of failing to honor the divine opportunity to honor the Messiah, says Eckardt, the Jewish people's non acceptance of him "remains among the most sublime and heroic instances of Israel's faithfulness to her covenant with God."

Second: the theme of Christian conversionism and the Jews. It can be argued that Christian efforts to convert the Jews to Christianity are a veiled attack, perhaps unthinkingly, upon the Christian Faith itself, for it is an implicit assault upon the Israel of God, the foundation of the Church.

Third: the theme of the covenant and the Trial of God. Eckardt asks whether the Holocaust cast judgement not upon Israel for betraying its covenant with God but upon God for not sustaining his covenant with Israel.

Fourth: the theme of the Crucifixion of Jesus. Eckardt asks if the experiences of the Holocaust have not transformed the Christian symbol of the Cross into a threatening presence.

Fifth: the theme of the Resurrection. If the Christian preaching of the Resurrection implies a setting aside of the Jewish legal tradition as a whole, because it is fulfilled in Jesus, then a triumphalism emerges with a historical relationship to the Holocaust.

Eckardt concludes that these flaws and failures in Christian self-understanding are not inevitable and can be corrected - a project he reserves for his second lecture.

CHAPTER TWO: PHILIP CULBERTSON

In the second essay, Fr Philip Culbertson, Rector of Christ Episcopal Church and member of the Episcopal Diocese of Ohio's Ecumenical Commission, outlines the history of discussions surrounding a resolution by the Commission drafted for the 1981 Diocesan Convention.

He gives first the text of the original resolution and the written amendments proposed because of objections to its clause concerning "the completeness and sufficiency of the Jewish faith." He then summarizes the discussion at the convention. He says that he was approached by a young priest there who asked him to amend the "whereas" clauses, and, when told no, then asked him to withdraw the whole resolution. Upon being refused, he said that he would present a substitute resolution "which would also deplore anti-semitism but without compromising the true biblical position that Jews cannot be saved until they accept Christ as their Lord and Savior." Thus was the battle clearly joined.

The substitute resolution was presented as promised the next day, confining itself to deploring anti-semitism mainly because of the attitude towards

2

the Jews expressed in St. Paul's Epistle to the Romans, Chs. 9-11.

Another speaker challenged this interpretation of Romans saying that St. Paul clearly understood that the role of the Jews in salvation history was not ended by the New Covenant. He urged support of the original resolution. Other speakers did so as well and the substitute resolution was defeated by an approximately two thirds majority.

Then an amendment was proposed concerning the section that implied that evangelism of the Jews was an anti-semitic act. Culbertson replied that "none of the inspired sources justified the notion that the Old Covenant of the Lord with his people had been abrogated or in any sense nullified." The amendment was defeated and the original resolution passed.

Culbertson then concludes with eight lessons to be learned from this debate, including the serious judgement contained in number eight that says that "the source of continuing anti-semitic thinking in a large part of the American population is the local preacher, who is all too unwilling to reexamine his or her personal theology."

CHAPTER THREE: VAN BUREN

Paul Van Buren started out as a student and disciple of Karl Barth, then turned to linguistic analysis as applied to religion. In this third essay, he explains how his work as Chairman of the Department at Temple University in searching for and appointing Jewish scholars led him to a realization of the fact that Judaism was very much alive and that Christian systematic theology was very much in need of reexamination in this area.

In brief, Van Buren noted that if Christian theology said that living religious Judaism "did not exist, then Christian theology, at least on this point, was simply wrong." So he asked himself what Christian theology would look like if corrected on so central a point. The task he set himself, therefore, was to discuss what God had done in Jesus Christ that had resulted in the Church and the Jewish people continuing to live religiously side by side.

Van Buren came to the conclusion that Christian theology needs to be done in full awareness not only of Jewish theology but of the theologies of other world religions. This task, while really theological, it also genuinely scientific and fully appropriate for a religion department in a state university. Such study implies no proselytism, only a search for understanding.

Jews and Christians, then says Van Buren, both need to listen to their Scriptures so that they can also listen sensitively to the Scriptures of other traditions.

In conclusion, Van Buren argues that Christian eyes will be opened not so much by the Holocaust, lying as it does in the past, as by the living reality of the Jewish people, the Israel of God.

3

CHAPTER FOUR: ROTTENBERG

Rottenberg begins by focussing on a debate between two Christians concerning "fulfillment" theology. Fr John T. Pawlikowski argued that the "fulfillment" concept was inaccurate and that a new Christological approach was needed, while Orthodox scholar Thomas Hopko responded that the abandonment of "fulfillment" theology would destroy the foundation of Christianity.

Rottenberg as a Reformed theologian then takes what he considers to be an intermediate position. He says that though "New Testament Messianic claims can be abandoned only at the cost of sacrificing crucial aspects of the Church's witness to the Gospel of the Kingdom . . . . Christians do need to abandon a good deal of 'fulfillment' theology that finds its source in ecclesiastical triumphalism."

The New Testament clearly contains fulfillment language about Jesus of Nazareth; in him the Law and the Prophets are seen as fulfilled and he is confessed as "Lord of all." (Rom. 10:12).

To these Christian claims, Judaism has traditionally responded with a question as to how the world can be spoken of as redeemed when a glance around at crime and selfishness shows that it obviously is not.

Christians respond to this charge in turn by spiritualizing redemption as an event in the "spiritual and inner realm." One of the products of this spiritualization of redemption is a lack of stimulus to reform the present inferior, material world.

Rottenberg says that a first way out of this dilemma for Christians is to confess their sins without abandoning their faith. Christian tradition is full of polemics that try to prove the superiority of Christianity over Judaism by saying that God rejected his Covenant with the People of Israel and constituted the Church as the New Israel.

Many of the Scriptural interpretations used to support this basic position are questionable: the Church as Israel (Gal 6:16); the fulfillment of the Law and the Prophets by Jesus (Matthew 5:17); and Law vs Love, Spirit vs Law (Rom 7:14; 2:13; 3:31). He says that these are interpreted as contrasting Law and the Gospel in a way that does not correspond to personal and historical reality.

Another area of Scriptural misinterpretation is the claim that while the people of the Old Testament lived by the promise, Christians live by the reality. The Bible from beginning to end gives witness to the reality of God's presence in the world. Promise applies to Jews and Christians alike, a promise for the final coming of the Lord and the partaking of the inheritance.

It is in Christology, of course, that this reality of redemption is claimed most clearly. And yet that redemption is an open force not a closed one, a broadening of the Covenant, a new foundation for the ultimate coming of the future Kingdom. All of these deal with our present life, not a remote spiritual one. The Spirit of God does not dehistoricize history.

4

And so, concludes Rottenberg, he agrees with David Flusser that Judaism and Christianity are "one faith." Differences remain, of course, but a common vision is shared and it is the light of that common vision that fulfillment theology can at last be discussed in respectful and fruitful terms.

CHAPTER FIVE: SPONG

Spong compares the relationship between Christianity and Judaism to the relationship between parent and child with its peculiar mixture of dependence and rebellion. Just as mutual appreciation between parent and child must wait until the child comes of age, so the coming of age of Christianity is seeing a new dawn in Christian-Jewish relations. In this context, Spong defines dialogue as "an interaction in which each participant stands with full integrity in his or her own tradition and is open to the depths of the truth that is in the other."

Spong sees three areas where Christianity, especially today, would be adversely affected without some important Jewish themes. The first theme arises out of the understanding of a God who is rooted in history. God is revealed in the ongoing events of life and there can be no escape into otherworldly piety before this God. And history here does not mean merely the past, it means that the God who meets us in the events of yesterday will meet us in the events of tomorrow. Faith then in the Hebrew sense is not intellectual assent to propositional statements, it is rather an attitude of expectancy in history, the courage to step boldly into tomorrow, since every day is seen as a meeting place with God.

Such an insight into the meaning of history is important to many Christians in this century overwhelmed as they are by rapid and fundamental change. One reaction is to cling to the past, even the dead past, but Jewish experience challenges all these fears and allows us to face the present and the future with confidence.

The second theme is a passion against idolatry. This is not the worship of graven images like money or success but the attempt to speak and act for God himself. The Jewish tradition emphasizes the "otherness" of God. The Bible and Creeds point towards God but do not contain him. The dark side of such idolatry is that those who believe in their absolute rightness find it easy to persecute those who differ from them. Some uncertainty even in religious matters is healthy for all concerned.

A third theme is that Judaism helps Christians to interpret the New Testament in nonliteralistic terms. An inability on the part of Christians to see the Scriptures in their original Jewish context has led to distortion and misuse of the Scriptures themselves. The Creedal phrase "he ascended into heaven," is a good example where the Judaic tradition in the New Testament calls on the image of Elijah as a means of describing the divine life and power in Jesus of Nazareth.

5

The rediscovery of their Jewish roots then will help Christians of today to lay down their fears and step boldly into tomorrow, to reclaim a sense of God's ultimacy and to better understand the Scriptures.

CHAPTER SIX: BERENBAUM

Berenbaum's essay is an attempt to deal with the concern felt by some that with the growth of memorials to the Holocaust in many communities throughout the United States the word Holocaust may come to mean simply mass murder and destruction. For Simon Wiesanthal, for example, the word refers "to the systematic murder of eleven million people, six million of whom were killed because of their Jewishness and five million non-Jews killed for a variety of reasons." For Elie Wiesel, on the other hand, the Holocaust is the "Mysterium Tremendum" and he fears that approaching it from Wiesenthal's viewpoint may set in motion a process that will erase its Jewishness.

The fact is, according to Berenbaum, that American memorials to the Holocaust are much more difficult to design than Israeli ones because they must address themselves to an audience for whom the Holocaust is an alien experience. Thus Yehuda Bauer, head of the Institute of Contemporary Jewry at the Hebrew University in Jerusalem seemingly attaches too much importance to President Carter's ceremonial words at Holocaust memorial inaugurations by saying that his view of the Holocaust as commemorating all the victims of Nazism would submerge its Jewish aspect. Berenbaum, on the contrary, believes that only by understanding the parallel fates of others can the distinctive character of the Jewish fate be shown. If the Holocaust is to have any ongoing impact it must enter the mainstream of international consciousness. This means exposing it to many eyes and pens, with all the dangers that that involves.

For Bauer, the uniqueness of the Holocaust resides in the organized and total annihilation of an entire community as well as in that apocalyptic element whereby the "death of the victims becomes an integral element in the drama of salvation." The very scientific and organized methods of destruction in the concentration camps are part of the Holocaust's uniqueness.

Ismar Schorsch responded to Bauer by saying that an overemphasis on the Holocaust in Jewish consciousness would diminish the totality of Jewish history. The essential uniqueness of it, he claims, is that the Jews were the only victims of genocide in World War II.

Berenbaum feels that there is an appropriate middle ground here based on a more comparative approach. In response to John Cuddihy's claim that the affirmation of uniqueness for the Holocaust may be a secular translation of Jewish Chosenness, he says that the Holocaust is "not only quantitatively but qualitatively different from other episodes of persecution in Jewish history." It is different because it was sustained, not episodic; legal, not

6

illegal; and biologically, not religiously based.

Other instances of mass murder do not obscure the Holocaust's uniqueness; they clarify it. For other peoples subjected to destruction, like the Poles, the aim was subservience, not annihilation, as it was for the Jews. Even the Gypsies went untouched in some countries. In this sense the Jews could be seen as occupying a kind of Dantean center of Hell. Proper comparisons and analysis then will enhance and not trivialize or dejudaize the Holocaust.

CHAPTER SEVEN: PAWLIKOWSKI

In this essay Pawlikowski examines the implications of the Nazi Holocaust for the relationship between Church and Society.

It would be a mistake, he says, to understand the Holocaust as only anti-Jewish. It was also anti-Christian. Its goal was a total transformation of human values. It was a decision to live fully within the limits of humanity without any moral restraints or religious hope. Before this kind of basic onslaught, the humanitarian values of our secular tradition were ineffective. The Holocaust then is the most evident and devastating example of modern man's alienation from "compassionate moral roots."

In the light of all this, Pawlikowski asks about the role religion ought to play in American society. Perhaps it is time, he says, to confront the dark side of separation of Church and State. Though otherwise very helpful, this separation can create dangerous side effects by overprivatizing religion. More exploration is needed into the ways "religion can be given a more public role without endangering the basic freedom of religion accorded to all by the U.S. Constitution." One of the great dangers is to relegate religion to an otherworldly sphere and thus make it irrelevant. In such circumstances, the unchallenged State can become too powerful. Religious groups have tried to keep religious conflicts out of the public sector, but can such a negative interpretation of religious liberty be enough for today?

In the light of Auschwitz we need to redefine our understanding of Church-State relations. In order to do this, Jews and Christians must learn how to cooperate. It is not enough for some Jewish writers to call for a period of shameful silence from Christians; active cooperation is now a moral imperative.

In tackling these public issues, it is helpful to keep in mind the salutary caution that there is another extreme to be avoided as well, namely an over-identification with a given social order. Among issues that need reexamination in this area, we have the just-war theory and the very concept of what history is. Christian withdrawal from worldly affairs and history in general affected their particular attitude towards what was happening to the Jews over the years leading to the "final solution." There are other final solutions facing us today including the nuclear sword of Damocles.

The Holocaust then has shattered a Christian ecclesiology that saw a Church existing apart from human history. This implies a reexamination of

7

the Messianic Age. No longer can it be claimed that the Messianic Age was fulfilled in the past. Since it is still being fulfilled today, the Church continues to be immersed in ongoing history.

Involved in all this is the question of power: its use and abuse. The Christian theology of the Cross should not be used to justify a weakness that allows demonic structures to flourish. Also related are such questions as the depersonalization of public language and the Holocaust potential of Mexican-American problems. In brief, the Holocaust introduces us to a new era of Church-State questions.

CHAPTER EIGHT: DAVIS

In this essay Stephen Davis rejects, as an evangelical, some conclusions drawn by Christian theologians about the Holocaust: that the Holocaust is some kind of theological absolute; that the traditional God of Christianity died at Auschwitz; and that Christians must give up religious themes with which Jews disagree. He then proposes his own views both for and to evangelical Christians.

He deals first with the theory that Christian successionism means a nullification of Judaism. He believes that there has been a literal succession but he rejects the idea that this implies Antisemitism or undermines Judaism's raison d'etre and integrity. According to Romans 9-11, Israel has a continuing role in God's plan. Jews on the other hand should not expect Christians to deny their belief in Jesus as the Messiah and Son of God.

Davis then defines Antisemitism as "active prejudice against Jews because they are Jews." The Christian Church has been responsible both directly and indirectly for much Antisemitism. This does not mean that the New Testament itself is Antisemitic, however. There is material there that can be twisted to Antisemitic uses, e.g. Jesus' attack, in the Synoptics, on "the Scribes and Pharisees." But this is really a conflict within Judaism itself. St. John's Gospel is ambiguous in its use of the term "Jews." But to even claim that all Jews, including those today, are responsible for Jesus' death is patently absurd. The anti-Jewish polemic of some of the Church Fathers, while at times excessive, can at least be understood in its historical context of Jews breaking away from a parent Judaism.

That the New Testament writers and Church Fathers failed to foresee the use to which their words would be put is unfortunate, but this is not a reason to blame them for subsequent Antisemitism and certainly not for genocide.

Christianity therefore should not be said to be necessarily Antisemitic, especially if just disagreeing with Jews is not itself Antisemitic. Davis then challenges Rosemary Reuther's claim that the real root of Christian Antisemitism is Christology. There are far too many counter examples in the history of Christian men and women to justify such a stand, especially when the High Middle Ages should have been, according to this theory, the most Antisemitic of all, and they were not.

Though Christian Antisemitism was a contributing factor to the conditions

8

that made the Holocaust possible, it was a minor factor compared to 19th century liberal criticism of the Old Testament. This severed the Church from its Jewish roots and the elimination of the divine authority of the Old testament left Jews as a dispensable residue.

Davis finds the suggestion that Christianity's survival depends on defining itself over against the Jews through Antisemitism an absurd one. Antisemitism is contrary to basic Christianity itself, not constitutive of it.

The question "Were Christians responsible for the Holocaust?" is poorly put since the word "Christian" can mean so many things, including even "Western Gentile." Cultural Christians were obviously involved in the Holocaust. However, they also sent many other Christians to the concentration camps and their horrors. What is true is that the work of these cultural Christians found some support in the implicit Antisemitic attitudes of many other Christians, in their idolatrous nationalism and in their silence before the Holocaust.

Committed Christians may have been guilty of passivity and silence before the Holocaust but they were not connected with or responsible for a genocide which is totally contrary to basic Christian belief.

Evangelicals, though they understand the suspicion of Jews about evangelism directed at them, still consider themselves urged to "Go and make disciples of *all* nations." Though this does not mean singling out Jews, it is a claim for freedom to preach the Gospel to anyone, including Jews.

Davis concludes that though Jews may not accept all that he has said above, he nevertheless feels that Jews and Christians should work together against a common enemy, a philosophy that says that the end always justifies the means and that "decisions about human affairs are to be made solely on the basis of power and cost efficiency."

CHAPTER NINE: FISHER

In the introduction to his essay "The Impact of the Christian-Jewish Dialogue on Biblical Studies," Dr. Eugene Fisher explains that it would be more accurate to speak of the impact of Biblical Studies on Jewish-Christian relations. New Biblical methodologies, especially after Divino Afflante Spiritu, developed neutral interpretative language that allowed Jews and Christians to approach the Scriptures together.

The first area to be enriched by such collaboration was exegesis itself. Text criticism was improved and a host of other related issues were clarified: problems in Genesis, first century Judaism, the "deicide" charge and Pauline, Synoptic and Johannine studies.

A second was the biblical critical enterprise itself. It is now seen as a collaborative effort among Catholic, Protestant and Jewish scholars. This means that much of the polemical uses of Scripture, including anti-Pharisaical polemics, are being put aside.

9

A third area was that of hermeneutics, and here Fisher examines first the question of the alleged anti-semitism of the New Testament. Earlier answers to the questions, "Is the New Testament Anti-Semitic?" tended to attempt a "defense" of the Gospel. A first shift from this, symbolized by Rosemary Reuther, was an understanding of anti-semitism as an *inevitable* consequence of New Testament anti-Judaism. But, more recently, this has been modified by a greater understanding of the polemical aspects of the New Testament and by a greater awareness of its positive portraits of the Pharisees, in Luke, for example. The question has now shifted to "Are the roots of anti-semitism in the Gospels? " To answer this question fairly and adequately something more than a few Matthean, Pauline or Johannine passages need to be taken into account. The basic structure and spirit of New Testament or Christian theology need to be considered, which is another matter.

Another major hermeneutical challenge of the contemporary Christian-Jewish dialogue is the question of the relationship between the Hebrew and Christian Scriptures. Most analyses of the past have ascribed a discontinuity between Old Testament Judaism and post-Biblical Judaism (which includes present day Judaism). This post-Biblical Judaism was seen as providing, through its legalistic inadequacies, the questions to which the New Testament had the answers, thus making itself ultimately irrelevant. Another way of putting all this was to see the relationship as "promise-fulfillment." This implied a supercessionist view. Two remarks need to be made about this: first, greater emphasis needs to be put on the continuity between Christianity, as part of the developing history of Second Temple Judaism and later Judaism, and second, that fulfillment or rather, unfulfillment is something which belongs to Christianity itself, for the great age is not yet fully here. In this inteptetation, "the two Testaments remain spiritually linked, in concrete historical terms and in the full sense of theological mystery." The link is one of dialogue not of absorption or supercession.

Finally, a newly developing hermermeutics of "suspicion" such as David Tracy's, allows scholars to recognize the presence of anti-Jewish polemics in the New Testament while relativizing them as historically conditioned. Divinity claims for Jesus, so central to Christianity need not be "accomodated" to avoid anti-semitism. What is needed is a "proleptic" christology, a messianic presence and power that is here yet not fully here. This would reaffirm on inner Christian gounds the Jews as God's covenanted people.

In conclusion, Fisher says that though much remains to be done in all these areas, he perceives "a healthy sense of progress at least in clarifying the questions that need to be addressed."

CHAPTER TEN: BOROWITZ

If, as Rosemary Reuther says, "Christology is "the other side of anti-Judaism," and if she herself mentions no contemporary theologians in this regard, it will be useful, says Borowitz, to examine the Christologies and their implications for Judaism of three relatively traditional theologians: Barth, Berkouwer and Pannenberg.

Karl Barth treats the Jewish people dialectically. First he insists that the Jews are still God's chosen people. Even though the Church is a member of the community of God in a quite different way, it is united to Israel as a living witness of the judgement from which God has rescued man. Furthermore, says Barth, "Anti-Semitism is a form of godlessness."

But then the dialectical side appears with the question of a Christian mission to the Jews. He sees the Synagogue as empty of grace and blessing because Israel denied its calling. Though there is no question for Barth of force, either physical or spiritual, the fact remains that for him, Israel is assigned a place irrespective of the religious life of the synagogue today or what Jewish practice might say about God.

Though highly biblical in his theological work, Berkouwer seems almost devoid of anti-Jewish sentiment. He universalizes those passages that speak of the Jews as the opponents of Christ, applying them to humanity as a whole. Though there are still traces of negativism in Berkouwer, they are focused more on "historical Pharisaism" than on the Jews. His treatment is generally fair and a good example of how a thoughtful exegete can go about interpreting Christianity from a biblical base while transcending anti-Semitism.

Wolhart Pannenberg, on the other hand, speaks of the collapse of the foundation of Jewish religion. He puts it starkly indeed, "either Jesus had been a blasphemer or the law of the Jews—and with it Judaism itself as a religion—is done away with."

Only Richard Neuhaus seems to have questioned this passage as "objectionable." Yet to say that Judaism died some 2000 years ago is to make it disposable. "To make this a pillar of a religion of love is contemptible. But to be a contemporary German and say such things is intolerable."

Pannenberg did disclaim this position in a later book, but it remains an obscure passage, while, in a later edition of his more popular work, he made no changes in the text, even attempting to justify this in an "Afterword." At best, then, this is giving the matter low priority through apparent unconcern and at worst is simple anti-Semitism.

Classical Christology, concludes Borowitz, can still lead some Christian theologians towards anti-Semitism, but not necessarily so, since Barth mitigated it and Berkouwer virtually eliminated it.

CHAPTER ELEVEN: WILLIAMSON

In this essay Williamson considers the relationship between one of the most important contemporary theological movements, liberation theology and anti-semitism as represented by one of its outstanding thinkers, Jon Sobrino, in his "Christology at the Crossroads." In this work he attempts to restate traditional Christology in the light of praxis and it is an intriguing question to ask how this affects his understanding of the relationship be-

11

tween Christ and the Jews.

It is wrong, according to Williamson, to say that any criticism of liberation theology arises only out of oppressive forces. Theology has its own life and rules and the Christological enterprise of Sobrino as a liberation theologian needs to and can be judged by generally accepted theological norms of self-criticism.

Generally speaking, he says, Sobrino's Christology may be criticized as repeating the standard anti-Judaism of Christian theology, ignoring both the effects this has had in history and the fact that it violates his own theory of praxis. Also, it is more related to German bookish sources than to his concrete situation in El Salvador.

Williamson begins his analysis by briefly examining this history of Christian theology for its anti-semitism. He says that "Anti-Judaism has long played a structural role in shaping the very articulation of the meaning of the Gospel. . . it is a mark of Christianity itself." He shows how all the major themes of Tertullian's theology: God, Jesus, the Law, are all constructed out of an Anti-Jewish model. Basically, this comes down to answering the question, "What does God demand of us?" with "Not what Jews did. More is required."

This anti-Judaic model found in Tertullian is also found in recent German Biblical scholarship. First, there is the characterization of Late Judaism, from the Exile to Bar Kokhba as inauthentic Judaism, constantly failing in its God oriented task. Second, the chief characteristic of this late Judaism is its legalism. Third, the Scribes and Pharisees are represented as the enemies of Jesus' teaching, even though other historical sources show that the polemical image of the Gospels does not correspond to reality. Fourth, Jewish guilt in the death of Jesus is still affirmed, even after Vatican II.

Williamson then examines Sobrino's theology point by point to show its anti-semitic elements: 1. God (greater than the God preached by the Rabbis); 2. Jesus (preaches a Kingdom unavailable on the terms of the Pharisees, 3. Law (Pharisaic clinging to it is obviously a way of saying "no" to the Kingdom of God, 4. Church: (it will call their very orthodoxy into question, 5. Jewish Exegesis (Jews were blind to the reality proclaimed by Jesus, 6. Prayer (the prayer of the Pharisees is a mechanical ceremony of self-deception—the interpretation of Jeremias in his *New Testament Theology*, 7. Late Judaism; 8. Legalistic Piety, and 9. The Pharisees (Jesus' attitude toward Sabbath worship is a "terrifying reversal" of the whole assumption that man is made for the Sabbath, 10. Jewish guilt for the death of Jesus ("It is the radical difference in their two viewpoints") (Jesus and the Pharisees) ("that explains the tragic end of the Jews.") He ignores the fact that there were "theological, apologetic and polemical considerations at work throughout the composition of each Gospel."

Williamson concludes that, theologically speaking, the Christology of Sobrino's liberation theology is a failure because it "cuts itself off from the liberation event of the Bible, the Exodus of a people from oppression."

Sobrino and many Christians, he says, need to rediscover the connection between Easter and Exodus.

CHAPTER TWELVE: SIEGMAN

Siegman sees far reaching changes in the relationship between the Roman Catholic Church and the Jewish people over the past decade or so. Triumphalism on both sides has diminished and the dialogue is deepening. The change is due not so much to theology as to history, a history in which both share the common predicament of nuclear danger and rapid technological change.

If greater dialogue is now possible, then, he asks, what kind of dialogue does this turn out to be? For many Christians it may seem disappointing at first sight. This is due to the fact that for a long time Christianity seemed to validate itself by seeing itself as the fulfillment of an earlier dispensation now moribund. When in the dialogue a living Judaism is encountered, Christians may feel some discomfort in facing the truth questions involved. Jews, on the other hand, faced nothing immanent in themselves in their confrontation with Christianity. They were brought to the dialogue more by historical reasons, by those evils that have come to them because of the Christian positions. At the same time, a bit further down the road perhaps, there remains for the Jews the further possibility of religious and theological enrichment from the dialogue. These different "agenda" then can create some initial disappointment.

A second reason why Christians may experience some disappointment is the reluctance of Jews to discuss questions of religious "truth." For them the supreme issue is "whether we are alive or dead to the challenge and expectation of the living God?" Theological reticence has always been a Jewish characteristic. Halachah is more sought after than theology. This issue, in fact, may lie at the root of Jewish divergence from Christianity, since Jesus is rejected as an incarnational medium between God and man on the grounds that God cannot be mediated and that the Torah is the proper way of interpreting divine-human relationships.

If all this is so, says Siegman, then the first practical step of the dialogue is to deal with a common history. For Jews that history is a continuing, haunting presence; for Christians, it is largely forgotten. The fact that a Holocaust was possible in a Christian nation of the 20th century is due to the way western culture was so long and thoroughly influenced by Christian hostility to the Jews. Christians must face up to and critique their own history. Recent Roman Catholic documents such as Nostra Aetate and the 1975 Guidelines still fall short of a full-scale, objective examination of Christian conscience in this regard. If antisemitism from the 1st to the 20th century is a Christian creation, then the Church should now clearly reject it, along with all the other inhuman intolerances it rejects.

The State of Israel is another historical issue. Whether one emphasizes

Israel's political or religious dimension, dialogical friendships would collapse if the possibility of Israel's demise were not rejected by Christians as well as Jews. Israel, furthermore, should not be seen negatively as the result of historical rejections, but as the result as well of inner Jewish affirmation. At the same time, it is necessary to make clear that religious reasons in themselves are not the only justification for political rights. Jewish political claims to Israel rest on a cluster of secular reasons, including an almost unbroken Jewish presence since the first Exile.

There are Christians who are embarrassed by these flesh and blood needs of Jews in Israel today and who oppose them being there because of this embarrassment. Part of this is due to a liberalism, secular as well as theological, that is predisposed towards a universalism hostile to particularity and earthiness.

Siegman then turns to Jewish responsibilities in the dialogue. If its first stage has been marked by a focus on Christian failings, one which a Christian sense of guilt and noblesse oblige has supported, then Jews must now also examine themselves.

The first stage of such a reexamination would focus on Jewish attitudes towards a pluralistic world and towards its traditionally defensive image of Christianity. Jews lose nothing of their own religious integrity by realizing that "Christians who are good and decent human beings are so not despite, but because . . . they profess Christianity."

Another major area of the dialogue which Jews could reexamine themselves on is that of Christian mission. There are some Jews who see the Church's insistence on its mission of preaching Christianity to everyone, including Jews, as destructive of the premises of the dialogue. Siegman does not believe this to be so. He sees the 1975 Guidelines, for example, as introducing qualifications that break sharply with the Church's past position. They demand that any mission include respect for the faith and conviction of others and that religious liberty be strictly protected. Also, the Guidelines make no mention of Jewish stubbornness. They speak, rather, of the difficulties that arise for Jews out of a pure notion of divine transcendence when encountering the Incarnation. Siegman makes a distinction between an active mission campaign directed against Jews and Christian eschatological hope for Judaism. "Witness," says Siegman, "is a legitimate religious exercise, as long as it fully respects the freedom of conscience of people of other faiths . . ."

The 1975 Guidelines are the first high level Catholic document that sees Judaism as a rich and vital religious movement. They call on Christians to study Judaism in all its aspects to learn how Jews define themselves religiously. Though familiar in the United States, such attitudes are revolutionary in many other nations. Since these are intended not to end but to begin a process, much needs to be done to lift the heavy historical burden of past mythological misunderstandings of the Jews.

CHAPTER THIRTEEN: FLANNERY

Fr. Flannery responds to Rabbi Siegman's Essay by praising his generosity of spirit and penetrating psychological insight into the Jewish-Christian dialogue, then goes on to suggest what he sees as inadequacies in his analysis.

He says that Siegman's view of the asymmetry in Jewish-Christian relations, with Christians concerned with theology and Jews with history, should not be overemphasized. Whatever the balance of interests, this should not offset the dialogue. Any and all dialogues, he says, should be based on the openness of both parties "to discuss fully whatever either of the parties wishes to discuss." Christians may be discouraged from dialoguing with Jews if there is Jewish reluctance to deal with the Christian agenda. In any case, Christians themselves are very much interested in history, a history in which, as a matter of fact, Jews and Christians share a great deal in common. Both the negative and positive aspects of that mutual history need to be explored.

Though attention to these historical dimensions of the dialogue should come first, can the theological dimension of the dialogue be avoided forever? If attention to history is seen as a first step in the dialogue then we are on the right track. But even this "first stage" of the dialogue, is a bit more complex than appears at first sight. As a matter of fact Jews have often been willing to take up theological questions while Christians have been reluctant to deal with such historical subjects as the State of Israel. Fortunately, these particular difficulties now seem to be behind us.

The reluctance of Jews to engage in theological discussion may have been due more to the awkwardness sometimes felt in the first developing stages of a more intimate relationship. It marked, perhaps, a fear that the hostilities so recently put aside should not be stirred up again, or, even, a fear of one's own intolerance.

When Siegman makes a distinction between theological issues and "ultimate truth," Flannery suggests he is merely emphasizing his personal preferences in dialogue, a normal procedure. Though Christians should respect his reticence and that of Jews who emphasize the Torah and the halachah, they also should be aware of the fact that there are other Jews who emphasize the Tanach, its commentaries and the Jewish philosophical and mystical tradition, which become a basis of what can only be called "theologizing." In any case, there is much more "theology" in common than would seem at first sight.

There is a fundamental unity of all serious religious experiences, as Western religious dialogue with the Eastern religions is making clearer all the time. This is not religious syncretism but a search for the unity of God in the unity of humanity. Flannery then gives an impressive list of theological considerations that need discussion by Christians and Jews.

If history is to be the first stage of the Jewish-Christian dialogue, then let

15

first mean only a temporal precedence which can then lead to the theological. Among these historical issues are antisemitism and the State of Israel. Flannery adds that his most rewarding personal experiences in Jewish-Christian dialogue have come after these historical stages were completed and the participants engaged in discussing vital areas of the inner life of Judaism and Christianity.

Finally, Flannery suggests that Siegman's refusal to accept a secularized understanding of the dialogue as one that would force all to abandon their absolutist religious claims to the truth is a courageous one. It helps to focus attention on this central issue. He concludes that Siegman's admonitions may help advance the Jewish-Christian dialogue more quickly than those who press the theological agenda too quickly.

CHAPTER FOURTEEN: DITMANSON

Ditmanson sees a new appreciation of Judaism in Christian circles with mutuality and dialogue becoming more important there than the old suspicions and enmities. Despite their close contacts over the centuries, it was the horror of the Holocaust that brought Christians to make amends for the past and give assurances for the future.

There have been dozens of ecumenical and denominational statements since the War condemning antisemitism. Many churches have institutionalized dialogue with Jews and worked at removing misrepresentations and negative attitudes in their educational materials. This does not mean that all negativism has been removed from Christian teaching materials but at least considerable improvement has been made.

The Christian impulse to make amends for the past is basically humanitarian in nature. But there remains the question whether instincts of fair play go far enough. "Peaceful co-existence may leave the dividing line between Judaism and Christianity as solid as ever." The problem is the tension that arises from regarding Jews with respect while considering their religion as rejected or defective.

What is needed is a new and decisive clarification by Christians of the theological premises for estimating the significance for the Church of Judaism today. Ditmanson then suggests as the basis for that theological clarification "a recognition by Christians of the reality and autonomy of Judaism."

The main obstacle to a Christian recognition of the reality of Judaism is the conviction that the "old" Jewish order has been displaced by the "new" Christian one. That would of course leave Judaism without either a mission or a message. This can be called the rejection-substitution theory.

Though there is doubt whether this traditional understanding of the relationship between Judaism and Christianity can be found in the New Testament, there is no question but that it can be found early in the Christian centuries and even more strongly in the medieval period. It was of course strengthened by an emphasis on the supreme curse of deicide and an

16

accusation of ritual murder. These ideas are what lie behind the torture and imprisonment, expulsions and massacres of Jews over the centuries.

Though Christians today have repudiated the negativities and hostilities of the past, the basic rejection-substitution theory has not been seriously affected. Because of this the curricula of most Christian seminaries have largely ignored Judaism as a living, active, spiritual entity. The bottom line argument in all this seems to be that if the rejection-substitution theory is abandoned or modified, the whole structure of Christian doctrine will collapse.

Many Christian theologians nevertheless argue today that this theory is in need of serious reform. Many major ecumenical statements repudiating the deicide charge and other false generalizations about the Jews have already undermined the theory. For the rejection of the deicide charge means that Christians no longer see Jews as being especially punished by God. Many Christians have come to the conviction that Judaism is alive and well today not out of stubbornness but out of God's plan for them and the world. This would mean that God has not abandoned his covenant with the Jews. Christians must therefore confront the validity of Judaism and begin speaking, as St Paul often implies, of two covenantal communities.

CHAPTER FIFTEEN: CAIRNS

In Germany, writes David Cairns, the bitter memories of the Holocaust have produced the following questions: Why were Christian protests against it so late and so ineffectual? Has the teaching of the Church over the centuries been in some measure responsible for it? Does the interpretation of Christian Scripture, especially St Paul, require reexamination?

A good example of the ferment in the German Church over these questions can be seen in the records of the meeting of the Provincial Synod of the Evangelical Church of the Rhineland held in 1980.

Cairns analyzes this voluminous and difficult documentation (it includes the official texts, and dissenting ''Commentaries.'') He discovers there contrasting outlooks on two questions: 1. Christian guilt and, 2, the relation between the Old Covenant and the New.

The Synodal material expresses a confession of shared responsibility and guilt of Churchmen in Germany for the Holocaust and says that only the common prayers of Christians and Jews will be able to find some meaning in these frightful happenings.

In the ''Bonn Reflections'' drawn up by thirteen professors of the Bonn University Theological Faculty, the Synod is commended for its desire to promote dialogue with Jews because of historical guilt. But the document then goes on to say that Nazi ideology was as anti-Christian as it was anti-Jewish, and that therefore substantive conversation with the Jews is not needed or wanted.

With regard to the second major question, the relation between the Old Covenant and the New, the Synod declares that the Old testament is a common foundation for further action for both Christian and Jews. It goes on to express a series of "creedal" statements all of which affirm the "indissoluble connexion of the New Testament with the Old" and says that "fulfillment" does not mean "replacement." It goes on to say that Christians have tended to misinterpret the Old Testament as a Book of Law and the New Testament, in contrast, as a Book of Love.

In their "Reflections," the Bonn professors refuse to accept the identification between modern Jews and the Israel to whom the promises were made. They propose a series of Scriptural interpretations to support this view.

A response on the part of the Synod challenges these specific Scriptural interpretations (especially that of Romans 11) as inadequate. It says that the Bonn professors express an attitude that is academic in the worst sense of the word, whereas the Synod, in trying to express an attitude issuing from historical experiences and challenges, is discovering the togetherness of Christians and Jews. The members of the Synod say that they and their Jewish associates had sought guidance in the Scriptures for ways of overcoming the fundamental schism that led to Auschwitz. The respondents also ask the Bonn professors how, after the Holocaust, some Christians can still speak of the Jews in a spirit of smug self-assurance.

This discussion, concludes Cairns, is important as an example of the self-examination going on now among Christians as they struggle for a renewal of the relationship between Christians and Jews, so devastated by the Holocaust.

PART TWO: *Systematic Synthesis*

THE THREADS OF CONSENSUS

Though these essays were written by many different authors and appeared in a variety of publications, some very interesting threads run through them. In this latter part of the introduction I will attempt to synthesize at least some of these threads of consensus. Though I tried to be as objective as possible in summarizing the fifteen essays, there is always the danger of misinterpretation. That danger is even greater when such a broad synthesis is attempted. I will attempt to introduce nothing substantial that has not appeared in one of the essays, but since the connections made are my own, it is difficult to avoid all subjectivity, for which I take full responsibility.

I shall divide this analysis into three parts: the first, the briefest, will look at those areas of the dialogue or dialogue situation on which there is general agreement; the second will consist of a series of reflections by Christians about the dialogue and their role in it; and the third will be made up of reflections by Jews about the dialogue and their role in it.

18

POINTS OF AGREEMENT

If there is one thing on which all the authors agree it is the fact that since World War II and the Holocaust a new era has developed in Jewish-Christian relations. Christians are seeing a new dimension of Jews and Jews have responded with an openness to discussion and dialogue. The old suspicions and enmities have been replaced, in many circles at least, with mutual respect and constructive conversation.

All are agreed also that though a good beginning has been made, there is still a considerable distance to go in order both to overcome the tragedies of the past and to shed more light on the complexities of the present in Jewish-Christian relations.

Finally there is wide agreement that progress will depend on the ability of both Jews and Christians to engage in a process of religious self-examination that, in a spirit of good will, will result in a genuine deepening of the dialogue.

REFLECTIONS FOR CHRISTIANS

In the spirit of religious self-examination then, what follows is a series of reflections by and for Christians as they prepare themselves for and engage in dialogue with Jews.

ANTISEMITISM

The first thing that Christians have to deal with in their own hearts and minds is the historical and theoretical problem of antisemitism. There is an ongoing temptation for Christians to look down upon post-biblical Judaism (which includes modern Judaism) because it is seen as having been superseded by Christianity on the grounds that it failed to live up to its Covenant with God.

Some of the traditional arguments put forward to sustain this position are as follows:

1. Biblical:

St Paul, especially in his Epistle to the Romans, says that the role of the Old Jewish Covenant was ended and abrogated by the New Christian Covenant. It was abrogated it is said, according to Paul, because the Jews failed to live up to their covenantal obligations which were then handed on to their successors in the New Covenant.

The rest of the New Testament, especially the Gospel of John, is filled with anti-Pharisaical and anti-Jewish language about their legalism and unfaithfulness.

All of this was reemphasized by nineteenth century liberal biblical criticism, one of whose consequences was the severing of the Old Testament from its Jewish roots, thus making modern Judaism even more irrelevant.

2. Theological

These biblical thoughts have been developed theologically into a supporting system. This is the way it goes: Post-biblical Judaism, the Judaism of the time of Christ and of subsequent centuries down to the present day, became irrelevant in God's plan because it was so legalistic. The Old Covenant between God and his people was therefore replaced by a new one instituted by Christ. The promises of God in the Old Testament were, because of the stubborness of the Jews, transferred to Christ who fulfilled them and to Christians who now continue to fulfill them under a new Covenant. Implicit in all this is the idea that the Israel of the Old Testament to whom these promises were made is not the same as later Israel.

This theory is called either the promise-fulfillment or the rejection-substitution theory. It is seen by some as the foundation of Christian self-definition and doctrine without which the very structure of Christianity would collapse.

Indications that this theory or attitude is still alive in some quarters can be seen in the fact that recent Roman Catholic documents, including Vatican II and subsequent Guidelines, fall short of a full-scale objective examination of conscience concerning antisemitism. And influential Protestant bodies such as the Lutheran Synod discussed in Chapter fifteen, are still trying to deal with charges of Jewish deicide, legalism and unauthenticity.

CHRISTIAN RESPONSE

To these theories, an ever growing number of Christians respond in the following way:

1. Scripture:

It is not at all clear, first of all, that St Paul in Romans and other places ever said that the role of the Jews in salvation history was ended by the New Covenant. This is an area that merits attention and further study.

What is involved here is a double misreading of Scripture. First, there is the misperceiving of post-biblical Judaism as qualitatively different from biblical Judaism. Second, there is the misinterpreting of the sins, shortcomings and failures of the people in the New Testament as those of Jews as Jews instead of those of ordinary human beings like all of us. The fact that they happen to be Jewish is only incidental. They stand as symbols of a common, sinful humanity.

The anti-Jewish polemic of the new Testament, especially in St John's Gospel, as well as that of the early fathers of the Church, has to be seen as an historically conditioned result of Jews breaking away from a parent Judaism. It needs to be interpreted as a strongly worded family fight where language should not be taken too literally. Most early Christians would be horrified to see the way in which their words, taken out of cultural and psychological context, have been used in later centuries to harm their Jewish brothers and sisters.

2. Theology:

The first thing that needs to be said is that a reinterpretation of the old promise-fulfillment, rejection-substitution theory does not imply an abandonment by Christians of their religious integrity or a dimunition of the importance of the role of Christ in salvation history.

The first, classic Jewish response to the Christian promise-fulfillment claim has always been, of course, that if one looks around the world today as well as in the past, one finds that it is still sinful and unredeemed. The traditional Christian response to this, on the other hand, has been that redemption is essentially an inward, interior spiritual reality that affects souls.

A more satisfactory answer to this dilemma of promise-fulfillment, however, is to admit that this dialectic remains valid but that it applies to Christianity as much as it does to Judaism. Christ has brought redemption, but that redemption is still in process and will continue to be so through the ages. Christ brought many promises and not all of them have been fulfilled as yet. Redemption remains open-ended as long as man in his freedom continues to rebel sinfully against God. Many speak of a "proleptic" Christology, one in which the gradual unfolding of God's plan in Christ means that in any given time in history before the eschaton, there will be spiritual incompleteness and longing for fulfillment. There is a "not-yet" in Christianity just as much as there is in Judaism. And it no more invalidates Judaism than it does Christianity. Both Christianity and Judaism, then, have a common vision of "promise-fulfillment," a mutual humility before God, a mutual dependence on his guidance and help.

Christians therefore need to become aware of Israel's living religious vitality, its ongoing autonomy and religiously significant presence. In the long run it is the perception of this reality that will remain influential even after the impact of the Holocaust begins to fade with the passing years and generations. Christians should stop failing to see the Jewish faith as complete and sufficient in itself. It is even possible for Christians to understand Jewish rejection of Jesus as the Messiah as arising not out of unfaithfulness but out of faithfulness to the transcendence in Israel's Covenant with God.

There is no need then to continue supporting a substitution-rejection theory on the grounds that it is essential to Christian self-definition. Christians are fully able to understand and develop their relationship with God through Christ as something that is in a constant state of growth out of sinfulness into light. One does not need to put other religious people down in order to build one's self up. As a matter of fact, if one steps back a bit and looks at the totality of Christian doctrine and life, it is difficult to see how the basic Christian doctrine of universal love, a love even to the death, can be reconciled with a process of self-identification based on hatred of or disdain for other human beings on the grounds that they are sinful, all the while ignoring the sinfulness in one's own heart. As Karl Barth said: Jews are still God's Chosen People and anti-semitism is a form of Godlessness.

There are a number of indications in official Christian circles that these principles of recognition of Israel's religious vitality are influential today. Besides the well known documents and decisions of Vatican II, there are a number of other statements by various Church bodies that are important.

21

Also there has arisen a whole spectrum of ecumenical groups whose discussions and deepening relationships have changed the climate. The deicide charge has already been largely repudiated in strong language and many more Christians are acknowledging publicly that Judaism is alive and well in its faithfullness to its Covenant with God.

This optimistic picture needs of course to be tempered and qualified by the fact that there are still Christians who cling to the older theories and there remain certain areas of the world where these ecumenical ideas, taken for granted in many ways in the United States, seem revolutionary indeed. Unfortunately, much still remains to be done in this area of antisemitism. This is an ecumenical task that needs to be pursued among Christians themselves.

THE HOLOCAUST

The clearest warning that rejection-substitution theories present not only an inaccurate picture of the overall development of God's plan for humanity, but that they can have very dangerous consequences, if pursued with a hardened heart is the Holocaust of the 20th century.

When talking about "responsibility" for the Holocaust, it is necessary to make a certain number of careful distinctions. It is necessary, first of all, to distinguish between "Christian" and "Committed Christian." If by "Christian" is meant, as is often the case, "Western Gentile" then of course "Christians" were responsible for the Holocaust. But if by "Christian" is meant "Committed Christian" then though these may have been guilty of passivity before the Holocaust, it is difficult to see them as consciously guilty of genocide. Though it changes nothing of the genocidal horror, the fact also remains that the Holocaust claimed 5,000,000 other victims, most of whom were Christian.

There does remain a Christian responsibility for the Holocaust, however, in the sense that as long as there was or is a view among Christians that Judaism is somehow defective because it rejected the Old Covenant, then a psychological climate is created where baser human passions can rise to the surface unchecked by profound religious convictions of respect for other faiths and traditions. If there has been a Christian cultural antisemitism then the terrible image of its disastrous consequences in the 20th century should make the abandonment of any rejectionist-substitution theory all the more urgent.

MISSION TO THE JEWS

The question of Christian "mission" to the Jews is a topic of perennial concern, especially among evangelical Christian bodies. It too is one that needs to have some careful distinctions made about it. There is general agreement between most Christians and Jews today that the sincere religious convictions and practices of others must be respected; also that both by conviction and by international and national law, the religious liberties of all to believe, to preach, to worship are protected. The problem in the past has often been that Christians, eager to spread their message of salvation, have violated one or another of the rights of Jews. When Christians therefore claim the right to "evangelize," the claim must be carefully examined to see whether it includes genuine respect for religious convictions of others as well as their rights to religious freedom. If these conditions are met, then Christians, like anyone else, are free to preach their beliefs to anyone who will listen, including Jews.

THE STATE OF ISRAEL

There are many Christians who seem embarrassed by Jewish claims to the land and State of Israel. Though they fully support claims of spiritual and religious freedom and though they express horror at any active persecution of the Jews, they often seem confused when all this turns into the flesh and blood (sometimes bloody) realities of the land of Israel and its wars of self-defense. Though there are many political reasons undergirding the State of Israel, including the continued presence there of Jews from the time of the First Exile, the religious reasons are most important and Christians should be more aware of the fact that most Jews expect Christians to be more sensitive to these religious reasons.

One of the purposes of Jewish-Christian dialogue, then, should be to clarify these issues concerning the State of Israel, so that, both sides being basically satisfied, the dialogue can then move on to more immediately religious and spiritual issues.

REFLECTIONS FOR JEWS

1. The First Stage

As Siegman suggests, a first stage of Jewish reflection and self-examination would be Jewish attitudes towards a pluralistic world on the one hand and towards a traditionally defensive image of Christianity on the other. As he says, Jews lose nothing of their religious integrity by admitting that "Christians who are good and decent human beings are so not despite, but because . . . they profess Christianity."

2. The Holocaust: Memorials and Dejudaization

Some Jews are disturbed by the great growth of memorials to the Holocaust, especially in the United States. The Holocaust is, for them, completely unique in its organized attempt at the annihilation of an entire community and in the apocalyptic, salvational role played by its Jewish victims. They fear that the growth of memorials to all the victims of the Holocaust may tend to dejudaize it and make it simply synonymous with mass murder and destruction. Other Jews, however, object to this interpretation on two grounds: first, that an overemphasis on the Holocaust tends to diminish the importance of the rest of Jewish history, and, second, that an

23

acknowledgement of the 5,000,000 non-Jewish victims of the Holocaust not only does not diminish its uniqueness for the Jews, but actually clarifies that uniqueness by showing the differences in the way that the two groups were victimized.

3. Church and State in the Light of the Holocaust

The direct cause of the Holocaust lay in the decision of many Nazis to live without moral restraint or religious hope, a philosophy of life where the end constantly justified the means. This implies that religion, including Christianity, was pushed deeply into a private ghetto of its own, where it had little impact on public policy, and which, unchecked, grew more and more demonic.

Perhaps it is time, say some, to reexamine attitudes and basic presuppositions with regard to the question of separation of Church and State in the United States. While religious freedom for all must be preserved at all costs, this must be done in a way that avoids overprivatizing or ghettoizing religion itself. Precautions need to be taken to prevent it from becoming irrelevant in the public domain. The unchallenged state can gradually become too powerful and morally blind and one of the first casualties could be religious freedom itself.

Some Jews are saying, therefore, that instead of calling for a shameful silence from Christians in the face of the Holocaust, Jews should seek to develop active collaboration with Christians against the public dangers of an omnicompetent state. Christians have their own problems in this area, namely, a reluctance to get involved in worldly, political affairs. Jews can help Christians to see the necessity of such involvement if greater dangers are to be avoided. Understandable Jewish concern about the impact of the state on religion needs to be tempered by Christian concern for the impact, or rather, the non-impact, of religion on the state.

4. Scriptures:

Jews can approach a fruitful examination of the Scriptures together with Christians now that advancing methodologies have developed a new, neutral interpretative language based on linguistic, archeological and hermenutical studies.

5. Mission:

Jews, in the name of their Covenant with a transcendent God, rightly resist any Christian mission or proselytism that fails to recognize their spiritual integrity or religious freedom. At the same time, given these protections, other religions, including Christianity, have the right to preach their beliefs to anyone.

6. Theological Discussion:

Many Jews are becoming aware that both sides approach the Jewish-Christian dialogue with differing expectations. Quite understandably, Jews want to deal first with the historical problems of Antisemitism, the Holocaust and the State of Israel. But what some Jewish participants in the dialogue need to become more aware of is that many Christians engaging in

24

the dialogue with good will are disappointed when it fails to move beyond these historical areas to more theological ones.

Though this may seem strange to Jews, Christians need help in dealing with the discomfort they feel in seriously encountering for the first time a living, vital Judaism rather than dealing with a straw man called legalistic post-biblical Judaism whose supposedly moribund tradition needed to be superseded by Christianity. A greater awareness by dialoguing Jews of this Christian problem, partly historical, partly psychological, partly theological, would help advance the relationship.

Christians are also disappointed at times at the apparent reluctance of Jews in the dialogue to discuss questions of religious truth. Such reluctance has been, of course, a Jewish characteristic over the ages in the sense that Judaism had always been more concerned with living properly before God than theologizing about it. But there are many Jews today who are less reluctant to engage in theological discussion in the dialogue. They are aware of the problems involved. They know that in the first stages of a newly developing relationship there is always a certain awkwardness in getting into more profound matters. They are also aware that there remains the danger of stirring up old hornets nests of hostilities. Nevertheless, they feel that both these dangers can be and are being overcome as the dialogue progresses with mutual trust. Both the traditions of the Tanach and its commentaries and the Jewish philosophical and mystical traditions offer solid precedents for theological discussion with Christians and members of other religions.

CONCLUSION

While these essays indicate that there are a number of presuppositional areas among both Christians and Jews that need some sorting out through self-reflection and that some of the rough spots in the dialogue need attention, the overall tone of the essays is optimistic. They indicate that these new agenda challenges can be met, that the dialogue is basically healthy and that the mystery of its deepening arises out of the mystery of God.

Richard W. Rousseau, S.J.
University of Scranton

Note: For reasons of accuracy, each author's critical apparatus has been preserved unchanged or with only minor changes.

I

Christians and Jews: Along a Theological Frontier

BY A. ROY ECKARDT

Lecture I: Faith Under the Judgment of History

I AM DEEPLY APPRECIATIVE *of being allowed a place in the Hugh Th. Miller Lecture series. I should like to dedicate my presentations to the memory of a dear friend, Heinz David Leuner of Breslau and London.*

It is now thirty-five years since I started to think about the Christian-Jewish relation. That may be a foolhardy announcement, in view of the limitations in what I have to say. The truth is that I can be of no primary aid in the historical and biblical areas; I may be of some help from ideational and moral standpoints.

I

In addressing ourselves to theological-frontier questions for Christians

---

A. Roy Eckardt (Ph.D., Columbia; L.H.D., Hebrew Union) is Professor and Chairman, Department of Religion, Lehigh University. Writer of many books on Jewish-Christian relations and holder of numerous Fellowships, his most recent study is Long Night's Journey into Day, written in collaboration with Alice L. Eckardt. His paper was given as the Hugh Th. Miller Lecture at Christian Theological Seminary in April of 1978. During this past year he has been visiting scholar at the Oxford Center for Postgraduate Hebrew Studies. It is taken from Encounter, Spring, 1979, pp. 89-127 and is reprinted by permission of the publisher and the author.

and Jews of today, we shall concentrate, first, upon "Faith under the judgment of history" and then in the second lecture upon "History under the judgment of faith." As a subtitle for both presentations (or, as I think about it, perhaps a substitute title for our whole time together), I submit "The Story of Some Children."

A passage of Elie Wiesel's work, *A Beggar in Jerusalem*, helps bring our whole problem into relief: " . . . the crowd keeps getting larger. Military personnel and officials, celebrities and journalists, all are streaming by in one continuous procession, along with rabbis and students, gathered from all over the city, from every corner of the land. Men, women and adolescents of every age, every origin and speaking every language, and I see them ascending toward the [Western] Wall, toward all that remains of their collective longing. Just like long ago, at Sinai, when they were given the Torah. Just like a generation ago, in the kingdom of night, when [the Torah] was taken back."[1]

Herein is focused our entire problem: The Torah, vehicle and treasure of faith, yet here taken back, evidently because of another event in time and place, an event called the kingdom of night. (Could it be that the kingdom of night saw, as well, the taking back of the Cross and the Resurrection?)

Is it so, then, that history — defined as realized event — is the judge of faith? Or is it so, contrariwise, that faith remains the judge of human history? Or, for that matter, are we obliged to sustain a dialectic between the two? When historical event is enabled to supervise and determine faith, will not the transcending and saving resources and norms of faith eventually dissipate? But when faith is permitted to determine the status and import of historical event, are not the values of a God-created humanity and of human obligation assailed? Conceivably, a worthful dialectic between faith and history will implement a required tension, or at least an unavoidable one, between spiritual affirmation and wordly humaneness.

The overall theological justification for the subjecting of faith to the judgment of history is the persuasion that God himself acts through the happenings of time and place. Here is exactly what it means to denominate Christianity and Judaism as historical religions. The judging of faith by historical event is nothing new in the story of Christianity. Indeed, this was precisely the method put forward by the church in her original evaluations of Judaism. We are met by the consequent paradox that the judging of faith by history may itself involve the work of faith. According to the Christian faith, the ultimate disposition of the dramas of history must come from beyond the stage of history. Nevertheless — to fill out our paradox — the critical assessing of history at the hands of faith is itself a historical act. As Martin Buber used to say, all religion is history.

II

A certain theological schema has intruded itself powerfully within the

Christian tradition, a schema according to which the triad of Cross-Resurrection-Parousia is made into a solely determinative series of faith-events. As Professor Heinz Kremers of Germany's University of Duisburg comments adversely, in the thinking of many Christians such a concatenation as this transcends the ordinary realm of history, with the consequence that it will forever marshall priority, soteriologically speaking, over all historical happenings.[2] It is in keeping with this outlook that Alan T. Davies of Toronto University identifies the Crucifixion and the Resurrection — lying as they reputedly do along "the margin of history" — as qualifying "the extent to which Christian faith can accept new revelatory moments. . . ."[3] A ready consequence of this schema is that Christianity itself becomes a wholly transcendent "reality," which moves in entirely "spiritual" ways above the flux and vagaries of history. Events of the in-between time are treated interstitially: history is remanded to a collection of interstices between the original truth-event of sacred history and a decisive, coming truth-event. These latter become the only truth-events that count. From this perspective, such a happening as the king of night, the German Nazi Holocaust of the Jews, possesses no significance for faith.

However, it would be most unwarranted to construe the dialogue between Christianity and Jewishness as involving, respectively, a transcendentalist outlook and a non-transcendentalist one. Jewish thinking and life are themselves not entirely devoid of the interstitial viewpoint — as witness those Jews who have identified their Holocaust as no different in kind from other evils that have beset the people of God throughout history. It is told, indeed, that certain pious Jews sang and danced their way into the gas chambers and crematoria — as though the Holocaust of their people were of no real consequence, were, in effect, a non-event.[4] Again, some ultra-Orthodox Jews, including, strikingly enough, certain ones who reside within *Eretz Yisrael* itself, wholly reject the legitimacy of today's Jewish state — for the reason that only the coming Messiah can implement a Jewish polity.

On the other side of the arena, the noted philosopher Emil L. Fackenheim recently confessed: "Authentic Jewish theology cannot possess the immunity I once gave it, *for its price is an essential indifference to all history between Sinai and the Messianic days.*"[5] Fackenheim has been brought up short, and shatteringly so, by the cruciality of the Holocaust of his people. And I remember well the day a non-religious Jewish friend at Kibbutz Yad Mordechai in the western Negev took my wife and me through their museum exhibit of the Holocaust of Polish Jewry. As we emerged into the sunshine, his arm swept across the surrounding countryside, and he said, "You have seen our crucifixion; now, please, behold our resurrection."

It is obvious as well that some spokesmen of the Christian faith are prepared to find decisive theological meaning in contemporary happenings — as examples, the United Methodist historian Franklin H. Littell, who characterizes the Holocaust of the Jews and the establishing of the Third Jewish Commonwealth as "alpine events" within twentieth-century Christendom,[6] and the Episcopalian Paul van Buren, who writes that Christian "theology can shut its eyes and pretend that the Holocaust never happened and that Israel doesn't exist. . . . But if there are prospects for serious theology, for a theology not hopelessly blind to matters that pertain to the heart of its task, then the time has come for a reconsideration of the whole theological and Christian enterprise of the most radical sort. . . ."[7]

If we are correct that today's Christian-Jewish dialectic cannot be identified in simple terms as an instance of transcendentalism versus historicalness, nevertheless the very fact that the Holocaust of the Jews and the inaugurating of the Third Jewish Commonwealth involve primarily the Jewish community means that through these very events the issue may be joined today between a transcendentalist faith that boasts imperviousness to worldly happenings, and a faith confessedly open to the wounding contingencies of time and space. Is it the case that the Jewish Holocaust and a reemerging Israel are special events for Christians, and if they are, in what explicit ways are we called to speak of, and to relate to, these events?

III

The possible Christian relevance of the Holocaust of the Jews is sometimes held to turn upon the charge that something in Christianity, in Christian teachings, and in the life and behavior of Christians helped to bring about and to implement the German Nazi *Endlösung der Judenfrage*, the "Final Solution of the Jewish question." In recent literature a most oft-cited historical aphorism is that of Raul Hilberg in his influential work *The Destruction of the European Jews:* The missionaries of Christianity had said in effect: You have no right to live among us as Jews. The secular rulers who followed had proclaimed: You have no right to live among us. The German Nazis at last decreed: You have no right to live."[8]

The British scholar and Anglican clergyman James Parkes, greatest historian of the Christian-Jewish relation, writes: The hatred and denigration of the Jewish people

> have a quite clear and precise historical origin. They arise from Christian preaching and teaching from the time of the bitter controversies of the first century in which the two religions separated from each other. From that time up to today there has been an unbroken line which culminates in the massacre in our own day of six million Jews. The fact that the action of Hitler and his henchmen was not really motivated by Christian sentiments, the fact that mingled with the ashes of murdered Jews are the ashes of German soldiers who refused to obey orders . . . ., the fact that churches protested and that Christians risked their lives to save Jews — all these facts come into the picture, but unhappily they do not invalidate the basic statement that

anti-semitism from the first century to the twentieth is a Christian creation and a Christian responsibility, whatever secondary causes may come into the picture.[9]

Why should Professor Littel characterize the Holocaust of the Jews and the reestablishing of political Israel as "alpine events" within contemporary Christendom? He declares:

> The cornerstone of Christian Antisemitism is the superseding or displacement myth, which already rings with the genocidal note. This is the myth that the mission of the Jewish people was finished with the coming of Jesus Christ, that "the old Israel" was written off with the appearance of "the new Israel." To teach that a people's mission in God's providence is finished, that they have been relegated to the limbo of history, has murderous implications which murderers will in time spell out. The murder of six million Jews by baptized Christians, from whom membership in good standing was not (and has not yet been) withdrawn, raises the most insistent question about the credibility of Christianity. The existence of a restored Israel, proof positive that the Jewish people is not annihilated, assimilated, or otherwise withering away, is substantial refutation of the traditional Christian myth about their end in the historic process. And this is precisely why Israel is a challenge, a crisis for much contemporary Christian theology.[10]

And why should Paul van Buren argue that the *Endlösung* necessitates a radical reconsideration of the entire Christian theological enterprise? He explains: "The roots of Hitler's final solution are to be found in the proclamation of the very *kerygma* of the early Christians. . . . (The command out of Auschwitz) is that we accept a judgment on something false lying close to the very heart of our tradition. . . ."[11]

Finally, the Canadian Catholic scholar Gregory Baum is cited: "What Auschwitz has revealed to the Christian community is the deadly power of its own symbolism." The "anti-Jewish thrust of the church's preaching" is not a historical, psychological, or sociological matter; "it touches the very formulation of the Christian gospel." Along with Parkes, Littell, and van Buren, Professor Baum concentrates upon the realities of Christian triumphalism and supersessionism in the presence of the Jews and Judaism, or upon what Father John Pawlikowski of Chicago calls "the theology of substitution," which (again citing Baum) "assigns the Jews to the darkness of history,"[12] rejected by God and man, in ways that could only end in the camps of murder. In the Nazi Final Solution "the theological negation of Judaism and the vilification of the Jewish people" within the Christian tradition were, at the last, translated into the genocide of the Jews.[13]

31

"Christianity and Judaism"

Of the multiplying of citations there is no end. And that practice may not settle very much. Historical analysis, however expert, does not end disputation — although in the present case the varied backgrounds of the many new historiographers (I have quoted only a few[14]) and the weighty consensus of their findings combine to demand careful and sober attention. One counterpoint may be inserted: That the anti-Jewish element in Christianity is not beyond exception is illustrated in the fact — if I may venture a personal note — that through all the years my wife and I were growing up actively in the Methodist Church, we never heard any such thing as Christian anti-Jewishness, and we did not really learn of it until Christian and other scholars apprised us of the phenomenon in our twenties.

The general question of the nature and *élan vital* of causation, not excepting historical causation, has been enigmatic for a long time — particularly since David Hume (though not "because" of him!). However, a salient fact travels as a silent and haunting partner with the new historiography: so large a number of the contemporary analysts are Christians. They are speaking of the historical fate of Jews. But in the very act of doing this, they summon attention to their own identity. For their identity as human beings is tied to someone who was himself a Jew, someone who, had he by some miracle been living in the "right" time and place, would have been dispatched to a Nazi gas chamber or crematorium. And, in all probability, his execution would have been brought off by men who were themselves Christians, and who were thus related to the very one whom they would have been destroying.

Thus does the new historiography of the church's place in the Holocaust of the Jews convey, *in and of itself, and quite independent of the specific historical theorization,* a metahistorical dimension, a dimension by means of which such categories as incredibility and revulsion and mystery inexorably gain entry, not to mention the categories of relevance, of moral decision, of culpability. "Jesus was a Jew" — in these four short words is established forever the bond between Christianity and the Holocaust of the Jews (as also the Third Jewish Commonwealth). These events become "alpine events" for Christians in a most elementary way: by the mere facts of the Jewish-ness of these events and, more importantly, by the very nature of Christian historical identity and destiny. How often are elementary and plain truths obscured by the artifices of history and the machinations of men!

The consequence indicated, the alpine character of the events under discussion, appears against the aura of an absolutely singular development within *Heilsgeschichte* (the story of salvation). For the effort was not carried forward to ensure that there would not be a single Jew upon Planet Earth.[15] The *ganze Einzigartigkeit,* the unique uniqueness, the only-ness of the Final Solution is disclosed in the fact that all Jewish babies were to be killed along with all children and grownups. This had never been the case, in 4,000 years. It is the historical *identity* of these victims that marks off this event from other horrible events, including other "holocausts." But the only-ness of the *Endlösung* is also, ultimately speaking, theological in nature. As William Jay Peck writes, after Auschwitz "the very being of God" is "tied up with the problem of murder."[16]

The Holocaust of the Jews splits the story of our world into two epochs: B.F.S., "Before the Final Solution," and F.S., "In the Year of the Final Solution." We are meeting in the year 38 F.S., since the traditional date 1941 is probably best identified as year one of the Holocaust of the Jews.[17]

IV

What are the possible judgments of the Holocaust of the Jews upon the life of faith? Earlier Professor Fackenheim was cited: Authentic Jewish theology can no longer be granted immunity to the history between Sinai and the messianic days; the *Endlösung* has intervened. And what about Christians? Can they permit themselves to retain an essential indifference to the history between Jesus of Nazareth and the End of days?

In order to face up to these questions, we shall single out five themes: the Jewish people and the person and claim of Jesus; Christian conversionism and the Jews; the Covenant and the trial of God; the Crucifixion of Jesus; and, lastly, the Resurrection.

In the first place, among socially fateful religious teachings has been the allegation that the Jewish people have failed to honor the divine opportunity to accept Jesus as the Messiah, and are deservedly chastised by God for the rejection.

What are we to say to this? Martin Buber has written: "Standing bound and shackled in the pillory of mankind, we (Jews) demonstrate with the bloody body of our people the unredeemedness of the world."[18] The Jew "feels this lack of redemption against his skin, he tastes it on his tongue, the burden of the unredeemed world lies on him."[19] The original, majority Jewish response to the possible messiahship of Jesus was, and stays so today, that his subjection to the Roman overlords, in contrast to his potential role of helping to destroy Rome, indicated the non-messianic character of Jesus. Jewish insistence that Jesus of Nazareth could not possibly be the promised Messiah of Israel, sustained as this conviction is by several thousands of years experience of the unredeemedness of the historical order, gained terminal authentication in the *Endlösung*. Climactic and, indeed, eschatological proof was furnished in and through the Holocaust of the Jews, administered as that event was by those who represented redemption of both a Christian and a non-Christian kind.

Jewish non-acceptance of Jesus as Messiah remains among the most sublime and heroic instances of Israel's faithfulness to her Covenant with God.[20]

V

A second theme is Christian conversionism directed at the Jewish people. This theme is a striking case of the convergence of faith and history, and a reminder that our present division between those two areas is analytical as much as it is substantive. On the one hand, it may be argued that any Christian attempt to missionize Jews comprises an implicit assault upon the Israel of God, the foundation of the church, and accordingly is self-refuting and self-destructive. If the Jewish people are not the elder brothers and sisters within God's family, it would appear that the gentiles as reputedly adopted younger brothers and sisters are still in their sins, and remain lost and without hope, "outside God's covenants and the promise that goes with them" (cf. Ephes. 2:1-13). The Covenant into which the gentiles are ostensibly led by the event of Jesus the Jew becomes a delusion.

From the standpoint of this reaction, the effort to convert Jews to Christianity is identifiable as a veiled attack, perhaps unknowingly, upon the Christian faith itself. Conversionism is a Christian impossibility — not for those pragmatic reasons so dear to the hearts of Americans, but for reasons of Christian theological principle.

On the other hand, the *Judenmission*, the organized effort to "save" Jews, is confronted by the judgment of history. The Final Solution helps to bring home the dreadful consequences of the entrenched program to convert Jews. Among some Christians of contemporary Germany, a shattering phrase has gained currency: *eine geistliche Endlösung*, "a spiritual Final Solution." Within the front rank of concerned Christian scholars in Germany today stands Rudolf Pfisterer of Schwäbisch-Hall. Dr. Pfisterer emphasizes that the *Judenmission*, the Christian mission to the Jews, is, in his words, "nothing more than the continuing work of the Final Solution." For, in the last resort, what is the moral difference between stuffing Jews into gas chambers and mass graves, and striking at the very heart of their religious integrity?[21] Here is a terrible reminder that Christian supersessionism and triumphalism, which helped ensure the Holocaust of the Jews, are also contemporaneous embodiments and fulfillments of the German Nazi program. Yet we should never have been led to think in these terms had it not been for the *Endlösung*. The judgments of history are strange, and sometimes they are saving judgments.

VI

A third theme is the Covenant and the trial of God.

We have referred to the taking back of the Torah in the kingdom of night. Could it be that it was God himself who withdrew the teaching and turned his face, because of the acts of his people? Did Israel betray the divine Covenant, and thus stand condemned? The Council of the Evangelical Church of

Germany meeting in Darmstadt solemnly asserted that the suffering of the Jews under the Nazis was God's punishment. The Council called upon the Jewish people to desist from their rejection of Christ and from their ongoing crucifixion of him.[22] The date of the meeting? Three years after the ending of the Holocaust.

The *Beggar in Jerusalem* speaks again to us. There is much laughter in that tale. For the most part, it is terrible, maniacal laughter. According to Rabbi Nackman of Bratzlav, somewhere in the world there is a certain city that encompasses all other cities. In this city is a street that contains all the other streets of the city; on that street is a house dominating all the other houses; it contains a room that comprises all the other rooms of the house. "And in that room there lives a man in whom all other men recognize themselves. And that man is laughing. That's all he ever does, ever did. He roars with laughter when seen by others, but also when alone."[23]

Is there something special for this man to laugh at now, in 1978? (By "1978," we mean, of course, 1933 to 1945, or 8 B.F.S. to 5 F.S.) Yes, there is a special occasion for laughter. The man is particularly laughing in this moment because of the context of the withdrawing of the Torah: it was *in the kingdom of night* that the Torah was taken back. Accordingly, it would appear that someone who identifies the *Endlösung* as God's act of condemnation of his people to subject to confinement, where he will be obliged to listen, without surcease, to the laughter of that man in that room in that house upon that street within that city which is the world. For, just a few pages earlier in *A Beggar in Jerusalem*, a young madman, one of only three survivors who had escaped the deportation, has put the ineluctable question: "How does God justify himself in his own eyes, let alone in ours? If the real and the imaginary both culminate in the same scream, in the same laugh, what is creation's purpose, what is its stake?"[24] The character Gregor in Wiesel's *Gates of the Forest* finally grasped the meaning of the Jewish Holocaust: the event implicated not only Abraham and his son Isaac, "but their God as well."[25] If, indeed the *Endlösung der Judenfrage* is an act of judgment, must not the judgment be addressed, in the very first instance, to God himself, as against the people of God? Could it be, then, that when the Torah was withdrawn, it was taken away, not from Israel, but instead from the King of the Universe?

In recent thinking, Jewish and Christian, no one has posed this kind of query more relentlessly than our colleague Richard L. Rubenstein. The question is here raised, not of the impossibility or objective negation of all divine-human covenants (as Rubenstein goes so far as to conclude), but instead of the obliterating of the Covenant of special demands upon Israel — this, in contradistinction to a Covenant of promise, of assurance.

From this standing-ground, a moral indictment is entered against the Lord of hosts — this God who, as Rabbi Eliezer Berkovits puts it, "is responsible for having created a world in which man is free to make history."[26] Once upon a time God mandated that his chosen ones be "a kingdom of priests and a holy nation'' (Exod. 19:6). As a consummation of this demand, in the kingdom of night his elect could be transubstantiated into *Unmenschen*, the bacilli from below. The original sin of God — a sin in which Christians, Muslims, and others were to become most ready and available accomplices — was the sin of applying the absolute divine perfection to the lives of ordinary human creatures. The accusation entered against God is no less than one of implicit Satanism. No plea of innocence appears open to him. No appeal seems available to him. He stands condemned, guilty as charged. All that is left for him is an act of penitence. In the shadow of the gas chambers and the crematoria, God is required, not alone to express genuine sorrow for his place in the unparalleled agony of his people, but to promise that he will not sin again, that he won't have anything to do with such suffering in the future. In Elie Wiesel's *Souls on Fire* Rabbi Levi-Yitzhak reminds God that he had better ask forgiveness for the hardships he has inflicted upon his children. This is why the phrase Yom Kippur also appears in the plural, Yom Kippurim; "the request for pardon is reciprocal."[27]

The consequence of the juridical-moral trial of God is the eclipse of the Covenant of demand. The myth of the Jews as "suffering servant" will surrender its loathsomeness only as that Covenant is granted a proper funeral.[28]

VII

Let us consider the theme of the Cross of Jesus. Could it be, the question was raised at the beginning, that with the advent of the kingdom of night, the Cross was also taken back?

A study by Jürgen Moltmann of the University of Tübingen, entitled *The Crucified God,* is of first importance, illustratively and substantively, to this our fourth theme. The theme has two aspects: on the one hand the historical-moral fate of the Cross as a Christian symbol, especially in its linkage to the Resurrection, as emphasized by Professor Moltmann; and, on the other hand, the historical-moral difficulty created by Moltmann's advocated link between the Cross and ultimate horribleness.

We are told by Moltmann that Christ's "death is the death of the one who redeems men from death, which is evil."[29] No, in the Nazi time the message of the cross assisted in *bringing* death, the polar contrary of the "pains of love." The "crucified Christ" simply cannot be separated from what has happened to, and been done to, the Cross. Professor Moltmann tries to argue that the Cross "does not divide Christians from Jews."[30] In truth, countless Jews of our world will never be enabled to distinguish the Cross from the *Hakenkreuz* (the "hook-cross," the swastika), nor can they be expected to do so. It was after the Holocaust of the Jews that a Jewish woman, catching sight of a huge cross displayed in New York City at Christmastime, said to her walking companion, Father Edward H. Flannery: "That cross makes me shudder. It is like an evil presence."[31] It was in and through the *Endlösung* that the symbol of the Cross was taken captive by ultimate devilishness. When asked by two bishops in 1933 what he was going to do about the Jews, Adolf Hitler could readily answer that he would do to them exactly what the Christian church had been advocating and practicing for almost two thousand years.[32]

Professor Moltmann declares: "The poverty and sufferings of Christ are experienced and understood *only* by participation in his mission and in imitating the task he carried out. Thus the more the poor understand the cross ... as the cross of *Christ,* the more they are liberated from their submission to fate and apathy in suffering."[33] No, in stark truth the millions of Jews[34] were *not* liberated, from death or from other suffering. They were not liberated at all, through "understanding" or any other factor. Moltmann goes on: " 'Resurrection, life, and righteousness' come through the death of this one man in favor of those who have been delivered over to death through their unrighteousness." No, history replies. The Jews did not "qualify" as unrighteous — nor, for that matter, as righteous. They were just murdered. And they were murdered just because they were Jews — not good Jews or bad Jews or any other kind of Jews, but just Jews. What does it mean to tell the inmates of Buchenwald or Bergen-Belsen, as this Christian theologian does, that "through his suffering and death, the risen Christ brings righteousness and life to the unrighteous and the dying?"[35]

However, the truly decisive consideration is that in the presence of Auschwitz, the claims that Jürgen Moltmann makes for Christian symbols and "virtues" have come to have the very opposite meanings and consequences from those he indicates. For now, within his own German history and within ours, the categories of "weakness" — he supplies them all — "weakness," "impotence," "vulnerability," "openness to suffering and love" "divine protection"[36] have all been transubstantiated into demonic structures. As Rabbi Irving Greenberg observes, in *our* world suffering only helps to "strengthen rampant evil and to collaborate in the enthronement of the devil."[37] The endlessly woeful consequence is that the Cross is robbed of its redemptiveness. All that remains upon the hill of Golgotha is unmitigated evil. After Auschwitz, a question mark is nailed to the Cross as the reputedly determinative symbol of redemptive suffering. From the point of view of the Holocaust of the Jews, God is not met on the cross — even in his "Godforsakenness." Once upon a time he may have been met there, but he is met there no longer. For as we seek to behold Golgotha now, our sight is blocked by huge mounds of torn bodies and their ashes.

The other aspect of the question of the Cross — Moltmann's effort to link the Cross with ultimate horribleness — is the more weighty of the two, because it is not eligible for the possible rejoinder that, after all, the Cross transcends and is immune to a certain historical-moral fate, and thereby is able to retain its redemptive power, come what may.[38] Professor Moltmann also puts the Cross of Golgotha in unique association with Jesus' (allegedly) total Godforsakenness. Jesus' abandonment and deliverance up to death are held to constitute the very torment of hell.[39]

It may be suggested that this particular abomination simply does not stand up as the absolute horror upon which the Christian faith can and should, dialectically, build its hope. It may be contended that in comparison with certain other sufferings, Jesus' death becomes relatively non-significant.

The tale is told of a scene in Auschwitz in the late Summer of 1944. The gas chamber near the crematorium was out of order; it had been wrecked in a Jewish commando operation in August.

> The other gas chambers were full of adults and therefore the children were not gassed, but just burned alive. There were several thousand of them. When one of the SS sort of had pity, he would take a child and beat the head against a stone before putting it on the pile of fire and wood, so that the child lost consciousness. However, the regular way they did it was by just throwing the children onto the pile. They would put a sheet of wood there, then sprinkle the whole thing with petrol, then wood again, and petrol and wood, and petrol — and then they placed the children there. Then the whole thing was lighted.[40]

How is it still possible, if it ever was possible, to make the passion of the Jewish man, Jesus of Nazareth, *the* foundation of Christian faith? Jesus was at least a grown man, a mature man, a man with a mission, and by all the evidence a courageous man, who set his face steadfastly to go up to Jerusalem (Luke 9:51). In contrast, there has occurred within this world and within the present epoch an evil that is more terrible than other evils. This is the evil of small children witnessing the murders of other small children, *whilst knowing that they also are to be murdered in the same way,* being aware absolutely that they face the identical fate. Jürgen Moltmann's claim concerning Jesus and his Godforsakenness reads like theology from before the Holocaust of the Jews. Though he writes today, Moltmann appears, at this juncture, to be living as though the events of the kingdom of night never transpired. The Godforsakenness of Jesus has proven to be non-absolute, if it ever was absolute, for there is now a Godforsakenness of Jewish children which is a final horror.

VIII

Our fifth and last theme, and the most crucial one, is that of the Resurrection. At the beginning we raised the question of whether not alone the Torah and the Cross, but also the Resurrection, were taken back in the kingdom of night.

James Parkes reminds us again and again that there is no way to build good theology upon bad history. Sometimes Parke's counsel causes no special difficulties, since many theological testimonies have a solid base in histori-

38

cal fact: the Exodus from Egypt did occur, the Crucifixion of Jesus did take place. But what about the Resurrection of Jesus? Is that a historical event, an event of time and place, *of the same order* as the Crucifixion?

To seek to grapple with this question by making reference to the Holocaust of the Jews would appear to be absurd. But is it actually so that there are no connections?

In a piece in the *Journal of the History of Ideas* entitled "The Nazi Holocaust as a Persisting Trauma for the Non-Jewish Mind," Emil Fackenheim argues that in the post-Holocaust time, *the* central question for Christianity remains the link between Christian affirmation and Christian anti-semitism.[41] No dogma is more central to traditional Christian affirmation than the Resurrection of Jesus Christ. It is as a means of facing up to such shattering allegations as this one from Fackenheim that some Christian theologians have been calling for a recovery of Jewishness within the church. But what is that recovery to mean? Christian spokesmen of today will sometimes be heard to stress that the scourge of Christian antisemitism demands a wholehearted rethinking of Christian teachings. Yet once these people have finished their presentations, they often have done little more than repeat, in attractive words perhaps, the very doctrines that have caused all the trouble. It seems to be a case of continuing Christian triumphalism — complete with guilt feelings.

The ultimate test case is the Resurrection — for three solid and related reasons. One of these was intimated just above. The faith of countless Christians has as its center the achieved Resurrection of Jesus. "If Christ has not been raised, ... your faith is vain" — so writes the Apostle Paul to the Corinthians (I Cor. 15:14). Second, and accordingly, the one place where a reaffirmation of Jewishness could occur, were it to occur at all, would be in conjunction with the Resurrection. For, thirdly, in this context the recovery of Jewishness can only mean a certain interpretation of the applicability of historical judgment to the Resurrection, the radical assertion that the Resurrection has not happened.

In the presence of historical judgment the Resurrection is made problematic, quite apart from the Christian-Jewish encounter, and problematic in a unique way that does not apply to our earlier themes. The same Apostle Paul who insisted that without the Resurrection of Jesus Christ the Christian faith is vain, did not himself believe in the Resurrection — in the way that the writer of Luke 24 did. To Paul, the body that is sown is not the body that is raised. "Flesh and blood can never possess the kingdom of God, and the perishable cannot possess immortality" (I Cor. 15:35-57). But according to Luke 24 — some are now arguing that Luke is the Earliest Gospel[42] — "Jesus himself stood among them. ... "See my hands and my feet, that it is I myself; handle me, and see; for a spirit has not flesh and bones as you see that I have.' And while they still disbelieved for joy, and wondered, he said to them, 'Have you anything here to eat?' They gave him a piece of broiled fish, and he took it and ate before them" (Luke 24:36, 39-43). The con-

"Christianity and Judaism"

troversy has never ceased. Christian Fundamentalism insists upon "the resurrection of the same body of Jesus which was three days buried."[43] Other Christians, unable to underwrite the resuscitation of a corpse, find consolation, or claim to, in some form of Pauline transformationism, often aided by mythologistic, spiritualist, or experientialist contentions. This latter view is most difficult to sustain from the standpoint of strictly historical judgment, or logical historicist judgment, which holding as it does that an event is either realized or unrealized, either happens or does not happen, will suggest that either the Fundamentalists are correct or the Resurrection has not occurred.[44] There is not, alas, any third choice. This state of affairs brings us back to the Christian-Jewish confrontation.

In the frame of reference of our present subject, a particularly serious question arises: Is it really possible for the Christian church to preach the Resurrection in a non-triumphalist way? From the very wording of this question, the traditional message of Easter Day and the German Nazi *Endlösung* are seen to be fatefully linked.

The overall Christian plight respecting the Jewish people and Judaism is brought into clear focus in the combination of ideas presented by Wolfhart Pannenberg of the University of Munich. Pannenberg asserts that "through the cross of Jesus, the Jewish legal tradition as a whole has been set aside in its claim to contain the eternal will of God in its final formulation."[45] The "law" is consummated, fulfilled in Jesus. Typifying as he does the accustomed (and false) allegation within German and other biblical scholarship that Jesus himself stood in opposition to a hardened Jewish "law,"[46] Pannenberg calls upon the Resurrection to prove his charge: Jesus came into fundamental conflict "with the law itself, that is with the positive Israelite legal tradition which had become calcified (*sic!*) as 'the law' after the exile." However, through the resurrection of Jesus "the emancipation from this law was confirmed by the God of Israel himself."

Professor Pannenberg employs exactly the same reasoning in the matter of Jesus' alleged claim for his own person, and he uses this opportunity to resort to the old canard of Jewish complicity for Jesus' death: Jesus' "claim to authority, through which he put himself in God's place, was blasphemous for Jewish ears. Because of this, Jesus was then also slandered by the Jews before the Roman governor as a rebel. If Jesus really has been raised, this claim has been visibly and unambiguously confirmed by the God of Israel. ..."[47]

In Wolfhart Pannenberg, we are supplied in a single package, with the major elements of the entire Christian historical-moral predicament vis-a-vis the Jewish people and Judaism: the Cross, the setting aside of "the law" through its "fulfillment" in Jesus, Jesus' own "opposition" to "the law," Jesus' "authority' as equal to that of God, and then the Resurrection[48] as the divine validation of these various points at which Christianity stands in judgment upon the Jewish people and their faith.[49] A value of Pannenberg's exposition is its pointing up the truth that the teaching of the achieved

40

Resurrection of Jesus lies at the heart of Christian opposition and hostility to Judaism and the Jewish people. For only with that teaching does Christian triumphalism reach fulfillment. Only here are the various human and divine-human claims making up the church's dogmatic structure furnished with the capstone of an event which is said to be exclusively God's and that in this way vindicates every other claim. The representative of this ideology declares, in effect: "It is not the Christian theologian to whom you Jews are to listen. The theologian is, after all, a fallible and sinful human being. Rather, let us have God decide the matter. But God's decision proves to be on the Christian side, not yours. *He* raised Jesus from the dead. Thus is the Christian shown to be right and you are shown to be wrong. In the Resurrection God himself *confirms* the Christian gospel, the Christian cause."

IX

The question is repeated, for it stands at the heart of history's judgment upon the Christian faith: Is it possible, or how is it possible, for the Christian church to proclaim the Resurrection of Jesus Christ in a non-triumphalist way? It is clear that although Professor Pannenberg is a Christian of Germany (or perhaps because he is a Christian of Germany?[50]), his theologizing is in no essential way affected by the Holocaust of the Jews. However, this is not the necessary fate of Christian thinkers and scholars in Germany or elsewhere. A passage from the young New Testament scholar Peter von der Osten-Sacken, Director of the *Institut Kirche und Judentum*, Berlin, will exemplify the opposite possibility and at the same time bring to summary-focus our initial lecture: "In view of the experience of history ... the Gospel's claim to exclusive truth must be open to theological criticism inasmuch as it lends the Gospel ... totalitarian features that are doom-laden and destructive. This and nothing else is the issue when we seek to come to terms with the matter of Christian anti-Judaism. Once the link between the Gospels' totalitarian claim and Christian hostility to the Jews is realized, a new light falls on the relationship between political anti-Judaism as a totalitarian ideology and Christian anti-Judaism. Both are then seen to be closely and unsuspectedly akin."[51]

It is evident that Professor Osten-Sacken has taken the *Endlösung* to heart. Is the destructive political-theological relation of which he speaks inevitable? I think not. That question will be among our concerns in the second lecture, as we reverse course and endeavor to subject history to the judgment of faith.

"Christianity and Judaism"

1) *Elie Wiesel, A Beggar in Jerusalem, translated from the French by Lily Edelman and the author, New York: Random House, 1970, pp. 199-200.*

2) *Heinz Kremers, communication to author, 19 November 1975.*

3) *Alan T. Davies, "Response to Irving Greenberg," in Eva Fleischner, ed., Auschwitz: Beginning of a New Era? Reflections on the Holocaust, New York: Ktav, 1977, pp. 61-62*

4) *Cf. Moshe Parger, Sparks of Glory, translated by Mordecai Schreiber, New York: Shengold Publishers, 1974, chap. 27 – "The Dance in the Shadow of the Gas Chamber."*

5) *Emil L. Fackenheim, "The People Israel Lives," in Frank Ephraim Talmage, ed., Disputation and Dialogue: Readings in the Jewish-Christian Encounter, New York: Ktav, 1975, p. 304.*

6) *Franklin H. Littell, The Crucifixion of the Jews, New York: Harper & Row, 1975, p. 2.*

7) *Paul van Buren, "The Status and Prospects for Theology," CCI Notebook (Philadelphia), 24 (November 1975), 3. Van Buren's article is based on a paper read before the annual meeting of the American Academy of Religion in Chicago, November, 1975.*

8) *Raul Hilberg, The Destruction of the European Jews, Chicago: Quadrangle Books, rev. ed., 1967, pp. 3-4.*

9) *James Parkes, The History of Jewish-Christian Relations, unpublished address to the London Society of Jews and Christians, p. 3.*

10) *Littell, The Crucifixion of the Jews, p. 2. An example of a New Testament passage sometimes utilized to support the view that the Jews were dispersed from their land in keeping with God's punishment is Luke 21:20-24, where it is adjudged that "this people will be taken captive "among all nations; and Jerusalem will be trodden down by the Gentiles, until the times of the Gentiles are fulfilled."*

11) *Van Buren, "The Status and Prospects for Theology," p. 3.*

12) *Gregory G. Baum, Christian Theology After Auschwitz (Robert Waley Cohen Memorial Lecture). London: The Council of Christians and Jews, 1976, pp. 8, 9, 11.*

13) *Gregory Baum, Introduction to Rosemary Radford Ruether, Faith and Fratricide: The Theological Roots of Anti-Semitism, New York: Seabury Press, 1974, p. 8.*

14) *Others include Charlotte Klein, Willehad P. Eckert, Edward H. Flannery, Eva Fleischner, Malcolm Hay, Friedrich Heer, Jules Isaac, Charlotte Klein, H. David Leuner, Guenther Lewy, Fadiey Lovsky, Reinhold Mayer, Rudolf Pfisterer, Léon Poliakov, Rosemary Ruether, Michael Ryan, Frederick M. Schweitzer, Marcel Simon, Martin Stöhr, and Karl Thieme.*

15) *Cf. Emil L. Facekenheim: "The Nazis were not antisemites because they were racists, but rather racists because they were antisemites" ("The Human Condition After Auschwitz: A Jewish Testimony a Generation After," Congress Bi-Weekly (New York),*

XXXIX, 7 *(27 April 1972)*, 9).

Any who doubt the singularity of the Endlösung may well reflect upon the current conspiracy to deny that it ever took place. Reference is made to the tacit murderers who are now engaged in killing the sufferers a second time, by taking away the victims' first death from them. Thus do these parties comprise a grisly witness to the distinctiveness of the Holocaust. The unique uniqueness of the event is validated through the pretense that it did not happen. Of what other monstrous event in human history has there ever been a plot by reputedly civilized people to say that the thing never transpired? (An example of the effort to deny that the Holocaust ever happened is a book by a professor of electrical engineering at Northwestern University, Arthur R. Butz, *The Hoax of the Twentieth Century*, Richmond, Surrey: Historical Review Press, n.d.)

16)   William Jay Peck, "From Cain to the Death Camps: An Essay on Bonhoeffer and Judaism," *Union Seminary Quarterly Review* (New York), XXVIII, 2 (Winter 1973), 159-160.

The only-ness of the Holocaust is likewise seen in its subjecting of the ultimate truth to the ultimate lie. In May 1933 Hitler said that "the Jew cannot be a human in the image of God, the eternal one; the Jew is the image of the devil" (as quoted in "Federal President honours woman who saved Jews," *Deutschland-Berichte* (Bonn-Holzlar), XIV, 3 (March 1978), 13).

17)   It was early in 1941 that the resolve was officially made to implement the Endlösung der Judenfrage in Europa ("the Final Solution of the Jewish Question in Europe"). The formulation was put forth on the 20th of January in that year, at a conference at Gross-Wannsee, although the actual decision was probably made sooner (so Gerald Reitlinger argues; of his *The Final Solution: The Attempt to Exterminate the Jews of Europe 1939-1945*, New York: A.S. Barnes, 1961, p. 102). Raul Hilberg speaks of the fateful step across the "dividing line" that inaugurated the "killing phase," and he refers to two all-decisive orders by Hitler in 1941 that were to doom all European Jewry (*The Destruction of the European Jews*, pp. 177ff.). The Wannsee agreement was simply the logical consummation of, or it merely gave expression to, a resolve whose roots are traceable to 1919, when Adolf Hitler declared that his ultimate objective was "the removal of the Jews altogether."

18)   Martin Buber, *Ereignisse and Bebegnungen*, Leipzig: Insel-Verlag, 1920, p. 20.

19)   Martin Buber, *Israel and the World: Essays in a Time of Crisis*, New York: Schocken Books, 2nd ed., 1963, p. 35.

20)   There is the allied question of the Jews and the fate of Jesus. The question of the "responsibility of the Jews" for Jesus' death rates no more than summary comment; the "charge" against them should have been placed long ago upon the refuse heap of historical falsehood. That the Jewish people of Jesus' time and their leaders had

nothing to do with any maltreatment or crucifixion of him is discussed in a definitive but predictably ignored study by Justice Haim Cohn of the Supreme Court of Israel, a volume entitled The Trial and Death of Jesus (New York: Harper & Row, 1971). Cohn shows the inconceivability of any Jewish legal or religious condemnation of Jesus. The very notion that Jesus was brought to trial by the religious authorities on a charge of blasphemy, was convicted on his own confession, and was given a capital sentence is wholly out of the question, on no less than seven fundamental provisions of Jewish law: 1. No Sanhedrin was permitted to try criminal cases outside the temple precincts, in any private home. 2. No criminal case could be conducted at night. 3. No one could be tried on criminal charges on the eve of a festival. 4. No one could be convicted on his own testimony or on the basis of his own confession. 5. A person could be convicted of a capital offense only on the testimony of two lawfully qualified eyewitnesses. 6. The eyewitnesses were required to have warned the accused of the criminality of his intended act and the legal penalties for it. 7. The meaning of "blasphemy" is the pronouncing of the name of God; and it is irrelevant what alleged "blasphemies" are uttered as long as the divine name is not expressed (pp. 95-96, 97-98, 105, 112, 116; cf. A. Roy Eckardt, Your People, My People: The Meeting of Jews and Christians, New York: Quadrangle/The New York Times Book Co., 1974, p. 34 and, in general, chap. 3).

On the basis of the foregoing considerations, plus such others as the falsity of the tradition that the Romans were accustomed to release malefactors at Jewish festival times (cf. the account about Barabbas), the thoroughgoing speciousness of the New Testament on the subject of Jesus' trial and death is underscored. It is necessary, however, to insert a caveat here, in the name of realism. Regrettably, historical analysis is a highly limited weapon in disposing of human emotional commitments and in counteracting volitional prejudices. The New Testament documents are not objective history; they are polemical, evangelical tracts. But this datum cuts two ways. On the one hand, it reflects the fact that the records cannot be trusted as bearers of objective truth. But, on the other hand, and lamentably, it points up the consideration that the Christian world is wedded to these documents. Scholarly analysis is severely restricted in its ability to overcome the human bias that is derived from, and sustained by, these sources. In a word, the Christian reformer has his work cut out for him. Insofar as he may be tempted to limit himself to the disseminating of historical truth, his chances of creative influence are not terribly great. It is most essential, therefore, that he not hamstring himself by adhering to one method alone. In a single sequence Ignaz Maybaumn points up this need for extra-historical strategies, and also authenticated the judgment made above that the alleged Jewish responsibility for Jesus' death rates only summary treatment. Maybaum writes: "the ancient tradition that 'the Jews killed Christ' ... has its origin in the twilight between myth and history and is therefore not accessible to historical research" (The face of God After Auschwitz: The Encounter of Jews and Christians, New York: Scribner, 1967, Schocken, 1973, pp. 157-158).

21)   *Alice and Roy Eckardt, "German Thinkers View the Holocaust," The Christian Century, XCIII, 9 (17 March 1976), 251.*

22)   *"Ein Wort zur Judenfrage, Der Reichsbruderrat der Evangelischen Kirche in Deutschland," Darmstadt, 8 April 1948, in Der Ungekündigte Bund, Neue Begegnung von Juden und christlicher Gemeinde, Dietrich Goldschmidt und Hans-Joachim Kraus, Herausgeber, Stuttgart: Kreuz-Verlag, 1962, pp. 251-254.*

Over the intervening years, the Evangelical Church of Germany has moved far from the position reported. In Christen und Juden, a recent official pronouncement from the Council of that Church, the authors reveal an acute awareness of the Endlösung; plainly it is much on their conscience. They speak of the deep trauma that the event created for Christians, of the church's latter day rediscovery of its Jewish roots, and of the abiding integrity of the faith of Judaism. They confess the appalling role of the Christian world in the historic persecution of the Jewish people, including the causative power of Christian antisemitism in the annihilation of the Jews of Europe. The contributors emphasize that a special obligation falls upon the Christians of Germany to oppose the new antisemitism that appears in the form of politically and socially motivated anti-Zionism. Christians have a particular duty to support the independence and security of the State of Israel – not alone as a political reality or human achievement, but also within the very frame of reference of the people of God (Christen und Juden, Eine Studie des Rates der Evangelischen Kirche in Deutschland, Gütersloh: Gütersloher Verlagshaus Gerd Möhn, 1975, pp. 25, 28-31).

23)   *Wiesel, A Beggar in Jerusalem, p. 30.*

24)   *A Begger in Jerusalem, p. 28.*

25)   *Elie Wiesel, The Gates of the Forests, trans. Frances Frenaye, New York: Avon Books, 1967, p. 168.*

26)   *Eliezer Berkovits, "The Hiding God of History," in Yisrael Gutman and Livia Rothkirchen, eds., The Catastrophe European Jewry: Antecedents-History-Reflections, Jerusalem: Yad Vashem, 1976, p. 704.*

27)   *Elie Wiesel, Souls on Fire: Portraits and Legends of Hasidic Masters, trans. Marion Wiesel, New York: Random House, 1972, p. 107.*

28)   *A. Roy Eckardt, "Is the Holocaust Unique?," Wordview (New York), XVII, 9 (September 1974), 34-35.*

29)   *Jürgen Moltmann, The Crucified God: The Cross of Christ as the Foundation and Criticism of Christian Theology, trans. R.A. Wilson and John Bowden, New York: Harper & Row, 1974, p. 51.*
51.

30)   *The Crucified God, p. 134.*

31)   *As cited in Edward H. Flannery, The Anguish of the Jews:*

Twenty-three Centuries of Anti-Semitism, New York: Macmillan, 1965, p. xi.

32)   Frederick M. Schweitzer, *A History of the Jews Since the First Century A.D., New York: The Macmillan Company, 1971, p. 222.*

33)   Moltmann, *The Crucified God, p. 52; emphasis added to the word "only."*

34)   *We must beware of falling into a numbers game. Taken in and of itself, there is nothing singular or impressive in the figure of "six million Jews." For example, out of five and a half million Russian prisoners of war in Germany, some four million were killed. Many more non-Jews than Jews died in the course of the Nazi period. The singularity of the Endlösung lies in the identity of the victims, not in their numbers.*

35)   Moltmann, *The Crucified God, p. 185,*

36)   *The Crucified God, p. 303*

37)   *Irving Greenberg, "Lessons to Be Learned from the Holocaust," unpublished paper at International Conference on the Church Struggle and the Holocaust, Hans Rissen, BRD, 8-11 June 1975.*

38)   *In answer we may point out that such a rejoinder is not able to overcome ideology, because, no matter how valiantly we human beings twist or turn, the "truth" always proves in the end to be our "truth."*

39)   Moltmann, *The Crucified God, pp. 148-151.*

40)   *This account is taken, with some minor changes, from a representation in the unpublished paper by Irving Greenberg, "Lessons to Be Learned from the Holocaust."*

41)   *Emil L. Fackenheim, "The Nazi Holocaust as a Persisting Trauma for the Non-Jewish Mind," Journal of the History of Ideas, XXXVI, 2 (April-May 1975), 375.*

42)   *Robert L. Lindsey contends for the chronological primacy of Luke (in, e.g., "A New Approach to the Synoptic Gospels," Christian News From Israel (Jerusalem), XXII, 2 (1971), 56-63. Lindsey is supported by David Flusser (in, e.g., "The Crucified One and the Jews," Immanuel (Jerusalem), No. 7 (Spring 1977), 25-37).*

43)   *J. Paul Williams, What Americans Believe and How They Worship, rev. ed., New York: Harper & Row, 1962, p. 105.*

44)   *If the one who was reputedly raised from the dead was not the psychosomatic Jesus of Nazareth, we are forced to ask: Who was he? But if he was the psychosomatic Jesus, we have to inquire: Where did he go? What became of him?*

45)   *Where has such a claim ever been made in the Jewish community? The real Jewish point of view is diametrically opposite to Pannenberg's caricature of it. The constant need to rethink and reformulate the legal tradition, a need that lies at the center of ongoing interpretations by scholars and rabbis, is itself the proof that the tradition does not "contain the eternal will of God in its final formulation."*

46) See Charlotte Klein, Theologie und Anti-Judaismus, Eine Studie zur deutschen theologischen Literatur der Gegenwart, München: Chr. Kaiser Verlag, 1975, espec. chaps. 2-3. A thoroughly documented and formidable work, written in a semi-popular way, is Jules Isaac, Jesus and Israel, ed. Claire Huchet Bishop, New York: Holt, Rinehart and Winston, 1971, espec. parts I-III on the wholly positive relation of Jesus of Nazareth to Judaism, Torah, and the Jewish people. Among other relevant works, see Ben Zion Bokser, Judaism and the Christian Predicament, New York: Alfred A. Knopf, 1967, espec. pp. 181-209; David Flusser, Jesus, New York: Herder and Herder, 1969, espec. pp. 44-64; Krister Stendahl, "Judaism on Christianity: Christianity on Judaism," in Talmage, ed., Disputation and Dialogue, pp. 330-342; and Joseph B. Tyson, A Study of Early Christianity, New York: Macmillan, 1973, pp. 373-380.

47) Wolfhart Pannenberg, Jesus – God and Man, trans. Lewis L. Wilkins and Duane A. Priebe, Philadelphia: The Westminster Press, 1968, pp. 67, 257, 258.

48) There is great irony in the fact that Pannenberg's own understanding of the Resurrection is a version of Pauline transformationism (Jesus – God and Man, pp. 75, 77).

49) Pannenberg writes that the Jewish people "represent humanity in general in its rejection of Jesus as a blasphemer in the name of the law." "In fact, the reproach of blasphemy (Mark 14:64) through the claim of an authority belonging only to God was probably the real reason why the Jewish authorities took action against Jesus. ... The rejection of Jesus was inevitable for the Jew who was loyal to the law so long as he was not prepared to distinguish between the authority of the law and the authority of Israel's God" (Jesus – God and Man, pp. 246, 247, 252, 253, 263). In the Foreword to a commentary on the Apostles' Creed, Pannenberg tells of a fundamental change in his views as against a position he had expressed in 1964, according to which the Resurrection of Jesus meant the end, in principle, of the Jewish religion. He has come to believe that a basic distinction is required between a religion of law and the Jewish faith. The God of Jewish history can surmount "the law" (Das Glaubensbekenntnis, ausgelegt und verantwortet vor den Fragen der Gegenwart, Hamburg: Siebenstern Taschenbuch Verlag, 1972, p. 6). However, in the same year Pannenberg wrote elsewhere that "Jesus Christ was not only the prophet of the coming Kingdom, but also became its Messiah and the pioneer and head of a new humanity" ("Zukunft und Einheit der Menschheit," Evangelische Theologie (München), 32. Jahrgang, Heft 4 (Juli/August) 1972, 389). On the other hand, several years later Pannenberg lamented the "eschatological exclusiveness of the Christian understanding of election" as a root cause of many wrong turnings in the history of Christianity. And he fully acknowledged that the Endlösung had antecedents in the Christian persecution of Jews (communication to author, 29 November 1975).

In a massive volume entitled Christsein (Christian Existence), München: R. Piper Verlag, 1974, identified by its author as a "smal

"Christianity and Judaism"

Summa," another German scholar, Hans Küng, includes a chapter on Christianity and Judaism in which he says many of the "right things" about Judaism and the Jews, e.g., that "all anti-Judaism is treason against Jesus himself" and that after Auschwitz, Christendom cannot avoid a "clear admission of its guilt" for the centuries of antisemitism, a guilt that contributed to the coming of Nazism. Yet even in this chapter – a quite brief one – Küng suggests that in the discussion between Christians and Jews today, it would be well for Jews to give heed to the question of the person of Jesus, and he concludes the chapter by emphasizing that it is "as the Christ, the finally decisive, critical, authoritative one" that Jesus of Nazareth makes Christianity what it is (pp. 161, 162, 164, 166). However, the real difficulties with Christein lie in Küng's analysis outside this particular chapter. To choose a few among a great many examples, we are told that Jesus set himself against the Mosaic "law" and its current interpreters; that the Jewish law "sought his death" and indeed "executed him"; and that "in the still-living crucified one" a disgraceful death has become a death "of redemption and liberation" (pp. 281-284, 328, 387). Küng's repeated efforts to soften some of these conclusions both in his book – for instance, we are assured in Christein that the Jews of today can hardly be held guilty for Jesus' death – and in a lengthy conversation with the writer and his wife (Tübingen, 5 December 1975) are not very convincing. He cannot avoid having presented these judgments as constituting the truth. Küng's problem may be associated with the fact that, as he granted to us, his rethinking of Judaism has been prompted not by the Holocaust itself but by the Second Vatican Council. Most fatefully of all, the reinterpretation of Jesus as das massgebende Grundmodell (the authoritative, basic model) for all human beings (Christsein, pp. 542-544) does not overcome the vice of Christian supersessionism in any way essentially different from the Christian claim of the divinity of Christ in the "from above" sense criticized by Küng. His reinterpretation may actually comprise a more dangerous kind of supersessionism than other traditionalist views, because it presents itself in a non-supersessionist spirit.

50)   Cf. Klein, Theologie und Anti-Judaismus.
51)   Peter von der Osten-Sacken, "Anti-Judaism in Christian Theology," Christian Attitudes on Jews and Judaism (London), No. 55 (August 1977), 6.

II

What Do We Really Think of Judaism?

BY PHILIP CULBERTSON

The Episcopal Diocese of Ohio may be seen as typical of Episcopal diocese across the United States. Its 114 parishes run the gamut from high church to low, from wealthy urban parishes to marginal rural missions. The diocese covers the northern half of Ohio, thus including the steelmills of Youngstown, the automotive assembly lines of Cleveland, the oil refineries of Toledo, and the rubber industry of Akron. Unemployment is high in the diocese, and many parishes have begun to suffer financial distress.

Like all Episcopal diocese, ours functions through administrative departments and commissions. I sit on the Diocesan Ecumenical Commission, made up of about a dozen clergy and laypersons drawn from across the diocese, to assist the diocese in keeping abreast of issues in ecumenical dialogue. Our commission is at least as devoted to Christian-Jewish dialogue as it is to dialogue with other Christian denominations. Over the past four years it has sponsored resolutions submitted to the annual diocesan convention, two study tours to Israel and a year-long study project for clergy and rabbis on the Second Temple period and modern Christian-Jewish dialogue.

Philip Culbertson is rector of Christ Episcopal Church, Oberlin, Ohio, and is a member of the executive board of the National Christian Leadership Conference for Israel. This essay is from Christianity & Crisis. May 25, 1981, pp. 147, 155-157 and is reprinted by permission of the publisher.

"Christianity and Judaism"

The 1981 annual diocesan convention was scheduled for early February. For several months members of the Ecumenical Commission had been concerned about reports of rising anti-Semitism across the United States, particularly in the urban East. It became our concern to present a resolution at the convention that would alert our clergy and laity to this returning wave of anti-Semitism and call upon them to oppose it, particularly within our church. The results of the process were revealing.

I was asked to compose a draft resolution for circulation among commission members before starting the resolution through regular channels leading to the floor of convention. The first draft read:

On Anti-Semitism

Whereas, the Christian Church has at times during its history been responsible for the promotion of anti-Semitic and anti-Jewish stereotypes in its theology, its art, its hymnody, and its lack of challenge of cultural stereotypes; and

Whereas, enthusiasm for the renewal of the church's mission and witness has frequently throughout history led to a rise in the persecution of the Jews, based on a narrow and exclusivist interpretation of the Johannine charge, "No man cometh unto the Father, but by me"; and

Whereas, theologians and scholars within the Church continue to grow into a deeper appreciation of the Jewish faith and values of our Lord and Savior Jesus Christ, a heritage underlined in the words of St. Paul, who wrote: "To them belong the sonship, the glory, the covenant, the giving of the law, the worship and the promises . . . . (Romans 9:4-5); and

Whereas, the faith of our Church holds that God does not break promises once made or covenants once sealed, a principle applying equally to the First and Ancient Covenant with Israel, as well as the Second and Newer Covenant with the Gentiles; and

Whereas, the 66th General Convention of the Episcopal Church, meeting in Denver in 1979, adopted a resolution calling upon "the leadership of the Episcopal Church, both clergy and laity, to deepen their commitment to Episcopal-Jewish dialogue and to interfaith cooperation in local communities"; therefore be it

Resolved, that the delegates to this 164th Annual Convention of the Episcopal Diocese of Ohio affirm their respect for the completeness and sufficiency of the Jewish faith, the source of our scriptural and theological heritage; and be it

Further resolved, that the delegates of this convention work to combat any apparent anti-Semitism among the clergy and laity of the church, and to eradicate anti-Jewish prejudice wherever it may be found to exist.

The resolution elicited several responses from members of the commission. One clergy member wrote: "My son is married to a Jewish girl whom we love and we also like her family, but I believe in John 3:3 — Jesus Christ is the only way to the Father and He will take care of the Jews because He chose them first. I would go along with this resolution, eliminating the phrase in the first 'resolved' — 'for the completeness and sufficiency of the Jewish faith.' "

'Doctrinal Extravagance'

Another clergy member wrote, "I am open to theological innovation, but the doctrinal extravagance of 'equal covenants' and the 'completeness and sufficiency of the Jewish faith' is unnecessary, inappropriate and self-defeating of the main purpose of the resolution. I would recommend the removal of the second and fourth 'whereas' clauses and the first 'resolved' clause containing these generalizations."

The chairperson of the Ecumenical Commission and the administrative assistant to the Bishop both phoned to say that while they wholeheartedly supported the resolution, they were afraid that the phrase "the completeness and sufficiency of the Jewish faith" was so theologically loaded for Christians that it would produce enormous dissension on the floor of convention, thereby bringing about the defeat of the entire resolution.

I wanted to make sure this resolution got to convention floor for consideration. I also knew that the Cleveland press covers diocesan convention and that a fight on convention floor over "the completeness and sufficiency of the Jewish faith" would project an undesirable image of the church. I agreed to change the phrase "affirm their respect for the completeness and sufficiency of the Jewish faith" to "affirm their re spect for the Jewish faith," hoping that the removal of this theological stumbling block would assure the passage of the resolution. The resolution thus amended was heartily, though not unanimously, endorsed by the Ecumenical Commission and recommended for passage by both the Diocesan Council and the Convention Resolutions Committee.

On February 7 the Episcopal Diocese of Ohio gathered some 200 strong — clergy and laity — for its annual convention at an elegant hotel in downtown Cleveland. We had all heard the buzz on several potentially controversial resolutions which would be presented: one calling for a change to nonsexist language in the canons and constitution of the diocese; one calling for bilateral disarmament in the US-Soviet nuclear arms race; one setting an embarrassingly low minimum clergy salary; one calling for the establishment of a full-time position at diocesan level for an officer for evangelism and renewal (evidence of the growing charismatic element in the diocese); and the resolution on anti-Semitism. The resolutions were to be discussed the following day, but the convention was already tense with lobbying, heated theological argument and pamphleteering.

Late that afternoon a young priest came to me to say that while he deplored anti-Semitism as a social phenomenon, he could not support a resolution which did not posit the exclusivity and centrality of salvation through Jesus Christ alone. Would I be willing to amend my resolution before its presentation by removing "whereas" clauses two and four? I declined. He then asked if I would be willing to withdraw my resolution, in order to save convention the embarrassment of voting on something that was clearly a betrayal of the central Christian message of salvation. Again I declined. He informed me, with cold politeness, that he planned to submit a substitute resolution which would also deplore anti-Semitism but without compromising the true biblical position that Jews cannot be saved until they accept Christ as their Lord and Savior.

Debate Begins

The next day the resolution was presented to convention with the recommendation for its passage. The first to address it was the chairperson of the Ecumenical Commission: "Very often we think about anti-Semitism and we look outside at the world around us; it's out there. But anti-Semitism can also be in here, within ourselves. I think we need to take a very careful look at ourselves in terms of our relationships with our Jewish brothers and sisters, the language we use, our intent, and exercise care and love in all of our relationships with them."

The next speaker, rector of a charismatic parish northeast of Cleveland, moved a substitute resolution:

Whereas, our Jewish brethren are often, even now as in times past, subject to anti-Semitic persecution; and

Whereas, we are reminded by our Lord to love our neighbors as ourselves; and

Whereas, we are told by our Lord in Matthew 25:31-46 to care for those in need; and

Whereas, the 66th General Convention of the Episcopal Church, meeting in Denver in 1979, adopted a resolution calling upon "the leadership of the Episcopal Church, both clergy and laity, to deepen their commitment to Episcopal-Jewish dialogue and to interfaith cooperation in local communities"; therefore be it

Resolved, that the delegates of this convention work to overcome any anti-Semitism wherever it is found, especially where it is found among clergy and laity of this church.

When debate resumed, the author of the substitute resolution spoke first: "I could not vote for the original resolution because of some of the 'whereas' statements, such as the one suggesting that the new covenant applies only to people who are Gentile by birth. The same problem applies to the passage from Romans 9; . . . the total context says that Paul would rather himself be accursed in order that the Jews might be saved, which assumes that they are not being saved. I would hate terribly to vote against a resolution decrying anti-Semitism, but I would be forced to do so on the basis of the 'whereases' in the original resolution."

The next speaker was the rector of the Episcopal parish at Kenyon

What Do We Really Think of Judaism?

College. "I find myself more bothered by the substitute than I do by the original resolution. My reading of Romans 9-11 does not suggest to me that Paul understands that the Jews are indeed accursed. The close of those three chapters is a clear statement by Paul to his readers of the role of the Jews in salvation history, a role which is not ended by the new covenant, but which is a part of it. This understanding of Romans is not inimical to the Christian proclamation.

"I understand also that confession has sometimes been said to be good for the soul. I think that Christians need to be continuously aware of the facts which are stated in the 'whereases' of the original resolution. It was some Christian teaching of Jews as Christ-killers that did so much to prepare the way for the Holocaust in Germany.

"One of the times that Jews get most concerned for their personal safety is those times of religious revival among Christians. You are aware of the concerns which were expressed in Key '73. There was great anxiety in the Jewish community about what might come of this, because their history told them that the pogroms of ancient times came when Christians really began to rev themselves up in spiritual renewal. Christians couldn't seem to do it without finding a scapegoat to persecute.

'Six Million Lies'

"I don't know about the rest of you, but down in our area we are getting newspaper letters to the editor saying the Holocaust never happened; it's 'six million lies.' We're getting people who are trying to rewrite history to say that the Jews are just trying to manipulate us again. I would like to see the substitute resolution defeated, the original passed, and to accept our role in this — not the role of breast-beating and beating ourselves to death — but to be mature enough to say Yes, we have sinned and fallen short. We do repent ourselves of our sin and seek to amend our lives, and here is one of the ways we'll try to do it."

The next speaker generated a murmur of shock with her opening statement. She was the Rev. Katherine Anne Levin, who spoke with tears welling up in her eyes;

"Ladies and gentlemen, many of you know that I am a Jew. In case there is any doubt about what the rector from Kenyon has said, anti-Semitism is on the rise again. I offer one incident of many. I was raised in the city of St. Paul, which until a very short time ago was known to sociologists as one of the three cities in this country in which there was no visible anti-Semitism. This summer the synagogue in which I worshipped was desecrated. That's one incident of many throughout this country.

"I urge this convention to adopt as strong a resolution opposing anti-Semitism as it can, and I do not believe this substitute resolution is sufficiently strong. First, it ignores the fact that Jews, and that includes Jews today, are the flesh and blood of Christ; and secondly, it ignores St. Paul's statement that the Jews as the people of God are the trunk of the tree of which

53

the church is but the branch. I urge the passage of the original resolution, for the sake of making as strong a statement as possible of the unity of all the people of God through time and through space."

The next speaker was a young lay woman from a Cleveland suburb. "The substitute resolution, if you will look at the third 'whereas,' borders itself on being an anti-Semitic statement. We are assuming that the Jews are in need of our help, urge the defeat of the substitute resolution and the passage of the original resolution."

After further discussion, including the presentation of some statistics from the 1970 study by Stark, Foster, Glock and Quinley, *Wayward Shepherds* (Harper and Row, 1971), which documents the extent of theological and cultural anti-Semitism among clergy in California, the question was called. By a voice vote of approximately two-thirds majority, the substitute resolution was defeated, and debate returned to the original resolution.

Evangelization of Jews

A young charismatic priest from a small parish east of Cleveland rose to address the original resolution:

"I would like to speak strongly in favor of a motion on anti-Semitism, and yet I have very strong concerns about this resolution. The difficulty I have with 'whereas' clauses two and four is that they imply that loving, committed and humble evangelism of Jewish people is an anti-Semitic act. This in turn raises the substantive issue of the finality of Jesus Christ. The Old Testament points directly to fulfillment in the Messiah, and the New Testament proclaims that our Lord Jesus Christ as that Messiah who is the fulfillment of the Old Covenant.

"St. Peter made it a pattern of his life to proclaim to the Jews the Gospel that Jesus Christ is the Messiah. St. Paul made it a pattern of his ministry to go to the synagogues all around the Mediterranean area and to start with the Jews. He stated again and again, particularly in Romans and Galations, that no man can be saved by the law, but only by faith in Jesus Christ. The finality of Jesus Christ is embodied in the creeds of the church and in the Articles of Religion of the Episcopal Church. I would hope that we could separate out the issue of whether evangelism of Jewish people is an anti-Semitic act and give that issue its due consideration in a proper forum.

"And finally, I would like to say that there is a lot of talk these days about human rights. It is my deep conviction that the basic human right of every single person in this creation is the opportunity to hear the Gospel of Jesus Christ preached by people who are committed to that Gospel, who live it with their lives, who share it with humility. I do not believe this to be an anti-Semitic act." '

A layman from a small charismatic parish in the diocese rose to amend the resolution by deleting these words in the second "whereas" clause: "Based on a marrow and exclusivist interpretation of the Johannine charge, 'No man cometh unto the Father, but by me'." He observed, "One of the reasons that

What Do We Really Think of Judaism?

I am limiting the amendment to the second 'whereas' is that I think the reference to Romans in the third 'whereas' is given in such a way that it leaves room for interpretation, and I hope it would not be offensive to those on either side of the theological question. But I find particular difficulty with the theological implications in the second 'whereas' and therefore propose this deletion."

I went to the microphone to address the proposed deletion. "I believe the amendment again begs the issue of addressing the theological concepts which feed the anti-Semitism of the church. I quote from Tomosso Federici, of the Vatican Office on Christian Unity: 'None of the inspired Christian sources justifies the notion that the Old Covenant of the Lord with his people has been abrogated or in any sense nullified. The covenant of the Jewish people is permanent. The church thus rejects in a clear way every form of proselytism. Also excluded are all hateful forms of comparison between Christianity and Judaism.'

"A previous speaker mentioned Key '73; I quote from the Rev. Billy Graham's response to that campaign: 'I believe God has always had a special relationship with the Jewish people. In my evangelistic efforts I have never felt called to single out the Jews. Just as Judaism frowns on proselytizing that is coercise, so do I.' I believe we must defeat this amendment in order to keep before us the memory that our theology, as it stands unexamined, holds out a false challenge to proselytize Jews, a challenge which I feel is a misunderstanding of the Gospel commission."

The vote was called on the amendment. It was deafeated by a vote of 162-111. A voice vote was called on the original, unamended resolution: It passed by an approximately two-thirds majority.

Finding the Moral(s)

The whole consideration of this resolution on anti-Semitism took no more than one-half hour out of a 36-hour convention. In my view, however, there are at least eight lessons to be learned from this all-too-brief discussion:

(1) The question of the relationship between Jew and Christian depends upon some particularly difficult passages of New Testament scripture. The standard exegesis of these passages is generally narrow and exclusivist, and the exclusion from salvation of all those who do not accept the Lordship of Jesus is widely assumed. Few clergy are trained to exegete these passages in a nonexclusivist manner, in spite of the current scholarship in "the teaching of contempt," particularly in the Gospel of John.

(2) It remains broadly held, particularly in charismatic religious circles, that the Old Covenant was a least nullified, if not abrogated, by the coming of Jesus and the failure of the Jews to recognize his true Messianic character.

(3) Proselytizing of Jews is not considered by many clergy to be an anti-Semitic act. They are particularly able to justify proselytism if it is conducted in an atmosphere of "Christian humility."

"Christianity and Judaism"

(4) The theological issues within the resolution on anti-Semitism were argued almost exclusively by the clergy, as opposed to lay delegates to convention. This was not the case with most other resolutions at convention, which were frequently addressed by the laity. Perhaps the laity find the issue of the salvation of the Jews too theologically complicated to address.

(5) The Episcopal Church has consistently, on a national level, affirmed its respect for Jews and Judaism as a living faith, beginning with its resolution on deicide at the 1964 General Convention in St. Louis. Most clergy delegates to convention seemed to be unaware of the Episcopal Church's commitment to Jewish-Episcopal dialogue conducted in an atmosphere of respect and forbearance.

(6) It is very easy for clergy to fall into anti-Semitic thought patterns, as witness the substitute resolution describing the Jews as being "in need." Even while ostensibly deploring anti-Semitism, the clergy tend to view Judaism as an inferior religion.

(7) Charismatics addressing this issue at convention repeatedly argued for a weaker resolution for the sake of "unity" and "not creating offense."

(8) While anti-Semitism may be deplored as a social or economic phenomenon, the clergy are unwilling to let go of the theological and scriptural roots of anti-Semitism, thus separating cultural anti-Semitism, which may be safely opposed, from theological anti-Semitism, which is God's word.

The source of continuing anti-Semitic thinking in a large part of the American population is the local preacher, who is all too unwilling to reexamine his or her personal theology. Anti-Semitism will continue to be subtly and unconsciously taught from church pulpits until clergy are taught to exegete New Testament scripture in a way which does not exclude from salvation the Jewish people, God's first chosen, the contemporary partners in service to God of the Christian faithful.

III

Probing the Jewish-Christian Reality

BY PAUL M. VAN BUREN

C *hristian theology has been wrong about Israel, the people of God, and therefore to that extent wrong about the God of Israel, wrong about the God and Father of Jesus Christ. IN MY LAST conversation with Karl Barth, in 1961 – a conversation that was for both of us in some ways painful – I asked him what he expected of his former students, seeing that he was so dissatisfied with what I was then doing (i.e. developing what was to be The Secular Meaning of the Gospel). Barth's answer was that every page of his Dogmatics was in need of improvement and that we should set to work to make it better. I took him to mean that we should be devoting ourselves to writing footnotes on his work. Instead, I took another path which led to some dozen years of working in analytic philosophy of religion, and that was where I was when the '70s began.*

By the end of the decade, however, I was at work at the task that Barth had asked of me, not as I then heard it, but as I now hear it. The dogmatic or systematic theological work of the church, of which Barth's *Church Dogmatics* is a distinguished crown, is indeed in need of serious correction on every page, and with the years that remain, I mean to continue the task of trying to improve it.

---

*   *Dr. van Buren is professor of religion at Temple University in Philadelphia. This essay is from the Christian Century, June 17-24, 1981, pp. 665-668 and is reprinted by permission of the publisher.*

57

"Christianity and Judaism"
Administrative Tasks

My change of mind in moving from the philosophy of religion to the task of systematic theology came roughly in the middle of the decade. The first third of the decade saw my last efforts at unsnarling the puzzles of religion, taken as puzzles of language. With *The Edges of Language* (1972) I had reached the limits of what I could do to understand religion with the help of the work of Ludwig Wittgenstein, and I was not impressed with the results. I was not impressed with the results which others had come up with either. Some were cleverer than others, but none of them seemed to make much of a difference. Philosophers in general — and so also philosophers of religion — were simply writing for each other, and their results seemed to me to have little to do with the real world.

The "real world" of the first third of the '70s, it will be recalled, included the ever-escalating Vietnam war and the ever-degenerating language flowing out of Washington. It was the Nixon era, the one that ended with Watergate. Perhaps in some indirect way of which I was not fully conscious, the degeneracy of language (and not only language) that was so evident a feature of the last years and final collapse of the Nixon presidency sapped my enthusiasm for the battle for clarity in analyzing the workings of religious language.

I could sympathize with the moral passion of Wittgenstein in the face of a similar situation of linguistic degeneracy in the last days of Hapsburg Vienna. It was the driving power of his philosophical work. I found instead that I was becoming increasingly bored by philosophical analysis. I therefore gave in to the urging of colleagues and accepted something I had carefully avoided all my life: administrative work. I took on the chairmanship of the religion department at Temple University in 1974.

For the next few years, I was engaged mostly with parenting: working to develop the cooperative spirit and patterns so necessary for a department of 20 specialists if we were to listen to and learn from each other in such a way that we could train graduate students together rather than at cross-purposes. Other university administrative tasks were also added, in the form of chairing a review of graduate programs in all of the colleges of the university. Teaching was reduced to a minimum and done mostly with the left hand. I found myself working almost exclusively as an academic administrator, and perhaps I would be doing that now, were it not for the fact that one particular administrative task played a central role in bringing about a change of mind.

Wrong About Israel

The first and primary job confronting me as chairman of the department was to shepherd the troops into making two appointments in Judaism to replace Jewish colleagues who had left us for other institutions. The process took us two years, and I spent a good deal of that time talking with Jewish scholars, reading about Judaism, and reading the works of and finally interviewing candidates. In the meantime, I had to make short-term appointments to keep our offerings in Judaism available for students. The first of these was Rivka Horwitz, visiting in the area from Israel. Just to see how things were working out, I visited her graduate seminar, and there I was introduced to Franz Rosenzweig's doctrine of creation, which struck me as exceptionally exciting and clearly a step ahead of what usually is said on the matter in the Christian tradition.

Rosenzweig, importantly, but also all those other contacts with the world of Jews and Judaism opened my eyes to something I had been looking at somewhat casually all along but had never really seen: Israel, the Jewish people, the people of God, was definitely alive. "The synagogue," "Jewish legalism," and all those old slogans of our theological tradition came tumbling down like the house of cards they were. In their place, actual Judaism, the living faith of this living people of God, came into view. I was fascinated.

I was more than fascinated. In the midst of administrative chores taking more and more of my time, I was set to thinking furiously. The Christianity I knew said that what I was coming to see so clearly simply did not exist, had not existed since Jesus Christ. What I was discovering was something of which I had heard nothing as an undergraduate, seminarian or graduate student. Yes, I knew that Barth had said some highly original and interesting things about ancient Israel and even about the continuing Jewish entity, but the latter was not real. It was but a ghost of ancient Israel, kept alive in the world as only a shadow of something else.

What I was coming face to face with, however, was no shadow, no "indirect witness to Jesus Christ," but a fully historical (certainly "warts and all") living tradition, constituting a quite direct witness to the God of Israel. If Christian theology said that this did not exist, then Christian theology, at least on *this* point, was simply wrong. It was wrong about Israel, the people of God, and therefore it was to that extent wrong about the God of Israel, wrong about the God and Father of Jesus Christ. I was far more than fascinated; I was back at my old discipline, wrestling with fundamental issues of systematic theology. What would Christian theology look like if it were corrected at so central a point? Would it even be recognizable as Christian theology?

Willing to Speak the Language

I thus found myself drawn deeply into the two linguistic communities of the church and the Jewish people. Whatever my earlier difficulties in understanding the use of the word "God", I found that if I were to get anywhere with the problems now confronting me, I had to accept myself as a member of one of those two linguistic communities and therefore to speak with them of the God of whom they both spoke. My older problems did not receive any direct answers. They simply receded into the background; or rather, the position from which I had been asking them was no longer one on which I could stand if I were to take seriously this new (or very old) problem.

Instead, seen from within this tension between the church and Jewish people, what before had been the problem of "God" now was the problem of *God* as the God of both these realities. By entering into their common problem and conflict, I found myself able and willing to speak their language. All the old problems remained, but they now appeared to be philosophical problems, not half so burning as the theological ones. I had run into a paradox and an incoherence that made the philosophical ones seem positively trivial.

The task confronting me — indeed, confronting the whole of theology and the whole of the church, if it were ever to notice it — was therefore to understand and interpret what God had done in Jesus Christ that had resulted in the concurrent existence and history of the church and the Jewish people. Both were there, side by side. I had to understand how this had come about.

No church history I had ever been taught had so much as hinted at the real historical situation. And what was that Judaism of the post-Exilic period, which had produced not only Jesus of Nazareth but also Yohanan ben Zakkai, and which was to flower in not just patristic Christianity but also, during precisely the same centuries, in rabbinic Judaism? Clearly I had much to learn. I therefore escaped at the first decent moment, at the close of my first term as chairman, and went off to read for a year — and think.

The last third of the decade of the '70s was spent digesting, digging deeper and formulating for publication the results of the change of mind that took place during the middle third. The prolegomena, or things to be said first, of the larger (and multivolume) systematic reflection on the matter, subtitled "a theology of the Jewish-Christian reality," has already appeared (*Discerning the Way* [Seabury, 1980]. Rather than speculate about what lies ahead, however, I would prefer to focus now on my perceptions of my context and my work, as these have been influenced by my change of mind.

The Context for Doing Theology

Let me begin with the interesting contextual situation. Here I am at present, and as a result of the change, a self-confessed Christian systematic theologian working in a large department of religion in a state university. Does that make sense? Is that any place in which to do a theology that openly addresses itself to the church? Is that appropriate to a religion department, in contrast to a school of theology or a divinity school? And is this proper, constitutionally, in a state-supported university?

I have not had to appeal to that oldest and best argument for the institution of academic tenure, the unqualified freedom of a scholar to move as his or her research and thinking lead, without being bound by past assumptions or present colleagues. As we have developed our department, we have intentionally left open the possibility that teaching about religion might be carried on by those committed to a religious tradition. Indeed, at least some colleagues outside of our department seem not at all opposed to the discussion and articulation of real theology — in their terms, real religion — within what is, after all, a department of religion.

My response to the question, therefore, will be more substantive. If Christian theology, which may or may not be listened to by the church, needs to be done in full awareness of Jewish theology, as I now believe, and then in due course in awareness of Islamic theology, and eventually surely also in awareness of Indian, Chinese and Japanese traditions, then where better can it be done than in a context in which it must be hammered out in constant discussion with Jewish (and then Islamic, and then Eastern) colleagues and especially graduate students, whose interests — and in some cases commitments — lie in these other traditions?

The history-of-religions point of view has no monopolistic right to be the only ground for the study of religion. If one is moved on *theological* grounds to take other traditions seriously, one has another and most fruitful approach to the study of one's own tradition in the presence of and in relation to other traditions. And where else but in such a department can a Christian theologian have the glorious if frightening responsibility of training, e.g., future Jewish theologians, as well as those who may contribute to turning the church toward new responsibilities?

As I see the matter, there is not in fact any constitutional issue at stake. When I conduct a seminar on, for example, Karl Barth's doctrine of revelation, none of my Jewish students need fear that I am trying to convert them to Christianity. Far from it. We are, rather, asking together how well Barth really understood *Torah* as good news to Israel (quite well, thank you), and how well he understood the teaching of the rabbis that Torah-living by the Jewish people was living by grace (quite poorly, I'm afraid), and whether the correction of his mistake could produce a better theology for Christian self-understanding and perhaps even something helpful for Jewish theology. *Mutatis mutandis*, in seminars on Franz Rosenzweig or Hermann Cohen, we are asking together about the adequacy and helpfulness of their work as theology for the Jewish people, and also what Christian theology has perhaps to learn from them. Does this in any way touch the constitutional prohibition of the establishment of religion?

My students are mostly Jewish and Christian, since the relationship between these two traditions is the center of my work, but we have given much thought to the relation of our traditions to the others, especially to Islam, which stands in a special relationship to ours for both historical and theological reasons. I think I might win some agreement from my students if I expressed a tentative understanding of the matter as follows. It may be that the God of Israel, as King of the Universe, is working his purposes out also in these other traditions — and in our situation, their reality confronts us regularly in the persons of faculty colleagues and graduate students.

We as Jews and Christians need in any case to work out our own self-understanding and understandings of God together, because we share the same name of God and largely the same canon of Scriptures, not to speak of subsequent history (although Jewish history in the world of Islam must be learned and not forgotten by Christians). We should do this, however, in such a way as to be open to the question of whether we can hear in these other traditions the voice we have been disciplined to hear by our own Scriptures. This is (with Schleiermacher *and* Barth) to deny the validity of the concept of natural or general religion, but (*with* Barth and *against* Schleiermacher) to learn to listen to our own Scriptures, in order (with *neither* Schleiermacher *nor* Barth) to listen to the Scriptures of other traditions with sensitive ears for the voice of the God we trust we know, perhaps even to hear a word that may correct our reading of our own Scriptures.

That, I am prepared to argue, is a fittingly scholarly investigation of religion in a department of religion in a state-supported university. May it go on elsewhere as well, but if not elsewhere, surely it can and should go forward where it is currently taking place.

A Christian, Not a Jew

To return to the theme of this series, let me conclude with three points, the clarification of which will help define how my mind has changed in the past decade. The points are that I am now a Christian, doing systematic theology, not "Holocaust theology." First, I am a Christian, not a Jew. The more I learn about Judaism and the Jewish people, the clearer it becomes that I am not a Jew, not an "honorary Jew," not a Jew by adoption or election. I am a gentile, a gentile who seeks to serve the God of Israel because as a Christian I share in the call of that God to serve him in his church, alongside, not as part of, his people Israel. As a gentile, I am bound to that God not by *Torah* but by Jesus Christ. That, as I see it, is not my decision but his, or it is mine only as an obedient acknowledgement of his.

Second, I have returned to the work I left off in the beginning of the '60s, the self-critical task of the church called systematic theology. I have now found a new lens, Judaism, through which to carry on this work, but I am finding Karl Berth once more to be a superbly stimulating and helpful teacher, especially at the points at which I must disagree with him. He is proving to be a better guide than Calvin, Luther, Thomas, Augustine, Athanasius or Irenaeus (with all of whom he was in continuous dialogue) because he was both more thorough and more rigorously systematic down to the smallest detail. He sets a standard for theological work for which we can only be grateful. When I disagree with him, he forces me to think hard and carefully. What more can one have from a teacher?

Finally, in the light of all that has gone on in the '70s, I must say that I do not in any way conceive of myself as a Holocaust theologian or a theologian of the Holocaust. The horror of the Holocaust has surely opened the eyes of many Christians to the reality of the Jewish people. I have told the story of how my eyes were opened, which was not by way of the Holocaust. What

Probing Jewish Christian Reality

Christians need to see, in my judgment, is not the Holocaust, but that which lives after and in spite of the Holocaust, the living reality, "warts and all," of the Israel of God, the Jewish people.

What concerns me as a Christian theologian is whether Christians will come to see that the God and Father of our Lord Jesus Christ is still loved, revered and obeyed by his original love, the people of God, the Jews. And if most of them do not love and serve God, what shall we say about most of those who have been baptized? The reality of the Jewish people, fixed in history by the reality of their election, in their faithfulness in spite of their unfaithfulness, is as solid and sure as that of the gentile church. That is what I ran into and had to see, and that is what accounts, as far as I can tell, for how my mind has changed in the past decade, and my agenda for the future.

IV

Fulfillment Theology and the Future of Christian-Jewish Relations

BY ISAAC C. ROTTENBERG

J*udaism and Christianity both point to the signs of God's active presence in history as the foundation of their hope. The book Auschwitz: Beginning of a New Era? (edited by Eva Fleischner [KTAV, 1977]) contains an exchange between two theologians – a Roman Catholic and a Russian Orthodox – on the question of "fulfillment theology" and its significance for future Christian-Jewish relations. John T. Pawlikowski, following other Catholic scholars such as Rosemary Radford Ruether and Gregory Baum, challenges the traditional "fulfillment" concept as basically inaccurate and calls for new approaches in Christology which he believes will "profoundly alter Christianity's self-definition and make possible a more realistic relationship to Judaism and to all other non-Christian religions." The basic implication of his proposal is that Christians ought to abandon the claim that in Jesus the messianic age has been inaugurated.*

Orthodox scholar Thomas Hopko responds to the challenge by expressing the hope that Pawlikowski's proposal will not be realized, because, he says, "the 'fulfillment' understanding of Christianity [cannot] be abandoned without the destruction of the Christian faith." He fears that the suggested changes in Christology will portend "the end of all meaningful religious and

---

Mr. Rottenberg, a writer and translator, is also a minister of the Reformed Church in America. This essay is from the Christian Century. Jan. 23, 1980 pp 66-69 and is reprinted by permission of the publisher.

"Christianity and Judaism"

spiritual dialogue'' and will result in a "sterile relativism, a monistic spiritual syncretism devoid of creative, truly pluralistic conflict and fruitful, truly creative tension.''

To this growing debate on "fulfillment theology'' I would add a contribution from a Reformed theological perspective: the thesis that New Testament messianic claims can be abandoned only at the cost of sacrificing crucial aspects of the church's witness to the gospel of the Kingdom, but that Christians do need to abandon a good deal of "fulfillment theology'' that finds its source in ecclesiastical triumphalism.

I

The New Testament everywhere contains fulfillment language. In christological context, fulfillment terminology is used to assert that in Jesus of Nazareth, God acted in an ultimately decisive way in history; used in this way, fulfillment language reflects the *fait accompli* aspects of the Christian faith.

According to the most ancient Christian confession, Jesus appeared when the time was fullfilled, and his coming meant nothing less than the breakthrough of the new age of the Kingdom of God (Mark 1:15). In this faith Christians came to see themselves as people who had "tasted the goodness of the word of God and the powers of the age to come'' (Heb. 6:5). In short, an encounter with Jesus as the living Lord was experienced as a foretaste of the future of the Lord proclaimed by prophets and seers. The emphasis in New Testament fulfillment theology is on foretaste, not on the full realization of divine redemption in present history.

Nevertheless, the christological claims of the New Testament can hardly be overestimated. We are told not only that time has been fulfilled, but also that in Jesus Christ the law and the prophets have been fulfilled. In Jesus, claim the early Christians, "all the promises of God find their 'Yes' '' (II Cor. 1:20). Jesus' death was intepreted as an act of atonement and as a victory over the forces of sin and death that hold humanity captive. Thus he was confessed as "Lord of all'' (Rom. 10:12), who has overcome the world (John 16:33).

II

Traditional Judaism has countered these Christian claims with some very fundamental questions. How can one speak of a breakthrough of the messianic era in light of the fact that the world is so obviously unredeemed? Does not the entire "Christian era'' provide one great testimony that the fulfillment of the prophetic promises is still a vision of the future? Some Jewish scholars maintain that empirical evidence shows a deterioration of the human condition since the death of Christ, rather than an improvement.

Redemption, as Martin Buber never tired of pointing out, will mean *Die*

Fulfillment Theology and the Future

Vollendung der Schopfung, a fulfillment of the creation which will amount to the re-creation of the whole world. That particular redemption surely has not taken place.

How then do Christians validate their "fulfillment theology"? A common Jewish view is that Christians seek to escape from the dilemma by spiritualizing redemption. "The thesis of historical Christianity has been 'otherworldliness.'" writes Steven S. Schwarzchild. The messianic idea, according to Gershom Scholem,

> is totally different in Judaism and in Christianity; Judaism in all its forms and manifestations has always maintained a concept of redemption as an event which takes place publicly, on the stage of history, and within the community.... In contrast Christianity conceives of redemption as an event in the spiritual and unseen realm; an event which is reflected in the soul, in the private world of each individual, and which affects an inner transformation which need not correspond to anything outside [*Auschwitz,* p. 218].

Once redemption becomes spiritualized and thus effectively removed from the realm of daily life, the danger of Christianity's becoming a status quo religion is real. Why try to change a world that is so obviously of inferior spiritual significance compared with the salvation of eternal souls for heaven?

Scholem's and similar views do not show the whole picture of Christianity through the centuries; nevertheless, the first response of a Christian to this kind of challenge should be one of *peccavi.* We finally ought to face up to the false claims made in some of our "fulfillment theologies" which have contributed immensely to the prevalent misconceptions about Christian views of redemption. In no way am I suggesting that we compromise our faith, but rather that we confess our sins.

For example, patristic literature is full of polemics that seek to prove the superiority of Christianity to Judaism. "Remember," said Paul, "it is not you that support the root, but the root that supports you" (Rom. 11:18). Faith in Christ's victory, however, was frequently turned into something quite different: ecclesiastical triumphalism.

As a result of this trend, "fulfillment" because interpreted as God's rejection of his covenant relationship with the people of Israel. When the church declared itself to be the "New Israel," it usually did so not in order to acknowledge in gratitude God's new initiatives in Jesus Christ, but rather to reinforce false imperialistic notions about the church's calling. Ecclesiastical claims that run counter to the biblical witness (for example, Paul's affirmation in Romans 11:29 that "the gifts and the call of God are irrevocable") became accepted as New Testament doctrine. The Jewish scholar Uriel Tal was mistaken when he wrote that the idea of God's continued covenant with the Jews "is of course contrary to the theology of the New Testament." That idea is only contrary to the church's false claims of being the "New Israel," replacing and superseding God's covenant relationship with the Jews.

III

Krister Stendahl has pointed out that the only New Testament passage claimed for calling the church by the name "Israel" rests on a mistranslation of Galatians 6:16, a text that really speaks of the original Israel as "the Israel of God." A careful reading of the Greek text, says Stendahl, "must lead to the translation: 'And as many as walk according to this standard [the new creation in Christ], peace be upon them — and mercy also upon the Israel of God.' The Revised Standard Version has suppressed the striking and strong *kai* (= also) before 'the Israel of God.' "

Equally unscriptural claims were made about the New Testament declaration that in Jesus' coming the law and the prophets were fulfilled. A text particularly significant is Matthew 5:17 — the opening words of the Sermon on the Mount. The church has struggled for centuries to gain a clear understanding of the meaning of these words. But the text makes unequivocally clear what Jesus did *not* mean to say. An interpretation this verse seeks to avoid is that the law of God, the law of the kingdom as embodied in the Old Testament, has been abolished, set aside or in any way declared defunct because of Christ's fulfillment. In fact, Jesus came to affirm and give a new foundation to the righteousness of God as embodied in the law. Another interpretation the text wants to make impossible is that the fulfillment of the prophetic promises means that Christians no longer live by promise, whereas the exact opposite is true: fulfillment implies that we live by promise more than ever.

The combination of law and fulfillment, as well as the combination of law and love, is mentioned repeatedly in the New Testament, particularly in the letters to the Romans and the Galatians. The New Testament leaves no doubt of its witness that something radical has happened in Christ's act of sacrificial love. Somehow, Torah, which certainly is more than a set of legal rules, and which refers to a dynamic reality — namely, God's righteousness as it comes to us in our historical existence — has been given embodiment. That embodiment is what Christ came to accomplish, and he continues to do so through the power of the Spirit. In this sense the law is called "spiritual" (Rom. 7:14), while at the same time we are told that only "doers of the law will be justified" (Rom. 2:13) and that through faith we do not overthrow the law but uphold it (Rom. 3:31).

Criticism of the law is not an exclusively New Testament phenomenon; it is found in the prophetic writings as well. In neither case does it reflect a disrespectful view of divine law (which both the Old and the New Testament see as grounded in divine grace), but rather it refers to what is bound to happen to the law when we start "handling" it and using it to establish our own righteousness rather than letting the rule and righteousness of God dwell and become embodied in our midst. Any suggestion that such misdeeds occurred among the people of Israel but are not happening among Christians would bespeak a self-righteousness that suffocates the very truth of the gospel message.

All Christian claims that Judaism confesses a God of law in the formal/ legal sense in contrast to a "Christian God" of grace are based on the false views of fulfillment; such views not only damage Christian-Jewish relations but are devastating for the life of the church itself. First we lose the law, then we lose the gospel of the Kingdom, and finally we end up with the spiritualism and/or moralism with scarcely a meaningful word to say to the modern world. Gerard Sloyan makes an important point when he states that "the teaching church cannot allow the confusion to continue with its grand- iose — and often quite wrong — contrast between the law and the gospel" *(Is Christ the End of the Law?* [Westminster, 1978], p. 101).

IV

Another false interpretation of "fulfillment" is the claim that the people of the Old Testament era lived by promise, while Christians possess the reality itself. I shudder when I read Lawrence E. Toombs's advice to preachers that they should see "the Old Testament related to the New as hope to fulfillment, as question to answer, as suggestion to reality" *(The Old Testament in Christian Preaching* [Westminster, 1961], p. 27). It is sheer heresy to suggest that those who believe in fulfillment are no longer saved by hope (Rom. 8:24).

Faith in Christ means that people have become "partakers of the promise with the people of Israel" (Eph. 3:6), and one of its main fruits is a rebirth of hope (I Pet. 1:3). How can we describe the Old Testament as "question" and "suggestion" and the New Testament as "answer" and "reality"? Does not the Bible from beginning to end witness to the reality of God's presence in the world, and does not an encounter with him always make people dreamers of the Kingdom of God?

Abraham Heschel expressed a basic insight found throughout the entire Bible when he wrote: "What lends meaning to history? The promise of the future. If there is no promise, there is no meaningful history. Significance is contingent on vision and anticipation, on living the future in the present tense" *(Israel: An Echo of Eternity* [Farrar, Straus & Giroux, 1967], p. 127). The Christian believes that in Jesus Christ, God's future has broken into our midst and that there is presence of the promised future in the power of the Spirit. But it is precisely through this presence of the Spirit, which is called "the Holy Spirit of promise" (Eph. 1:13), that the whole creation is made pregnant with longing for the final coming of the future of the Lord (Rom. 8). The Holy Spirit is also called "the guarantee of our inheritance until we acquire possession of it" (Eph. 1:14). To receive the fullness of the Spirit means to be filled with expectation.

69

"Christianity and Judaism"

Jakob Jocz wrote some years ago that "a bridge theology" between Judaism and Christianity "can be accomplished only at the point of a diminution of traditional Christology." This process is being attempted only by a number of theologians, but more promise may be found in a reexamination of the New Testament pneumatology.

Rosemary Radford Ruether repeatedly (in *Faith and Fratricide* and elsewhere) makes the point that the church preaches a fulfilled messianism whenever it forgets the Parousia, losing its vision of the future. Historically, many false claims of fulfillment have indeed found their basic source in a loss of the eschatological perspective. On the other hand, the New Testament witness to fulfillment is rooted precisely in the eschatological vision and in the belief that the future of the Lord, albeit in a hidden and fragmentary way, is present in our midst in the form of signs, first fruits, foretaste and so on. These are all pneumatalogical categories. The key concept of *pleroma* (fulfillment, fullness of the Spirit) in the New Testament illustrates that fulfillment is essentially an eschatologically charged reality.

"God was in Christ reconciling the world to himself" (II Cor. 5:19). In the incarnation and the act of atonement, according to Christian confession, reconciliation has taken place and the possibility of forgiveness is offered to humankind. Christ's work is seen in *fait accompli* terms. But the act of reconciliation does not mean that redemption of the world is now a reality. For Christians it means a renewal and broadening of the covenant (gentile branches are grafted onto the tree of Israel — Rom. 11:17) and a new foundation for hope in the ultimate coming of the future Kingdom. Through the presence of the Spirit, signs of that Kingdom are established in the world. In faith, first fruits of the eventual harvest of the new age are experienced; we receive a foretaste of the fullness of history that is yet to come (Eph. 1:10).

These occurrences take place through the presence of the Holy Spirit; they are spiritual realities. But it is a tragic misunderstanding of the Christian message to interpret that truth as meaning that redemption becomes "spiritualized." One must exercise major portions from the New Testament in order to claim that redemption and the life of faith have nothing to do with the poor, justice, the state, and other earthly realities.

Gregory Baum states that "the redemption brought by Jesus to mankind in the present is prophetic or anticipatory of the future glory; it is a token, a pledge, a first installment of the complete redemption promised in the Scriptures." This assertion is correct, but the christological and pneumatological aspects of such a statement, while intimately related, should not be confused with each other.

Rosemary Radford Ruether rightly rejects an "illegitimate historicizing of the eschatological." The church is not the Kingdom of God; sanctification is not yet glorification; in the first fruits we taste the promise of the harvest but do not possess the harvest itself, and the fulfillment of time is not the same as the consummation of history. Yet the presence of God in history through the Spirit is real. In sum, there must not be an illegitimate dehistoricizing of the *inhabitatio Spiritus sancti* either.

V

Martin Buber used to speak of Judaism and Christianity in terms of "two types of faith." Today a noted Hebrew University scholar, David Flusser, who has a profound knowledge of early Christian literature, in his book *Jews and Christians Between Past and Future* advocates the view that Judaism and Christianity are "one faith." Says he: "When both Judaism and Christianity acknowledge that it is fundamentally one religion, one faith, and do *not* deny it, as still happens so much either out of ignorance or out of dogmatic prejudices — then they can really debate with each other." Flusser's statement seems closer to the truth than Buber's arguments in his book *Two Types of Faith.*

Flusser does not wish to ignore the real differences between Judaism and Christianity. Nor do I. But Jews and Christians share a vision concerning the new heaven and the new earth. They also share some basic perspectives on the nature of God's redemptive presence in the world today, even though the Christian view of history "between the times" is influenced in a decisive way by its christological confession.

At a time when Christians of various traditions are wrestling with questions of political theology, it does not seem to make sense for Jews to insist that Christianity holds an essentially ahistorical view of salvation. That would be tantamount to saying that the Sattlemer Rebbe and his followers, who deny any form of historical realization of eschatological expectations, represent Judaism as a whole. We must move beyond caricatures of each other's faith. When Seymour Siegel notes that "the State of Israel is salvation but not redemption," he seems to come very close to what many Christians mean when they speak about "signs of the Kingdom" in historical existence. Such signs are an embodiment of the promise — fragmentary and constantly threatened by the sinful impulses of humanity, but nevertheless the beginning of the dawn of our redemption. Of course there are also the birth pangs of the Messiah. Both Jewish and Christian literatures have much to say about positive as well as negative signs of the approaching end.

Emil Fackenheim has pointed out that "all attempts to link the precarious present with the absolute future are themselves precarious. . . . Yet, unless the Messianic future is to become ever-elusive and thus irrelevant, its linking with a *possible* present, however precarious, is indispensible. . ." The Jewish scholar here touches on a basic issue with which both Jews and Christians struggle as they seek to read the signs of the times and to approach their historical responsibility with a sense of honesty as well as hope.

Judaism and Christianity both point to the signs of God's active presence in history as the foundation of their hope. The role of Jesus in God's historical-eschatological dealings with the world remains a point of radical difference between the two faiths. Distorted Christian interpretations of "fulfillment" have had destructive consequences for meaningful dialogue. The debate on "fulfillment theology" is therefore of crucial importance, both for Christian-Jewish relations and for the life and mission of the Christian church itself.

The Continuing Christian Need
for Judaism

By John Shelby Spong

W hen Christianity severed itself from Judaism the Christian
faith itself became distorted.
BETWEEN every parent and child there is always a
combination of emotions—one that includes love and hate, dependence and rebellion. Judaism is Christianity's parent; that is a fact of
history. Unfortunately, it has been the negative side of the combination that has marked most of the relationship between these two faiths
through the centuries. Ofttimes the hate and rebellion have reached
inhuman and murderous proportions. Both overt and covert acts of
anti-Semitism have soiled the pages of history with unforgettable
amounts of both blood and shame which stand forever on the Christian church's record.
The negative emotions between the parent and child, however, never
exhaust that relationship. The other side of hate is love, and the other side of
rebellion is dependency. But in the parent-child relationship it frequently
appears that love and dependency cannot be celebrated, and mutual appreciation, acknowledgement of indebtedness and the willingness to learn anew
from the witness of the parent cannot be experienced, until children come of
age.
In our generation, a new dawn may be breaking in Jewish-Christian

*The author is bishop of the Episcopal Church's diocese of Newark. This
essay is from the Christian Century Sept. 26, 1979, pgs. 918-922, and is
reprinted by permission of the publisher.*

"Christianity and Judaism"

relations. I cannot forsake or even modify my deepest convictions about the one I call Lord and Christ, but I can respect and treasure the tradition in which my Lord was born and from which he and the entire Christian movement have sprung. I can also learn from Judaism past and present and find my Christian life enlightened, enriched and deepened by Jewish insights.

It is the reality of this conviction that creates for me the only possible basis for true dialogue between Christians and Jews. Dialogue can never be an attempt at conversion, nor can it occur if one party assumes an objective ultimacy or a superiority for his or her point of view. Dialogue must be an interaction in which each participant stands with full integrity in his or her own tradition and is open to the depths of the truth that is in the other.

In this dialogue I as a Christian want first to acknowledge, then to express my gratitude for, and finally to bear witness to the continuing insights of Judaism that challenge, stimulate and enrich Christianity. If Judaism were to cease to be, if Christianity were to lose that peculiar Jewish witness and these insights were to lose their power or have their distinctiveness blunted, then Christianity would be poorer, more open to distortion. I as a Christian need Judaism to be Judaism lest the ultimate truth of God be compromised or even lost in the shallowness of a rootless Christianity.

Three major themes are rooted in Judaism without which Christianity, especially at this moment in the life of the church, would be adversely, perhaps fatally, affected: the Jewish sense of history as God's arena, the Jewish passion against idolatry, and the Jewish background which illumines the New Testament.

The God of History

At the very heart of Judaism is the understanding of a God who is rooted in history. God for the Hebrew is not an idea to be contemplated but rather a living force to be engaged. God's arena for the Jewish mind is history. The mystery of God is revealed in the ongoing events of life, and any people who would know, serve or worship this God must be willing to plunge into life.

There can be no escape into otherworldly piety if one is to worship Yahweh, for this is the God who brought his people out of Egypt and for whom bondage and slavery are an abomination. This is the God who parted the waters, who led his people by cloud and fire, who covenanted with them at Mt. Sinai, who guided them in their homeless wanderings in the wilderness, who established them beyond the Jordan, who was known in victory and in defeat, in sustaining power and in vengeful judgment, who worked even through Israel's historic enemies to purge his people. This God the Hebrews encountered even when their nation was destroyed and they were exiled. For even in Babylon—a captive people once again—they discovered that Yahweh was still the God of history and that they could still sing the Lord's song in a strange land. The same God, said Jeremiah, who brought you out of Egypt will also bring you out of the north country.

The Continuing Need for Judaism

When the Hebrews told the story of their God, they also told the story of their history, for the history of Israel was the history of their meeting with the holy. They looked at their history not as a museum in which God was encased but as a chronicle of their experiences that empowered and enabled them to press on into the unknown future, for the God who had met this people in the events of yesterday would also meet them in the events of tomorrow.

Holding this conviction, one will always appreciate the past but will never worship it. One will always treasure history but will not be immobilized by it. The God who constantly is doing new things in history can always be trusted to be consistent.

Faith (*emunah* in Hebrew) was not understood to be intellectual assent to propositional statements. "The Faith," that handy phrase which dogmatic religious folk use to designate a body of organized creedal convictions fully worked out with footnotes by C. B. Moss and implying that all revelation has been concluded, was not a concept that the Hebrew mind could embrace. Rather, faith meant an attitude of expectancy in history. Faith was the call to step boldly into tomorrow, to embrace the new—with confidence that every new day would prove to be a meeting place with the holy and enternal God. The opposite of faith was to cling desperately to yesterday, fearing that if one ever left it, one would leave God.

It was because of this conviction about the meaning of faith and history that the Hebrew tradition could produce prophets. Prophets were not predictors of future events. They were those who had the eyes to discern the presence of the holy God in the living moments of history, and they spoke to that insight, opening the eyes of the people of their generation to the realization that God was active in their lives. Security for the Hebrews did not reside in an unchanging tradition. It resided only in the holy God who was always in front of his people calling them to step boldly into the future.

No insight into the nature of God is more vitally needed by our generation of Christians. In this century, change has come more rapidly than the average person's emotional system is able to absorb. We have moved from a horse-and-buggy mentality to space travel, from a pony-express communication system to instant satellite communication; from thousands of separated, independent, local communities to one deeply interdependent society; from enormous distances and the resulting security-fostering provincial prejudices to a globe so small that I have had breakfast in Tel Aviv, lunch in Paris and dinner in New York all in the same day.

The result of this rapid rate of change has been to frighten many persons into seeking some unchanging "security blanket" which they can wear or under which they can hide. For many, yesterday's religious certainty provides that blanket. So they artifically respirate the corpse of yesterday's insights, yesterday's convictions, yesterday's religious experience; they feel secure and they defend their security system with the vehemence of the

Inquisition. This attitude, so prevalent in the Christian church today, is not to be attacked or condemned; rather, it desperatly needs to be understood. These people are looking for God, but faith, as the Hebrew mind understood it, has died.

The living God of history is our true security, not some reflection of this God or some unchanging tradition. This biblical God was and is and is to come. This God of history enables us to lay down our false religious security blankets and plunge into life. We engage history, we risk, we venture, we live. By faith, Abraham could leave the security of Ur of the Chaldees. He left home, kinspeople, security—and went into the unknown in the confidence that God had promised to meet him there.

It is the Jewish tradition that has kept this insight alive—an insight which today contradicts and challenges all of those Christian fears that, in fact, deny belief in the living God of history. These fears manifest themselves in the revival of an anti-intellectual oldtime religion that was not adequate yesterday and gives no promise of being adequate for today or tomorrow. Judaism teaches Christians the value of being theological and religious wanderers and pilgrims. In an age of intense anxiety and rapid change, it counters the yearning to locate our security in anything less than the holy God of history.

A Welcome, Frightening Challenge

The second major conviction of Judaism so clearly needed by the Christian church today is a passion against idolatry. I do not mean what most people mean by idolatry. I am not concerned either with graven images or the kind of idolatry against which so many of my profession rail: the substitution of something like wealth or success for God. I mean rather the idolatry of religious folk who seem to believe that they can speak, act and judge for God himself. I mean the idolatry that successfully tempts so many religious people into thinking that they possess the ultimate truth of God—the idolatry of the evangelical tradition that equates the words of Holy Scripture (usually the King James Version) with the eternal, life-giving Word of God. This is the idolatry of the Roman tradition that believes the truth of God can be or has been captured in the ex-cathedra utterances of the bishop of Rome—the idolatry of many who like to pretend that ultimate truth has been captured in the ecumenical councils of the early church, in the historic creeds, or in the "unbroken tradition of the catholic faith," which usually is the same thing as the speaker's special prejudice.

A major theme of Judaism is the "otherness of God"—the God who can say, "My ways are not your ways, nor are my thoughts your thoughts." This God of Judaism can never be fully symbolized; he can only be pointed to. This is a God whose being is beyond the human capacity fully to comprehend, whose name is beyond the human capacity even to utter. This God is ultimate. His ultimacy cannot be captured by things made by human hands or with words shaped by human lips or with concepts designed by human minds.

The Continuing Need for Judaism

God is ultimate; the church's understanding of God is *not* ultimate. When the church substitutes its understanding of God for the reality of God, we have become idolatrous. Nothing besides God is ultimate, no matter how scared. The bible and the creeds point to God but do not capture him. The tradition of the church may point to the ultimacy of God, but it will never capture him either—and sometimes it may amount to nothing more than sanctified prejudice or pompous ignorance.

Something dreadful happens to religious people when they mistake their understanding of God for God himself. Inevitably, those who believe that they possess the absolute truth of God find it quite easy to persecute those who do not share their point of view. When God's truth is "possessed," wagons are inevitably placed in a circle, for that ultimate truth must be defended. Nothing is quite so evil as fanatical religious people who in the name of God carry out inquisitions, pogroms, heresy trials, witch-hunts, holy wars and crusades. We have ample evidence of this perversion in Christian history, and today's Muslim leader Ayatollah Kohmeini in Iran is absolutely true to his historic prototypes.

The Jewish condemnation of idolatry stands as a constant guard against this mentality. It serves forever to remind us that God, blessed be his name cannot be captured in symbols, words, creeds, Bibles, traditions. Certainly we cannot live without these symbols and traditions; they are enormously important, but their task is always to point beyond themselves to that which is ultimate. If they are ever invested with infallibility or ultimacy, they will become idolatrous—a fact for which Christian history provides ample evidence.

If God alone is ultimate, if he cannot be captured in either words or symbols, then one can never be secure or at peace with faith. But the absence of religious security or religious certainty is a virtue, not a vice. I agree with the wag who said, "If you can keep your head while people all around are losing theirs, you probably don't understand the issues." For me, any religious system that gives or promises to give peace of mind is idolatrous; the price we pay for "peace of mind" will be nothing less than the sacrifice of something basic to our own humanity. We would have to stop questioning or growing.

A major task of the Christian church today is to call people out of religious idolatry into an exciting and fearful religious insecurity. We should shake at the wonder of the vision of God that is always beyond us; we should welcome a future filled with frightening challenges. With its passion against idolatry, Judaism serves as a guide toward this goal.

A Loss of Perspective

Christians have paid a fearful price for their anti-Semitism—a price quite different from the much greater one that Jews have paid. It has not come in physical persecution, in the creation of a ghetto mentality, in insults to personal dignity. Rather, when Christianity severed itself from its Jewish roots, the Christian faith itself became distorted, for it removed itself from the prophetic correction of Judaism. This development produced a Christian inability to interpret our own Scriptures because we failed to see them in their original Jewish context. Such distortion can be observed in the Christian art that portrays our Jewish Jesus as a northern European complete with blond hair and blue eyes. Every New Testament writer save Luke was Jewish, and Luke was a gentile proselyte; surely their Jewishness would have shaped their stories.

Much of the misuse of Holy Scripture, much of the creedal literalism that has caused bloody inter-Christian warfare, is part of the price Christians have paid for the loss of a Jewish perspective in Scripture and doctrine. We severed our roots from Judaism and victimized our own understanding of Christ. This could be illustrated in many ways; one example involves both biblical exegesis and traditional doctrine. It appears in the creedal phrase, "He ascended into heaven."

No story in the New Testament gives literalistic people more difficulty than this one. The first point to note is that the content of the ascension story comes from Luke, and Luke alone. Matthew and Mark have no ascension content unless one counts the last verse of the Markan appendix, which biblical scholars are unanimous in declaring to be a later addition. The fourth Gospel speaks of Jesus' ascension only in the strange Easter morning confrontation between the risen Christ and Mary Magdalene in the garden of Gethsemane. "Touch me not," says Jesus, "for I have not yet ascended to my father. But go tell my brethren," he continues, "that I am ascending to your Father and my Father, to your God and my God." When the risen Christ appears to the disciples on Easter Sunday afternoon, he breathes on them, and they receive the Holy Spirit. The clear Johannine understanding is that the already ascended Lord is appearing; Luke, in contrast, carefully places the ascension at the end of the resurrection appearances.

The second noteworthy feature of Luke's ascension story is its pre-Copernican world view; Luke expresses clear commitment to the truth of a literal three-tier universe. The earth is flat; hell is under the earth, so to get there one must descend. Heaven is above the earth, and to get there one must ascend.

Doctrinal development has tended to ignore the Johannine order, to concentrate on Luke and to literalize the account. In medieval art forms the Christ is portrayed as rising from the earth and disappearing behind the clouds. From our 20th century scientific perspective in which we have seen space vehicles that rise into the atmosphere, we might suppose that the ascension placed our Lord into orbit rather than into heaven.

Had we been in touch with our Jewish roots, however, we might have understood Luke's account in a nonliteralistic manner. We would recognize first that literal human words can never capture the reality of God. If one cannot even speak the name of God, one can hardly assume that human words have the power to capture God's truth.

The Continuing Need for Judaism

We would also see this account in terms of the biblical antecedents. Luke looked to the Old Testament tradition for images that he could heighten in his attempt to describe the divine life and power he perceived in Jesus of Nazareth. One image he used was that of Elijah, conceived of by Israel as the father of the prophetic movement, and whose life in the biblical accounts was surrounded by enormous miraculous power. It was Elijah who had been "received up" into heaven, and it was Elijah who after his ascension poured a double portion of his human spirit on his disciple, Elishah. So Luke, drawing on this Old Testament material, tries to heighten the Elijah story to stretch his language sufficiently to speak about Jesus.

The Gospel writer portrays Jesus as setting his face to Jerusalem where he too will be "received up" into glory. The followers of Jesus assumed that this meant the glory of a re-established Israel, and so they hailed their hero with hosannahs and palm branches. But for Luke, this Jesus was a new and greater Elijah, who like the Old Testament prototype would be "received up" literally into heaven; then, in stark contrast to the Elijah prototype, who bestowed his enormous but still human spirit on Elisha, this Jesus would bestow his infinite spirit upon the church, giving it life to all ages. For that infinite spirit of Jesus would be nothing less the the Holy Spirit of God, which, says Luke, conceived Jesus in the first place.

So the ascension becomes for Luke not a literal event that baffles scientists and historians, but a symbolic event lifted out of the Old Testament and told to open the eyes of faith, to behold this Jesus as he really is—God of God, light of light, begotten not made.

A Fruitful Dialogue

Like the ascension story, many other sections of the New Testament are clarified through examination of Hebrew counterparts. The confusion of languages at the Tower of Babel illumines the story of the overcoming of all language barriers at Pentecost. The feeding of the 5,000 is elucidated by the Old Testament story of manna in the wilderness. The flight to Egypt by the holy family to avoid death leans on the story of the flight to Egypt by the people of Israel to avoid death by famine. The dreaming character of Joseph in Matthew is clearly shaped by the dreaming character of Joseph in Genesis. The murder of the Hebrew children by Pharaoh, from which Moses was spared, is retold by Matthew as the murder of the Hebrew children at Bethlehem by Herod, from which Jesus was spared. Jesus' baptism parallels the Red Sea experience. Jesus' 40-day temptation in the wilderness parallels the 40-year wilderness wanderings of Israel. Moses delivering the law from Mt. Sinai illumines Matthew's Jesus dispensing the new law from the mountain. These and many other parallels could deeply enrich New Testament study and preaching.

To recapture the Jewish sense of a God who is made known in history, a God who calls us to lay down our fears and step boldly into tomorrow, to reclaim that Jewish sense of God's ultimacy so that we can see all other religious symbols as less than ultimate and therefore subject to change, to rediscover our Jewish roots which time after time unlock the doors of the Holy Scripture—all of these can become the fruits of the dialogue between Christian and Jew.

VI

The Uniqueness and Universality
of The Holocaust

BY MICHAEL BERENBAUM

The question of the uniqueness and universality of the Holocaust is being considered with increasing frequency not only in scholarly quarters with a focus on historiography but also in communities throughout the United States where Holocaust Memorials and commemorative services raise a consciousness of the Holocaust, which then enters the mainstream of American culture. In the process the word *Holocaust*, shorn of its particular reference along with its article, threatens to become a symbolic word connoting mass murder and distruction, whatever the magnitude. The debate over the place of the Holocaust in human history is being conducted within the academy, in the streets among political activists and community leaders, in schools by educators developing curricula, among a cultural elite in literature and the arts, and in religious and philosophical circles.

Perhaps it is as much the force of personality as of circumstance that has brought the definition of the Holocaust to the fore. The chief protagonists for alternate conceptions, Elie Wiesel and Simon Wiesenthal, are both survivors, both European Jews, both men of towering stature and magnificent accomplishment in bringing the Holocaust to the attention of the world. Yet these two men differ markedly not only in their achievements but in their

Michael Berenbaum is on the faculty of George Washington University in Washington, D.C. This essay is taken from the American Journal of Theology and Philosophy, Vol 2, n. 3, Sept. 1981, pp. 85-96 and is reprinted by permission of the publisher.

"Christianity and Judaism"

personal histories, their legacy and destiny. For Simon Wiesenthal, the word Holocaust refers to the systematic murder of eleven million people, six million of whom were Jews killed because of their Jewishness and five million non-Jews killed for a variety of reasons in an apparatus of death and destruction designed for mass extermination: the *Einzatsgruppen*, the concentration camp, and the extermination camp. Wiesenthal maintains that although all Jews were victims, the Holocaust transcended the confines of the Jewish community. Other people shared the tragic fate of victimhood.

As a person Wiesenthal personifies two self-characterizations of the Jewish people, *din* (justice) and *am kisheh oref* (a stiff-necked people); he has been tenacious in his pursuit of law demanding that the European nations bring their Nazi war criminals to trial. He has stubbornly refused to abandon the quest for justice after some thirty-five years, when its meaning may have been tarnished by international disinterest and by the absence of appropriately severe sentences. (One war criminal was recently sentenced to the equivalent of 1.5 minutes in jail for every person he killed.) He has also declined to resort to revenge as a swifter, more primitive form of punishment. Wiesenthal hounds both the criminal and the state to remember and reaffirm the value of justice in a world that would prefer to forget.

Wiesenthal's perception of the Holocaust may reflect his most basic post-Holocaust commitment, the prosecution of Nazi war criminals. When apathetic governments are reminded that their non-Jewish citizens were also killed, a greater measure of their cooperation can be enlisted. By more broadly defining the Holocaust, Wiesenthal can intensify the political pressure he can exert. Wiesenthal's more universal predilection may also reflect his present status as a European Jew, namely, that of belonging to a demoralized community that may be psychologically incapable of taking a Judeocentric perspective in the public domain--preferring instead the aphorism of Gordon, ''be a Jew in your own home and a man in the street,'' even if in this instance the choice of a wider definition is more efficacious. Yet lest we lose perspective here, we should remember that in over 200 panels in the museum of the Simon Wiesenthal Center for Holocaust Studies in Los Angeles, less than 7% mention the five million non-Jews, and half of those displays center on the righteous among the nations who lived with the Jews, fought beside them, helped rescue Jews, and eventually died with them. Those who would contend that there is a major dilution of the Jewish meaning of the Holocaust in the work of the Wiesenthal Center had better look elsewhere for the substantiation of their accusations.[1]

Wiesenthal himself, it should be added, is not the only person who has included non-Jews among those killed in the Holocaust nor has he become an active participant in the debate over definition. Rather, his general position and his stance in the past have led to his being seen by others as the representative of a ''universalist'' posture that some interpret as an affront to the unique experience of the Jews in the Holocaust.

Uniqueness and Universality of Holocaust

By contrast, Elie Wiesel is the poet laureate of the Holocaust, a man who has become, in the words of Steven Schwarschild, "the defacto high priest of our generation," the one who speaks most tellingly in our time of our hopes and fears, our tragedy and our protest.[2] If Wiesenthal represents justice and the tenacity of the Jewish soul, Wiesel stands as the embodiment of *shirah* (poetry) and *Rachamim* (compassion). Wiesel relates to the Holocaust as the *mysterium tremendum* (sacred mystery) that can be approached but never understood, the *PARDES*, a world that one can only apprehend at great peril and that should not be approached without preparation and extreme caution. Elsewhere I have written at great length of Wiesel's abiding significance as a thinker and his impact on contemporary Jewish consciousness.[3] Wiesel's contribution as a writer and story-teller toward keeping the memory of the Holocaust alive and transmitting it to my generation and beyond should not be underestimated. Wiesel fears that Wiesenthal's definition of the Holocaust may set in motion an irreversible process by which the memory of the six million Jews will be erased. First, he argues, people will speak of 11 million people, 6 million of whom were Jews, then of 11 million people some of whom were Jews, and finally of 11 million people without any reference to Jews.

Wiesel is the only American Jewish author of reknown who writes solely from a Jewish perspective and for whom the process of Americanization was never central to his tale or to his literary contribution. Even though Wiesel has been an American citizen for close to two decades, he continues to write in French and, unlike other of his literary contemporaries, he has not reflected upon the American Jewish experience in any significant way. His novels are primarily set in Europe or Israel, and few American characters ever appear. (*The Accident*, a lone exception, is set in New York but deals with the psychological scars left by the Holocaust on a survivor, and in that sense the American setting is irrelevant.) Nevertheless, it was as an American figure that Elie Wiesel was appointed Chairman of the President's Commission on the Holocaust and its successor body, the United States Holocaust Memorial Council, which is charged to create a national museum to tell the story of the Holocaust, to transmit the legacy of Jewish suffering to a general American audience. In my opinion, the task of the Holocaust Memorial Council involves the Americanization of the Holocaust; that is, the story must be told in such a way that it resonates not only with the survivor in New York, his son in Houston or his daughter in San Francisco, but with the Black leader from Atlanta and his child, the farmer from the Midwest, the industrialist from the Northeast, and the millions of other Americans who each year make a pilgrimage to Washington to visit their nation's capital. The Americanization of the Holocaust is an honorable task provided that the story told is truthful, faithfully representing the historical event in a way that can be grasped by an American audience. Each culture inevitably leaves its stamp on the past it remembers. Israel, for example, has retold the story of the Holocaust as *Shoah ve Gevurah* (Holocaust and

Resistance), emphasizing the pockets of armed rebellion along with the victimization that was in fact more prevalent. The intersection of the historical event and societal need, what happened and what can be understood, leaves neither history nor society unchanged. Indeed, this process is integral to the formation of what sociologists have termed the civil religion of a given society.through the Holocaust/Resistance tale, Israelis have linked their origins to the heroic warriors who defied the mighty powers of the world in order to affirm the honor and dignity of the Jewish people. Charles Leibman, who has written eloquently of the civil role of the Holocaust in the Israeli consensus, has shown the degree to which the Holocaust tale has been shaped by societal need.

The task of the National Memorial Council in America in designing a museum is far more difficult than was Israel's endeavor at Yad Vashem (the Israeli Holocaust memorial museum), for the Council must address itself to an audience that finds the tale itself alien and not directly a part of the American experience. The Council also runs the risk of creating a magnet for antisemitism if others who perceive themselves, rightly or wrongly, as victims of the Holocaust feel excluded from the memorial and/or sense that their suffering has been trivialized or denied. The museum must grapple intelligently and painfully with the problem of complicity with the Nazis in the destruction of the Jews by people who were themselves the victims of Nazism, and it must struggle with the dilemma of the bystander in a way that makes sense of the few successes and many failures of American policy toward the Holocaust during and following the war.

Enter the historians--Yehuda Bauer, the prominent historian and Head of the Institute of Contemporary Jewry at the Hebrew University in Jerusalem, distinguished between two definitions of the Holocaust offered in speeches by the then President of the United States, Jimmy Carter. Carter twice defined the Holocaust, once speaking of the memorial to "six million Jews and millions of other victims of Nazism during World War II" and on another occasion decrying the "systematic and state-sponsored extermination of 6 million Jews and 5 million non-Jews." Bauer comments:

> the memorial as seen by the President [not the Commission] should commemorate all the victims of Nazism, *Jews and non-Jews* alike and should *submerge* the specific Jewish tragedy in the general sea of atrocities committed by the Nazi regime (emphasis added).[4]

Bauer attributed what he perceived as a submersion of the specific Jewish tragedy to pressure from ethnic groups within America and warned that an Americanized, non-Jewish memorial would misrepresent the Holocaust. Professor Bauer marshals three highly emotional arguments to foster his claim. He invokes the Russian attempt to deny the Jewishness of the Holocaust, which resulted in the abomination of the memorial at Babi Yar, where no mention of Jews is made either in the content of the sculpture or in an inscription on the memorial. Secondly, Bauer refers to the Western denial of the particular "War Against the Jews," which led to the failure to rescue. Thirdly, Bauer alludes to the international antisemitism that seeks to deny the Holocaust altogether.

We must separate the emotional elements of these arguments from their substantive components. It is ironic that Bauer should focus on the President's words when Carter had delegated responsibility for designing and implementing the museum to the Holocaust Memorial Council, which consistently and conspiciously chose over and over again to emphasize the uniqueness of the Jewish experience and the centrality of Jewish suffering. For Bauer, displaying an almost mythical regard for the power of a president, Carter's words on a ceremonial occasion or in a message to Congress were viewed as all-important, while the deliberations of the Commission, its *Report to the President*, which is the central document of the legislative history of the Holocaust Memorial Bill, and indeed the work of the Council in implementing its recommendations were seen as secondary. Notice also that *inclusion* of others (non-Jews) is transformed in Bauer's logic to *submergence* in the general sea of atrocities. Why, indeed, must inclusion become submergence if, as was argued in the Commission Report and in what follows, the uniqueness of the Jewish experience can only be detailed and documented by comparing it with the Nazi treatment of other subservient populations persecuted by the Nazis? Only by understanding the fate of others who suffered, where it paralleled the Jewish experience and more importantly where it differed, can we demonstrate the distinctive character of the Jewish fate as a matter of historical fact.

With respect to Bauer's fear of Americanization, the question of audience should not be confused with content. The Holocaust is only "Americanized" in so far as it is explained to Americans and related to their history with ramifications for future policy. Insights can be gained from the study of the Holocaust that have a universal import for the destiny of all humanity. A Presidential Commission funded at taxpayers' expense to design a *national* memorial does not have the liberty of creating an exclusively Jewish one in the restricted sense of the term, and most specifically with regard to audience. Such is the task of the American Jewish Community operating with private funding and without government subvention. In the final analysis, private Jewish memorials and the national Holocaust museum (along with work of scholarship, art, and media productions) will speak a message that will endure in America far longer than the words of an American President.

There is a fundamental paradox that reflects itself in an ambivalence expressed by many survivors and shared by other Jews about bequeathing the story of the Holocaust. For the Holocaust to have any sustained impact it must enter the mainstream of international consciousness as a symbolic word denoting a particular, extraordinary event with manifest moral, political, and social implications. The moment it does enter the mainstream, however, it becomes "fair game" for writers, novelists, historians, theologians, and philosophers from all backgrounds and with unequal skill. Some lesser minds or insensitive talents are bound to disappoint, dilute, and misrepresent. Transmitting the Holocaust entails a degree of uncontrolled dissemination. We cannot simultaneously maintain the Holocaust as a horribly sanctified topic untrespassed and inviolate while complaining that the world· is ignorant of its occurrence. Even for Wiesel, the decision to run the risks of exposure began the day *Night* was published in French rather than remaining in its Yiddish original, which was printed five years earlier. Nonetheless, Bauer does provide his readers with a valuable definition of the uniqueness of the Holocaust, which he sees as containing two central elements: the planned, total annihilation of an entire community and a quasi-apocalyptic, religious component whereby the death of the victim becomes an integral ingredient in the drama of salvation. Bauer adds that "to date such an act has only been directed against the Jews." As we shall see, Bauer presents us with two necessary but perhaps not exhaustive conditions for the uniqueness of the Holocaust.

Bauer displays no discomfort with the word *Holocaust* even though the term itself is not without its problems. Holocaust is a theological term in origin rather than a historical one. It is an English derivative from the Greek translation of the Hebrew word *olah* meaning a sacrificial offering burnt whole before the Lord. Some serious students of the Holocaust have maintained that the word itself softens and falsifies its impact by imparting religious meaning to the events.[5] The Yiddish word *churban*, meaning destruction, is far more stark and refers to the results of the event itself. The Hebrew word *Shoah* shares much in common with its Yiddish antecedent. Bauer's views are essentially supported with but minor modifications by scholars such as Lucy Dawidowicz, Uriel Tal, and George Mosse. Their work centers on intent and ideology. There is another argument for the uniqueness of the Holocaust that focuses not on its purposes or ideology but on the mechanisms of destruction and the creation of concentration and extermination camps. This argument is culled from the work of Raul Hilberg who centers his research not on the philosophy that underscored the destruction but on the processes by which Jews were executed. In fragmented form, Hannah Arendt, Lawrence Langer, Richard Rubenstein, and Joseph Borkin also examine this dimension of the Holocaust. Its importance should not be overlooked, for its implications are far too critical.

Joseph Borkin has argued that Auschwitz represented the perverse perfection of slavery. In almost all previous manifestations of human slavery, including the particularly cruel form practiced in NORTH America, the slave was considered a capital investment to be protected, fed, and sheltered by the master and generally permitted the opportunity to reproduce and hence increase his master's wealth. In contrast, under Nazism the human being was reduced to a consumable raw material, expended in the process of manufacture, from which all material life was systematically drained before the bodies were recycled into the Nazi war economy, gold teeth for the treasury, hair for mattresses, ashes for fertilizer. At I.G. Auschwitz the average slave lived for ninety days, at Buna, thirty. As one survivor put it, "they oiled the machines, but they didn't feel the need to feed the people." These corporate decisions, Borkin hastens to remind us, were made in Frankfurt and *not* in the field, made for "sound" economic reasons and not under the exigencies of battlefield conditions.

Yet it was not only slavery that reached its most demonic, absolute expression at Auschwitz. The need to eliminate surplus population, as Rubenstein explains, was also carried to its logical conclusion. Bureaucracy was perfected to tackle ever more difficult problems in the machinery of destruction. The coexistence of demonic evil with banal evil in a bureaucratic mechanism points to another unique dimension of the Holocuast.

The camps themselves represent a society of total domination, one which Langer has called the universe of choiceless choices. Langer has explained that Auschwitz was a world apart, shattering our conceptions of language and meaning and remaining with us, now some three-and-a-half decades later, for it eludes the inner space or time in which to bury it:

> The fault lies not in our own deficient vision but in the nature of the experience, which challenges our imagination with a nearly impossible task. Confrontation with the springs of conduct in the death camps represents less a recollection of times past (with the observer imposing a Proustian order on chaotic material) than a collection of past moments, whose intrinsic chaos urges us to invent a new moral and temporal dimension for its victims to inhabit.[6]

No theory of the uniqueness of the Holocaust that refuses to probe the inner dimensions of the mechanisms of destruction will suffice, for it is in the inner world of how the terrible crime was committed, as much as in the conception of the deed or its importance, that an understanding of the unparalleled world of the Holocaust must be sought.

In response to Bauer, the prominent Jewish historian and Dean of Graduate Studies at the Jewish Theological Seminary, Professor Ismar Schorsch, entered the dialogue. Schorsch joined with those advocating a limited role to the Holocaust in the civil religion of American Jews, fearing a lacrymose theory of Jewish history.[7] The history of Jew as victim threatens to dominate Jewish consciousness, to diminish the totality of Jewish history in which the Jews were the authors of their own destiny, and to overwhelm the vital, energizing celebration of life or the hope for redemption. Moreover, Schorsch argues, the consequence of an overemphasis on the Holocaust has been an "obsession with the uniqueness of the event as if to forgo the claim would be to diminish the horror of the crime."[8]

"Christianity and Judaism"

The truth, Schorsch argues, is that Jews were the only victims of genocide in World War II. "To insist on more is to imply or overindulge in invidious comparisons" either of which evokes earlier or later genocide. When used indiscriminately the argument for the uniqueness of the Holocaust is a "throwback to an age of religious polemics, a secular version of chosenness."[9] This argument is seen most clearly in the writings of the orthodox Jewish theologian Eliezer Berkovitz in which he writes:

> The metaphysical quality of the Nazi-German hatred of the Jews as well as the truly diabolical, superhuman quality of the Nazi-German criminality against the Jews are themselves testimonies to the dark knowledge with which a nazified Germany sensed the presence in history of the hiding God.[10]

For Scorsch the claim of uniqueness is both historically unproductive and politically counterproductive, for it "impedes dialogue and introduces issues that alienate potential allies from among other victims of organized depravity," i.e. other victims of Nazism, Armenians, Gypsies, Blacks, etc. Schorsch recommends that Jews translate their experience into existential and political symbols meaningful to non-Jews without "submerging our credibility." What for Schorsch is the process of translation appears to Bauer as Americanization and dejudaization. When the Holocaust is properly communicated to Americans, it can assume its rightful place as a symbolic orienting event within human history, pregnant with meaning and implications for our common destiny.

II

While I find Bauer's characterization of the uniqueness of the Holocaust inadequate and Schorsch's resistance inappropriate, both Bauer's assertions and Schorsch's reticence could be informed by a more comparative approach to understanding the Holocaust. The fruits of such consideration are amply apparent in important works such as Irving Horowitz's study of the Holocaust and the Armenian Genocide, *Taking Lives*, Helen Fein's *Accounting for Genocide*, and the literary analysis of Terrence Des Pres. A search for uniqueness need not alienate potential allies for it might properly sharpen our insights into areas in need of greater research and additional scholarship. Nevertheless, Schorsch's inhibiting cautions, like Bauer's misplaced fears, should be taken as warning signals of what must be avoided in order to secure serious scholarship and responsible application.

Professor John Cuddihy of Hunter College is an informed, brilliant, yet eccentric critic of contemporary American Jewry. His insights often glisten even if they do not long endure deep introspection--his information is wide-ranging and his comparative understanding of modernity and the Jewish condition original and innovative, exciting even if not entirely accurate or friendly. Cuddihy probes critically not the history of the Holocaust but its historiography. To his credit, Cuddihy had the courage to present the original version of some of his work to a faculty seminar of Holocaust scholars from the Northeast to sharpen his thoughts through dialogue and open exchange.[11] He first cites a number of scholars, all of whom are making similar points regarding the Holocaust as unique in its character, in its systematic, senseless, and non-instrumental organization, in its totality and its focus on death. For Henry Feingold, perhaps the most important historian of the Roosevelt Administration in relationship to the Jews, the danger is that we may rob the Holocaust of its horrendous particularity. We may generalize and modulate Nazism by treating it not as a uniquely demonic force but as the dark side of the human spirit that lurks in all of us. For A. Roy Eckardt, a Christian theologian of the Holocaust, the event is "uniquely unique," a category apart from even those historical events one would classify as unique. In his critical work *The Cunning of History*, Richard Rubenstein projects the precedent of the Holocaust toward its present and future ramifications, as noted by William Styron both in his introduction to Rubenstein's work and in his novel *Sophie's Choice*. For both Rubenstein and Styron the Holocaust looms as the extreme technological nightmare, the manifestation extraordinaire of the potentialities of Western civilization. Emil Fackenheim, by contrast, believes that the uniqueness of the Holocaust is found in the uniqueness of its victims. The Holocaust was directed against Jews who were "not the *waste products* of Nazi society but its *end product*,"[12] (italics added). In reviewing these claims of uniqueness, Professor Cuddihy has remarked that the distinction between Jews and non-Jews is the key element that unites Fackenheim and Feingold, Bauer and Wiesel. The "residual category" of non-Jews that continues to divide the world serves three critical functions for the Jews. It preserves the sacred particularity of the Jews, freezing the presence of antisemitism in the consciousness of the Jew and thus eliminating the Sartresque question "Why remain a Jew?" It continues to separate the Jew from the Gentile not as the free choice of the Jews but the imposed decision of Hitler who divided Jews from non-Jews and caused the ultimate separation of their fates. Thirdly, according to Cuddihy, uniqueness functions not so much for preventing historical fraud, denials, or dejudaization, but as a continuing device for conferring status.

In fairness to Cuddihy, me must stress that his concern is not history but sociology, and he is writing something of a cryptosociology of historiography. Often one can dissent from his views with much ease, especially when his statements are flip and inaccurate. Yet one must examine his claim that inherent in the desire to affirm the uniqueness of the Holocaust, apart from the issue of its factual validity, may be a secular translation of Jewish choseness wherein the specialness of the people, once formulated in terms of spiritual descent from the recipients of the divine revelation at Sinai, is now recast as the inheritance of those wronged by the most demonic, the anti-

God, so to speak, which acted at Auschwitz.

In response to the arguments of Cuddihy and others, it is incumbent upon us to consider the factual arguments for the uniqueness of the Holocaust and the resistance to the centrality of the Holocaust in contemporary Jewish consciousness that is currently surfacing in discussions among Jewish historians and theologians. Questions about the uniqueness and universality of the Holocaust in world history are accompanied by queries regarding the place of the Holocaust in Jewish history. The current discussion centers on three major questions: whether the Holocaust is indeed unprecedented within Jewish history; whether it occupies an all too prominent position in contemporary Jewish consciousness, threatening to obscure and perhaps even exclude the promise of Sinai, the triumph of Israel, and the totality of previous Jewish history; and whether the Holocaust has normative implications for Jewish history and theology. To rehearse the parameters of the dialogue and summarize the discussions between Jacob Neusner and Irving Greenburg, the *New York Times* article by Paula Hyman, the theology of Michael Wyschogrod, the writing of Robert Alter, and both the public and printed debates between Arnold Wolfe and myself would sidetrack us at this juncture.[13] Suffice it to say that essential to the general argument for the uniqueness of the Holocaust is the more specific conclusion that the Holocaust is not only quantitatively but qualitatively different from other episodes of persecution in Jewish history, a point not universally accepted by some scholars in the field, whose objections are often motivated by the politics and aesthetics of Holocaust commemoration rather than by specific historical data.

Elsewhere I have indicated my own conviction that the Holocaust is unprecedented in Jewish history; it was not simply a continuation of traditional antisemitism for four fundamental reasons. The Holocaust differs from previous manifestations of antisemitism in that the earlier expressions were episodic, non-sustained, illegal (they took place outside the law), and religiously rather than biologically based. (That is, Jews were killed for what they believed or practiced; conversion or emigration were possible alternatives.) By contrast, Nazism was unrelenting; for twelve years the destruction of the Jewish people was a German priority. Trains that could have been used to bring soldiers to the front or transport injured personnel to the rear were diverted to bring Jews to their death. The persecution of Jews was geographically widespread throughout Europe from Central Russia to the Spanish border. Furthermore, it was legally conducted, the legal system serving as an instrument of oppression. The persecution of Jews and their annihilation was a policy of state, utilizing all facets of the government. Most importantly, Jews were killed not for *what* they were, for what they practiced or believed, but for the *fact* that they were--all Jews were to be exterminated, not merely the Jewish soul. Jews were no longer considered, as they were in Christian theology, the symbol of evil; rather, they had become its embodiment and as such were to be eliminated.

Uniqueness and Universality of Holocaust

Even the traditional category of Jewish martyrdom was denied to the victims of the Holocaust, for they lacked the essential element of choice in their deaths. Since they did not die because of their beliefs but due to the accident of their biological birth as Jews (or the children or grandchildren of Jews), a new category of martyrdom, a new language, had to be invented.

The Jewish uniqueness of the Holocaust can also be considered a matter of historical fact, not of theological faith, the case for which becomes even more apparent when the fates of other victims of Nazism, such as the Poles, are included. Undoubtedly, the Nazis planned to destroy the Polish intelligentsia and to Germanize the elite Polish youth by arranging for their adoption and assimilation into the dominant culture. This plan for destruction and assimilation was part of the overall effort to make the Poles a subservient yet useful population for Germany. For the Jews subservience was insufficient; the aim was annihilation, the killing of every Jew regardless of his or her potential usefulness to the Germans (as Mordecai Chaim Rumkowski, the leader of the Loaz Judenrat who predicated the survival of his ghetto on its undeniable utility and absolute subservience to the Nazis, learned to his ultimate dismay). The Nazis wished to eradicate all Jews from the face of the earth.

When we consider the fate of the Gypsies, who share with the Jews the unfortunate distinction of being targeted for destruction, we discover more differences between the fate of the Jews and others in the Holocaust. While the Gypsies were killed in some countries, they remained relatively untouched in others. The fate of rural Gypsies often differed. By contrast, the murder of Jews was a priority in every country the Nazis invaded. In country after country the Nazis pressed the bureaucracy to process the Jews for the complete implementation of their "final solution."while the Gypsies were murdered as asocials, the destruction of the Jews had an apocalyptic, religious character to it that made it psychologically central to the Nazi drama of salvation for the German people. Even though Gypsies were also subject to gassing and other forms of extermination, the number of Gypsies killed was not as vast and individual death by gassing was far less certain than it was for Jews. I stress these comparisons not to diminish the loss to these communities or the significance of each death. Jewish tradition teaches that every death shatters creation. However, the distinctness of the Jewish fate cannot be understood except in contrast with and relationship to the fate of the other victims of Nazism.

Like Gypsies, homosexuals were arrested and incarcerated, and many Ukrainians were sent to concentration camps where they were jailed as prisoners of war, yet a Ukrainian or a gay could hope to outlive the Nazis merely by surviving. In contrast, all Jews lived under the sentence of death. The ovens and the chambers were primarily restricted to Jews. An apparatus originally designed for the retarded and the mentally disturbed consumed the Jews, though in all likelihood it would not have ceased its operation had the Nazis won both the World War and the War Against the Jews.

"Christianity and Judaism"

Bohdan Wytwytzky, a young philosopher from Columbia, has offered a compelling image for describing the Holocaust when he refers to the many circles of hell in Dante's Inferno. The Jews occupy the center of hell with the concentric rings extending outward to incorporate many other victims much as the waves of water spread outward with diminishing intensity from a stone tossed into a quiet lake. In order to comprehend the Jewish center, we must fully probe the ripple effects as well as the indisputable core.

In arming themselves to protect the uniqueness of the Holocaust, many defenders of the faith (rather than the fact) have shied away from comparisons with other instances of subjugation or mass murder. Such comparisons do not innately obscure the uniqueness of the Holocaust; they clarify it. Inclusion of the Armenian experience, for example, in commemorating the Holocaust does not detract from the uniqueness of the Holocaust but deepens our moral sensitivity while sharpening our perception. Additionally, such inclusion may intensify our moral worth since it displays a generosity of spirit and an ethical integrity. We let our sufferings, however incommensurate, unite us in our condemnation of inhumanity rather than deride us in a calculus of calamity.

The exploration of the analogies between the Armenian Genocide and the Holocaust establishes several themes that are central to the moral lessons of the Holocaust. For example, Hitler used the excuse of the world's indifference to Armenian suffering to silence his Cabinet opposition and as a license to proceed at will with the destruction of the Jews without the fear of permanent negative consequences. If our aim is to teach that remembrance of the Holocaust might prevent future catastrophe not only to Jews but to other people as well, then what better example is there than the Armenian one? Similarly, one can probe with fruitful results the influence of Henry Morgenthau, Sr., the American Ambassador to Turkey during the Armenian massacres, on his son and namesake, the courageous Secretary of the Treasury who confronted President Roosevelt with undeniable evidence of American inaction, if not complicity, with the extermination of European Jewry. The Jewish resistance fighters at Bialystok invoked the memory of Mesudah, the Armenian uprising, in fighting for freedom and honor.

Common to all these examples are three principles for dealing with events analogous but not equivalent to the Holocaust. The analogies must flow from history, they must illuminate other dimensions of the Holocaust and/or the analogous event, and finally, they must be authentic. If these three principles are followed, then we need not fe .ar engaging in analogies that illumine our scholarship and our memory. They will not trivialize nor dejudaize the Holocaust.

Uniqueness and Universality of Holocaust

1) *Oral Communication, the Simon Wiesenthal Center for Holocaust Studies, Los Angeles, California.*
2) *Steven Schwarzchild, "Jewish Values in the Post-Holocaust Future,"* Judaism *Vol. 16, No. 3 (Summer, 1967):157.*
3) *Michael Berenbaum*, The Vision of the Void *(Middletown: Wesleyan University Press, 1979.*
4) *Yehuda Bauer, "Whose Holocaust?"* Midstream, *Vol. XXVI, No. 9 (November 1980):42.*
5) *Walter Laqueur,* The Terrible Secret *(Boston Little Brown and Company, 1980, p. 7.*
6) *Lawrence Langer, "The Dilemma of Choice in the Death-camps," a presentation to Zachor: Holocaust Resource Center's Faculty Seminar, January, 1979 (unpublished manuscript), p. 19.*
7) *Ismar Schorsch, "The Holocaust and Jewish Survival,"* Midstream *vol. XXVII, No. 1 (January, 1981):3842.*
8) *Ibid.*
9) *Ibid.*
10) *Eliezer Berkovitz,* Faith after the Holocaust, *(New York: Ktav, 1973), p. 118.*
11) *John Cuddihy, "The Holocaust: The Latent Issue in the Uniqueness Debate," a presentation to Zachor: the Holocaust Resource Center's Faculty Seminar, January, 1980 (unpublished manuscript).*
12) *Emil Fackenheim,* The Jewish Return into History: Reflections in the Age of Auschwitz and a New Jerusalem *(New York: Schocken Books, 1978), p. 93*
13) *Robert Alter, "Deformations of the Holocaust,"* Commentary *(February, 1981). Arnold Jacob Wolfe and Michael Berenbaum, "The Centrality of the Holocaust: An Overemphasis?"* The National Jewish Monthly *(October, 1980).*

VII

The Holocaust: Its Implications for the Church and Society Problematic

BY JOHN T. PAWLIKOWSKI

AN IN-DEPTH EXAMINATION of the Nazi Holocaust raises some challenging questions relative to the relationship between church and society. In the following essay it will be possible to delve into only a few of the major ones with some indications of their various dimensions.

Before tackling the specific questions at hand it is necessary to set a basic context for the discussion.[1] As with any precedent-breaking event in human history commentators on its significance move in many varied directions. It is not possible here to discuss all the divergent approaches. All I wish to do is offer some indications of the interpretations that seem best to me after

John T. Pawlikowski, OSM is a member of the Servite Order and Professor of Social Ethics at the Catholic Theological Union, a constituent school of the Chicago Cluster of Theological Schools at the University of Chicago. Author of six books including Catechetics and Prejudice *1973;* Sinai and Calvary *1976;* What Are They Saying About Christian-Jewish Relations, *1980. Recently published a major new work in Christology and Christian-Jewish relations entitled* Christ in Light of the Christian-Jewish Dialouge, *1982.*

This essay is taken from Encounter, *Spring 1981. Vol. 42 N-2 pp. 143-154 and is reprinted with the permission of the publisher and author.*

"Christianity and Judaism"

several years of study and reflection on Holocaust materials.

Auschwitz has emerged in my mind as the beginning of a significantly new era, one in which the extermination of human life in a guiltless fashion becomes thinkable and technologically feasible. It opens the door to an age when dispassionate torture and murder of millions has become not just an action of a crazed despot, not merely an irrational expression of xenophobic fear, not just a drive for national security, but a calculated effort to reshape humanity supported by intellectual argumentation from the best and brightest minds in a society. The Holocaust was not the product of 101 Idi Amins. It was the brainchild of some of the most sophisticated philosophers and scientists Western society has known to date. While the attempt to liquidate the Jewish People had everything to do with the legacy of Christian anti-Semitism, the Nazi "Final Solution" was not aimed at the Jews alone. It would certainly be an unconscionable evasion of moral responsibility for Christians to forget the many believing members of the church who collaborated with the Nazi attack on the Jews. Yet it would also be shortsighted to view the Holocaust merely as directed against the people Israel.

Nazism was as much opposed to Christianity in the final analysis as to Judaism; it was as much a product, perhaps even more so, of fundamental trends in Western society as it was of traditional Christian anti-Semitism. As the Israeli historian Urial Tal strongly maintains,[2] it was meant to answer a universal crisis of the human person. Its expressed goal was the total transformation of human values. Liberation of humankind from what the Nazi theoreticians looked upon as the "shackles", imposed by conventional ideas about God, moral responsibility, redemption, sin and revelation — that was the ultimate hope. There existed a clear and deliberate attempt to restate classic theological notions in purely anthropological and political categories.

The Holocaust also represented a deliberate decision on the part of the Nazi leadership to live within the condition of finitude while asserting for itself total power within this condition. As the theologian Michael Ryan has put it,

> Hitler's worldview amounted to the deliberate decision on the part of mass man to live within the limits of finitude, without either the moral restraints or the hopes of traditional religion — in his case, Christianity.[3]

Thus the basic moral question that emerges from a study of the Holocaust is how we today grapple with a new sense of freedom and power within humankind in a context of a highly sophisticated technological capability with the capacity for massive destruction. And in dealing with this question as the people of the Western world we will need to recognize that the basic humanitarian values of our secular tradition also proved ineffective in the face of the Nazi onslaught. Irving Greenberg has made this point forcefully and quite correctly:

The Holocaust: Church and Society

How naive the nineteenth-century polemic with religion appears to be in retrospect; how simple Feuerbach, Nietzsche, and many others. The entire structure of autonomous logic and sovereign human reason now takes on a sinister character . . . All the talk in the world about "atavism" cannot obscure the way in which such behavior is the outgrowth of democratic and modern values . . . . This responsibility must be shared not only by Christianity, but by the Enlightenment and democratic cultures as well. Their apathy and encouragement strengthened the will and capacity of the murderers to carry out the genocide.[4]

The Holocaust thus must be seen as the most devastating example to date the fundamental alienation of men and women in the Western world from compassionate moral roots. This condition has been well described by Dr. Jay Forrester in a volume called *Towards Global Equilibrium*. He argues that the Western person has experienced a separation from important segments of authentic humanity. This has resulted from the fact that the multidimensionality of human existence has virtually shrunk to the level of a single dimension — that of technology and economy. Forrester writes that

> Western society requires the individual to choose without values (repression of the normative); to work without meaning (repression of the spiritual); to integrate without community (repression of the communal dimension). One could add: to think without feeling (repression of the affective) and to live without faith, hope, myth, utopia (repression of the transcendental dimension).[5]

Irving Greenberg raises the same questions in his reflections on the Holocaust's impact on Western society to which reference was made earlier. He claims that after Auschwitz it has become all the more important for believing people to resist the absolutization of the secular. He writes:

> Secular authority unchecked becomes absolute. Relative values thus become the seedbed of absolute claims, and this is idolatry. This vacuum was a major factor in the Nazi ability to concentrate power and carry out the destruction without protest or resistance.[6]

For Greenberg the Holocaust serves as an advance warning of the demonic potential in modern culture.

All this serves to introduce us to the fundamental question as to what role religion ought to play in American society in light of the Holocaust experience. In an address to the 1974 American Academy of Religion Convention in Washington, Congressman Robert Drinan of Massachusetts directly challenged some of the traditional notions of church-state separation in this country. As a lawyer and a Roman Catholic priest, Fr. Drinan expressed great appreciation for what the dis-establishment of religion in the United States had done to promote religious freedom and civil liberties for all citizens. But he likewise felt that it was time Americans began to confront the dark side of this separation, namely the overprivatization of religion. It was important for Americans to discuss ways in which the cherished sense of religious liberty for all could be protected in this country while allowing religion and religious organizations a greater influence in the shaping of national policy, both domestic and foreign. As an example, he cited the problem faced by the leadership of the National Council of Churches which tried in vain for two years to secure an appointment with President Nixon to discuss the Council's concern about United States military policy in Vietnam. There needs to develop in this country, according to Drinan, some new models for allowing religious groups a greater voice in shaping the public values of our society. America's soul cannot sustain the continued privation of religion.

This same sentiment has been voiced by the well-known, albeit controversial, pastor and social commentator Richard John Neuhaus. In a 1976 article in *Worldview* magazine he wrote the following:

> Realizing that the visions and values of a religious people cannot be excluded from the public realm requires major readjustments in the way we conduct our public business. Realizing that faith can no longer be isolated from public reason requires major readjustments in the ways Jews and Christians understand their religion. The politics of enlightenment rationalism divorced from religious vision becomes sterile and alienating, and that is what has happened in modern America. The politics of religious vision untempered by public reason becomes fanatic and divisive, and that is what must not be permitted to happen.[7]

While not in complete agreement with the stated positions of either Drinan or Neuhaus, I do second their call for a re-examination of the church-state tradition in this country, especially when we seriously confront what took place in Nazi Germany. Though I fully recognize the pitfalls inherent in opening up the question, there is need in my mind to explore ways in which religion can be given a more public role without endangering the basic freedom of religion accorded to all by the U.S. Constitution. That there are religious groups in the land wanting to impose their highly doctrinaire interpretation of the Scriptures on the entire body politic is a fact I cannot deny. Certainly opening up the church-state question means the possibility of unlocking doors, if we are not continually vigilant, for the kind of relogous domination of the public sector that would prove harmful and offensive to all serious minded Christians and Jews. But such a danger is in my view insufficient excuse for supporting an unbending "no re-examination" policy. The threat that the continued exclusion of religion from the public sphere will result in the dominance of a secular, anti-justice approach to policy issues constitutes an even greater danger to the well-being of America.

This threat has been accurately perceived by several recent writers repre-

The Holocaust: Church and Society

senting a broad spectrum of religious and academic backgrounds. The noted church historian Professor Franklin Littell has warned that the

> disestablishment of historic religion(s) may, unless accompanied by an affirmation of the temporal values of pluralism and open interreligious dialogue, create a vacuum which will be filled sooner or later by a new coercive orthodoxy. . . .[8]

Professor Littell is especially worried about this possibility because of his extensive study of the effect of such a movement in Nazi Germany.

At the 1975 Woodstock Symposium celebrating the 10th anniversary of the II Vatican Council's Declaration on Religious Liberty, the Jewish scholar Manfred Vogel addressed what he considered to be a deep-seated danger in the modern Western cultural situation — the desire of this culture to confine the domain of religion exclusively to the sphere of vertical relations, making it the private affair of the individual's inwardness. In this way religion is excluded from the horizontal relations among people, an area which in this conception remains the exclusive prerogative of the state. To the extent that organized religion has accepted such confinement, friction and tension with the modern cultural ethos has been sharply curtailed. But the question, Vogel insists,

> is whether in doing so religion does not really commit suicide or, to change the metaphor, whether in doing so religion does not succeed in merely smoothing and gracing its own exit from the state; for the arena of concern for modern man is overwhelmingly the horizontal domain, the concrete temporal world, the domain of the relations between man and man.[9]

What Vogel is saying is that in relegating religion to an otherworldly sphere and excluding it from involvement in the concerns of this earth, one in effect pushes religion to the borders of irrelevancy. And a religion that is irrelevant for all intents and purposes belongs on the ash heap.

The church historian Clyde Manschreck also raises some concerns similar to those expressed by Vogel. He is especially bothered by the possibility that continued reduction of religious influence in the public sector might well lead to the development of what he terms "naked state sovereignty." Certainly for him there is little doubt that the state cannot allow one religious group to infringe on the religious freedom of others and must be careful that no one religious group subvert its own legitimate sphere of authority. But, on the other hand, he clearly warns that

> state sovereignty cannot be allowed to be idolatrous. Therein is the church-state tension as I see it for the future. Ancient Rome was tolerant of many religions; however, it demanded worship of the Emperor as divine, emperor worship being symbolic of imperial unity. The early Christians could not do that. Hitler led Germany into a similar situation. A few resisted; millions of Jews died. Whether such an impasse will develop in the United States remains to be seen.[10]

"Christianity and Judaism"

From the above quotations it seems obvious that a growing body of serious Catholic, Protestant and Jewish scholars see a potentially dangerous situation developing in the frequently subtle but real attempt to totally divorce religion from the creation of societal values and norms. This trend becomes even more worrisome when we reflect on the consequences of such a divorce during the Nazi period. This trend is forcing us seriously to ask, what role do we wish religion and religious institutions to play in our present and future society? Do we want to turn over the sector of public values exclusively to the technocrats, the media and the advertising specialists? If not, how do we establish the formal and informal channels whereby religion can exercise a constructive influence on public morality without imposing a particular moral perspective on the body politic.

Our problem here remains in part one of trust among the religious groups themselves. There is yet no widespread conviction in this land that promoting the authentic development of religious traditions other than my own with their systems of moral values contributes to the overall well-being of the society. The pervasive spirit among religious groups in this country has been to try to keep the hands of their religious confreres out of the public sector with the underlying assumption that any such influence will harm the general social fabric. Given the early history of the United States, it is relatively easy to understand how such apprehension developed. But can we continue to survive as a healthy and just nation if we insist on maintaining only a negative interpretation of religious liberty? Franklin Littell who has studied the church struggle with the Nazis as thoroughly as any Christian historian has cautioned that we cannot: "Religious liberty," he writes, "cannot survive as a negative concept alone. Both philosophically and practically its continuance depends upon a certain respect for the dignity and integrity of the human person — in both communal and individual commitments."[11]

So the task before us in the latter part of the twentieth century, in the period after Auschwitz, is to begin the process of redefining our understanding of church-state relations, moving towards a situation where religions are clearly recognized as indispensable parts of public value creation in our society. This re-definition, if it is to prove successful, must be done within an interreligious context, with the awareness that non-theistic humanists also have a role to play. But as this is being done, a watchful eye must always be kept on the religious fanaticism that stalks so many quarters of this nation. Despite the real dangers the process must begin. The only alternative is a society in which a-morality is king and where despotism and fascism will sooner or later triumph.

In order to prevent the emergence in our nation of the kind of naked state sovereignty that developed in thought and in action during the Hitlerian period there will need to be unprecedented cooperation between Christians and Jews in the coming years. Yet some Holocaust interpreters such as Eliezer Berkovits have urged a period of silence in Christian-Jewish dialogue in light of the Holocaust. While I can understand the feelings behind such a viewpoint, it is ultimately shortsighted and dangerous for both faith communities. The Holocaust has clearly demonstrated that our respective covenants are not automatic guarantees of happiness and safety on the earth. It has shown how totally interrelated we both are with each other and with all humanity in the face of demonic power. If some part of the human community decides to misuse the creative power that human freedom gives them, as was the case with the Nazis, all may suffer. God will not intervene to spare any special group. Our joint mission is to bring the knowledge and the experience of the loving/transcedent God and the value system it implies to all humankind as the only effective curb against the violence of Auschwitz. But if Christians and Jews refuse to cooperate, if we take Auschwitz to mean we must remain silent and in separation from one another, this opposition will be an obstacle to the humanization of the world and will create the potential for even greater destruction and suffering. The Holocaust has elevated interreligious cooperation to the level of a moral imperative for both Christians and Jews.

One cautionary note must be sounded, however, with respect to the above call for a re-thinking of the church-state separation question in light of the Holocaust experience. It is one raised by the Catholic sociologist Gordon Zahn, one of the first Christians to grapple with the significance of Auschwitz for the post-war generation. The danger is, in Zahn's eyes, that the church can become *too* identified with a given socio-political order in the process of value construction. Zahn feels that one overriding lesson to be learned from the study of the Holocaust is that all religiously-motivated communities must never become so enmeshed with a particular socio-political experiment that they lose their potential for constructive dissent and disobedience. He writes as follows:

> In other, more familiar terms, the church must recognize that it has a stake in maintaining a separation of church and state as that separation is defined from its own perspective. It is a serious mistake to see that separation, as Americans are so prone to see it, only in terms of protecting the purity and independence of the secular order from unwarranted intrusions or domination by the spiritual. The problem as it developed in Germany (and as it may exist here to a greater degree than we are aware!) is also one of preserving the purity and independence of the spiritual community and its teaching from domination by the national state, with its definitions of situational needs and priorities.[12]

While I cannot totally endorse Zahn's underlying ecclesiology, his warnings need to be seriously considered in any restatement of the church-state problematic.

Zahn also believes that as a consequence of the experience in Nazi Germany, the church must re-evaluate its traditional position relative to the "just war" theory, that it must more thoughtfully grapple with the resistance

"Christianity and Judaism"

to authority as a possible moral option for Christians, and that a new hard look is needed at the idea that as a temporal social institution the church can accommodate itself to any regime which affirms its willingness to respect church property and prerogatives, something that has been virtually an unchallengeable truism in Catholic political philosophy and Vatican diplomacy.[18] A similar analysis can be found in Guenter Lewy's *The Catholic Church and Nazi Germany.*[14]

One of the theological issues the church will have to re-examine is its concept of history. This imperative applies in a special way to Roman Catholicism, but has significance for all branches of Christianity. On the Catholic side, the philosopher Frederich Heer has spoken of this "re-historization" of the church in extremely blunt terms. For him, Catholicism's failure to challenge the Nazis in any effective way is symptomatic of how the Roman church has dealt with other manifestations of evil, in particular war and the possibility of a nuclear holocaust. For him, the main problem springs from the church's withdrawal from history:

> The withdrawal of the church from history has created that specifically Christian and ecclesiastical irresponsibility towards the world, the Jew, the other person, even the Christian himself, considered as a human being — which was the ultimate cause of past catastrophes and may be the cause of a final catastrophe in the future.[15]

As Heer sees it, anti-Semitism is the product of a long-standing and deep-seated cancer within Christianity that began to grow in its classical period. The disregard on the part of Christians for the well-being of the Jewish people throughout history, especially between 1918 and 1945, can only be understood as part of a general disregard for humanity and the world. He attributes this attitude to the dominance in Christian theological thinking of what he calls the "Augustinian principle." This attitude views the world under the aspect of sin and ultimately leads to a sense of fatalism and despair about the world. Heer is convinced that this fatalistic tendency constitutes as much a danger today as it did in the period of the incubation of Nazism. In fact, he argues that millions of contemporary Christians share the responsibility for preparing the suicide of the church and of humankind in a new holocaust which may be brought about by nuclear warfare while the churches remain silent bystanders. He writes:

> There is a straight line from the church's failure to notice Hitler's attempt at a "Final Solution" of the Jewish problem to her failure to notice today's and tomorrow's endeavors to bring about a "Final Solution" to the human problem. The murder of millions of Jews during the Hitler era anticipated the murder of millions and perhaps hundreds of millions of human beings who would die if the great war returned — a war that could only end in mass murder and genocide.[16]

102

The Holocaust: Church and Society

The only cure for this centuries-long pattern in Christianity, according to Heer, is to abandon the "Augustinian principle" and replace it with a return to the Hebrew Bible's roots of Christ's own piety and to even older roots — namely, to the original faith in which people felt themselves to be both God's creatures and his responsible partners in the development of the earth.

In highlighting the fatalistic tendency in Christian theological thinking, Heer is on to something quite significant. The one drawback in his analysis is that he does not carry it far enough. His search for the origins of this destructive tendency stops short of probing its ultimate source. The origins of this tendency really lie in the assumption by the early Christian community that the Christ Event had launched the Messianic era, had pushed history to its final culmination. When the anticipated characteristics of the Messianic age failed to be seen, the church's theology tended to push the sense of fulfillment into an inner, spiritual dimension. Rosemary Ruether, though I do not fully subscribe to her interpretation, has rightly pinpointed some of the serious problems created for the church's relationship with the world as a result of this "spiritualizing of the eschatological" as she terms it.[17]

The end result of this impulse was a theological approach to the world which described the church as a wholly complete entity essentially existing apart from human history. The Holocaust has shattered such an ecclesiology. The church now cannot be viewed as anything but an incomplete community, still struggling for salvation within the confines of the flow of history. An imperative therefore exists for Christian theologians to rethink the whole meaning of the Christ Event relative to the fulfillment of history. Some theologians have already begun this process.[18] Its completion still requires considerable work and research because of its central role in Christian meaning.

These theologians are beginning to assert that Christianity must take a fresh look at its long-standing contention that the Messianic age, the time of fulfillment, took place with the coming of Christ. It has become obvious that Christian theology can no longer simply claim that the Jewish notion of the Messianic age was realized in the Death-Resurrection of Christ. Such a conclusion does not imply a total discarding of traditional Christology, but it does demand significant restatement and clarification. Only by reversing the process of the "spiritualizing of the eschatological" that took place in the first century can the church finally remove the fatalistic tendency identified by Heer and insure that it will not cause some future, far greater holocaust.

In short, what is demanded by the Auschwitz experience is the creation of an ecclesiological vision in which the church is clearly seen as immersed in history despite its transcendental dimensions, recognizing as well that it is only within the flow of history that its still incomplete nature can be perfected. One must understand that the salvation process is directly inhibited by regimes such as Nazi Germany and that the church can never reach its ultimate goals while non-Christians suffer and die in crematoria, prisons and torture chambers. Only such an ecclesiology can have legitimacy after the Holocaust.

One of the more concrete facets of the church-society problematic in the post-Auschwitz era is the power question. It is certainly not a new dilemma. Richard Rubenstein in his recent writings[19] and Irving Greenberg have insisted that the use of power becomes a moral imperative for human survival after Auschwitz. This is also implied in the writings of Emil Fackenheim who insists that after the Holocaust the 614th commandment of the Torah becomes Jewish survival. This conclusion on the part of sensitive Jewish religious scholars such as Greenberg, Rubenstein and Fackenheim must be taken seriously by Christians. Yet a dialogue needs to take place here about necessary curbs on power, a dialogue that is not yet adequately present in their writings even though part of Greenberg's call involves the recognition that power needs to be redistributed in the light of the Holocaust:

> No one should ever be equipped with less power than is neces-
> sary to assure one's dignity. To argue dependence on law, or
> human goodness, or universal equality is to join the ranks of
> those who would like to repeat the Holocaust. Anyone who
> wants to prevent a repetition must support a redistribution of
> power. Since this, in turn, raises a large number of issues and
> problems with regard to power, we will not analyze it here. But
> the analysis of the risks of power and the dialectic of its redis-
> tribution is a central ongoing task of religion and morality, and a
> vast pedagogical challenge to all who are committed to prevent a
> second Auschwitz.[20]

Without seeming haughty as a Christian here is an area where the Christian tradition and its discussions on power and morality may make a genuine contribution to Jewish self-reflection in a dialogical context. Because of its minority status for so long a time, Jewish thought has not yet been able to develop a social ethic that grapples with such issues as power in a comprehensive fashion.

In this context, however, it is important to caution against easy acceptance of some Christian theological attempts to link the sufferings of the Jews at Auschwitz with a theology of the Cross, a process at work, for example, in the writings of Jürgen Moltmann.[21] I cannot go into this question in depth here. But it touches on the power question. A. Roy Eckardt is to be listened to in his critique of Moltmann in this regard. Eckardt rightly fears that Moltmann's emphasis on the categories of "weakness," "impotence," "vulnerability," "openness to suffering and love," and "divine protection," only pave the way for the creation of demonic structures. He cites Irving Greenberg to the effect that in the world today suffering only helps to "strengthen rampant evil and to collaborate in the enthronement of the devil."[22] In light of the Holocaust liberation theology's approach to the church and the use of power represents a more adequate response than does Moltmann's position. But let me state clearly that in my judgment the liberation theological perspective also requires much clarification and re-

The Holocaust: Church and Society

formulation, especially on the Jewish question.

Finally, I would call attention to two other problems as symptomatic of the situation we are facing in light of the Holocaust. The first is the development of depersonalized public language. It is fascinating to see how the Nazi theoreticians tried to neutralize the moral impact of their death camps, to reduce them to mere technical activity, by the creation of totally depersonalized terms to describe their work. The daily work output of a camp was described in much the same fashion as one might report the daily production line activities of a Detroit automobile assembly plant. Some see this as the beginning of a whole new phase in the dynamics of mass destruction. It is one that continues to affect our society today, both in the United States and elsewhere. The reporting by the Pentagon during the Vietnam War and the way many governments in Latin America describe torture operations are cited as cases in point.

There is likewise the southern border problem facing the United States caused by poverty and population explosion in Mexico, which Richard Rubenstein sees as the next potential Holocaust in which America may be directly involved. And it is relevant to the depersonalized language problem. Will the religious communities of this land sit back and allow this growing problem to be defined by our governemnt in purely technical and economic terms? Or will they insist that the government make clear in its language that it remains first and foremost a human problem?

From the above analysis, it should be clear that the Auschwitz experience introduces a new era in our handling of the church-state problematic. How we answer it will determine whether our nation, whether religion, whether humanity will survive. Without exaggeration I am convinced it is as momentous as all that.

1)   *I elaborate this more fully in my monograph*, The Challenge of the Holocaust for Christian Theology *(New York: ADL, 1978)*.
2)   *"Forms of Pseudo-Religion in the German* Kulturbereich *prior to the Holocaust,"* Immanuel, *No. 3 (Winter, 1973-1974)*.
3)   *"Hitler's Challenge to the Churches: A Theological-Political Analysis of* Mein Kampf," *in Franklin H. Littell and Hubert G. Locke, eds.,* The German Church Struggle and the Holocaust *(Detroit: Wayne State University Press, 1973), pp. 160-161*.
4)   *"Cloud of Smoke, Pillar of Fire: Judaism, Christianity and Modernity After the Holocaust,"* in Eva Fleischner, ed., Auschwitz: Beginning of a New Era? *(New York: KTAV, 1977), p. 17*.

5) (New York: Harper & Row, 1976), p. 7.
6) "Cloud of Smoke," p. 29.
7) September, 1976, p. 30.
8) "Foundations and Traditions of Religious Liberty," Journal of Ecumenical Studies, Vol. 14, No. 4 (Fall, 1977), p. 10.
9) In Walter J. Burghardt, S.J., ed., Religious Freedom: 1965 and 1975: A Symposium on a Historic Document, Woodstock Studies 1 (New York: Paulist Press, 1977), p. 68.
10) "Church-State Relations – A Question of Sovereignty," in Clyde L. Manschreck and Barbara Brown Zikmund, eds., The American Religious Experiment: Piety and Practicality (Chicago: Exploration Press, 1976), p. 121.
11) "Religious Liberty," p. 112.
12) "Catholic Resistance? A Yes and a No," in Littell and Locke, eds., The German Church Struggle, pp. 234-235.
13) Cf. German Catholics and Hitler's Wars (New York: Sheed and Ward, 1962), pp. 208-234.
14) (New York: McGraw-Hill, 1964), pp. 325-41.
15) God's First Love (New York: Weybright and Talley, 1970), p. 406.
16) "The Catholic Church and the Jews Today," Midstream, Vol. 17 (May, 1971), p. 29.
17) Cf. Faith and Fratricide: The Theological Roots of Anti-Semitism (New York: Seabury Press, 1974). For my critique of Reuther and her response, cf, my essay, "The Historicizing of the Eschatological: The Spiritualizing of the Eschatological: Some Reflections," in Alan T. Davies, ed., Anti-Semitism and the Foundations of Christianity (New York: Paulist Press, 1979).
18) Cf. my essay, "The Contemporary Jewish-Christian Theological Agenda," Journal of Ecumenical Studies, Vol. 11 (Fall, 1974), pp. 602-606; also What They Are Saying About Christian-Jewish Relations (New York: Paulist Press, 1980).
19) Cf., for example, The Cunning of History (New York: Harper & Row, 1978).
20) "Cloud of Smoke," p. 54.
21) Cf. The Crucified God: The Cross of Christ as the Foundation and Criticism of Christian Theology (New York: Harper & Row, 1978).
22) Cf. "Christians and Jews: Along a Theological Frontier," Encounter, Vol. 40, No. 2 (Spring, 1979), p. 102. Cf. Irving Greenberg, "Lessons to be Learned from the Holocaust," unpublished paper from the International Conference on the Church Struggle and the Holocaust, Hans Rissen, BRD, 8-11 June 1975.

VIII

Evangelical Christians and Holocaust Theology

A growing and influential number of Christian theologians in the United States are being decisively influenced by Jewish thinking and by the Holocaust. They are convinced, as I am, that Christians ought to think long and hard about the theological and religious implications of that event. Some such theologians are proposing radical revisions in Christian thought. (1) Some seem to regard the Holocaust as a kind of *theological absolute*, almost as if it were on a par with divine revelation as a basic datum of Christian theology.[1] (2) Others hold that *the traditional God of Christianity died in the Holocaust* or at least, less metaphorically, that given Auschwitz it is no longer rationally possible for Christians to believe that God is both all-powerful and perfectly good.[2] (3) Some even suggest that in the light of Antisemitism and the Holocaust *Christians must give up Christian themes that are offensive to Jews*, e.g., the notion that Jesus is the messiah or the notion that Christians ought to engage in evangelism.[3]

Although I am not a fundamentalist or a "moral majority"-type, I am an evangelical Christian, and thus I am unwilling to accept any of the above suggested revisions in Christian thought. In the light of such a commitment,

Stephen T. Davis is on the faculty of Claremont Men's College. This essay is taken from the American Journal of Philosophy and Theology, Vol. 2, n. 3, Sept 1981, pp. 121-129 and is reprinted by permission of the publisher.

107

"Christianity and Judaism"

how should I, as an evangelical, think about the Holocaust? That is the question I shall consider here. I suspect my suggestions will seem unimpressive to the Christian thinkers who are pioneers in this field — what might be called Holocaust theology. Most of them seem to be rather liberal or even radical in their approach to Christianity, and they probably will not like what I am about to say. Doubtless I will be accused of "not taking the Holocaust seriously enough" — that seems to be the charge such people level at those who find their proposals too extreme.

Nevertheless, someone from the evangelical ranks ought to try to say something in this area. Let me try. In what follows, I shall both speak *to* evangelical Christians, recommending what our position should be on these matters, and *on behalf of* evangelicals, letting others know what I at least think our position is.

Successionism

Many theologians who reflect on the Holocaust single out for criticism the traditional Christian notion that it succeeds or supersedes or fulfills Judaism. Christian successionism comes in many forms, and some of them I agree are clearly unacceptable. However, as an evangelical Christian, I do hold and am not prepared to give up the notions: (1) that Jews were once God's sole elect people and that Christians are now chosen too, and (2) that all people should believe in Jesus.

Do these propositions entail that Judaism is a religious relic, that it has been nullified, that it has no *raison d'etre,* that Jews no longer have any standing before God and should have disappeared? Apparently Franklin H. Littell thinks so. In *The Crucifixion of the Jews,* he argues that "the cornerstone of Christian Antisemitism is the superseding or displacement myth." This myth, he says, "already rings with a genocidal note," having "murderous implications which murderers will in time spell out."[4]
Most evangelicals would find these remarks by Littell not only false but outrageous. In the first place, they do not think the notion that Christianity succeeded Judaism is a myth. In the second place, they will point out that there is no necessary connection whatsoever between believing in successionism and being an Antisemite, let alone a condoner of genocide. Antisemitism and genocide are both about as clearly contrary to the Christian ethic as anything is. It just is not true that successionism has murderous implications. In the third place, it does not follow from successionism, as I have defined it, that there is no longer any justification for the existence of Judaism. St. Paul argues in Romans 9-11 that Israel has a continued role to play in God's redemptive plan, and evangelical Christians follow Paul in affirming that it is so. Furthermore, as we all know, for very understandable reasons most Jews find it psychologically impossible to believe in Jesus. This being so, I believe they should continue to practice Judaism. In the fourth place, we cannot hold Paul and the other "successionist" biblical writers morally guilty of the later murder of Jews even if it is true (which

Evangelical Christians and the Holocaust

certainly can be doubted) that theological successionism helped motivate the later murderers. The crucial point is that Paul and the others had no intention of supporting genocide, nor any reason to suspect their words might later be used to support genocide.

Jews should not expect Christians, even in their desire for good relations with Jews, to surrender crucial Christian notions. Some liberal Christians seem eager to do so, but evangelical Christians will not do so. What evangelical Christians must say to Jews, then, is I imagine something like this: "We love you as Jews and not just as candidates for baptism; we affirm your freedom to believe and practice Judaism without any sort of coercive interference from us; we will cooperate with you and stand shoulder-to-shoulder with you in areas of agreement (e.g. opposition to Antisemitism), but we believe that Jesus is the messiah and Son of God and that those who deny it are mistaken."

Antisemitism and Christianity

Let us define the word "Antisemitism" as active prejudice against Jews just because they are Jews. I include the word "active" because we normally think of Antisemitism as involving words or deeds as well as just attitudes; Antisemitism would not be nearly as morally objectionable as it is if it only involved attitudes. I include the phrase "just because they are Jews" because it is possible for someone to be prejudiced against a group of Jews for reasons other than the fact that they are Jews, e.g. because they are all graduates of UCLA or because they are all left-handed. And that would not count as Antisemitism.

There is absolutely no doubt that the Christian church must plead guilty for being directly and indirectly responsible for much Antisemitism. The Old Testament makes clear, of course, the fact that Antisemitism antedates Christianity; nevertheless, it cannot be denied that the record of Christian treatment of Jews is *at best* very mixed indeed. By their own admission and even insistence, Christians are fallible and sinful human beings. Here, *par excellence,* we find the most conclusive confirmation of that admission. Christians have grievously sinned against Jews.

Is the New Testament Antisemitic? Despite the arguments of certain Jewish thinkers and Christian Holocaust theologians, I remain unconvinced. What certainly is true is that there is material in the New Testament which Antisemites can twist in order to buttress their Antisemitism. Jesus' attack on "the scribes and pharisees" in the synoptic gospels is scathing indeed (see Matthew 23), but it does not necessarily constitute an attack on Pharisaism per se. Furthermore, it has all the earmarks of a conflict within Judaism rather than an exercise in Antisemitism. Much as the apostle Paul criticized the Jews who rejected Jesus and (as he saw it) misinterpreted the Mosaic law, he remained till his death a Jew, proud of his heritage and training (see Phil. 3:7-8; I Cor. 11:21-22; see also Acts 25:8; 26:5; 28:17). The Fourth Gospel uses the term, "the Jews" in an equivocal way — at times it refers to the entire Jewish nation, especially where Jewish customs are being explained (see John 2:13; 3:1; 5:1; 6:4; 7:2; etc.) and at times it refers to Jesus' enemies, those who plotted against him (see John 5:15-18; 7:1, 13; 9:22; 10:31-33; 18:12; 19:7, 12, 38; 20:19, etc.). Thus, the evangelist can be and sometimes is mistakenly interpreted as implying that the entire Jewish nation was somehow responsible for Jesus' death, which was not his intent at all.

Are the Jews, i.e. all Jews including Jews today, responsible for Jesus' crucifixion? Of course not.[5] Certain Jews of Jesus' day must apparently bear considerable responsibility for that crime, but so must certain Romans. Thus, to claim that the whole Jewish nation was responsible is ridiculous; to claim that all Jews, even those born afterwards, were responsible is perfectly absurd. The claim would not even be worth commenting upon except for the sad fact that there have been people who have accepted it. Perhaps there are occasional events where the shadowy notion of "collective moral responsibility" for a crime makes sense, but certainly not here.

Much has been made by Holocaust theologians of the *Adversus Judaeos* tradition in Christian theology, especially the anti-Jewish polemic of some of the church Fathers. Certainly there are statements made by the Fathers that are wrong-headed and mistaken — not to mention ill-advised in the light of later events. Here again we find points where the church must plead guilty of Antisemitism. But while we cannot condone the excesses of the *Adversus Judaeos* tradition, perhaps we can understand its existence. The earliest Christians were Jews and wanted to make no break with Judaism. When they were later forced by events to see the Christian movement as quite separate from Judaism, it was natural that they and their spiritual descendents try to work out the meaning of Christianity in terms of its opposition to Judaism. A crucial factor here, of course, was Jewish persecution of the earliest Christians (see I Thess. 2:14-16), who like European Jews during the Holocaust, were largely powerless. And although Christianity's early persecution by and competition with Judaism led certain Christians to regrettable excesses of polemic and outright mistakes in theology, it is also perhaps understandable that the early Christians felt a strong need to establish the superiority of Christianity over its disapproving parent Judaism.

But we can hardly blame the New Testament writers and church Fathers for failing to foresee the future. Unfortunately, their words were (and are) used by later Antisemites; we (knowing what we now know) would rather in places they had expressed themselves differently. There are things said by some of the Fathers and later theologians (Luther particularly) that can be considered Antisemitic. But we can hardly blame them for later acts of genocide. (Naturally, we are less inclined to excuse contemporary Christian leaders who make Antisemitic statements, including the sad case of Bailey Smith, the president of the Southern Baptist Convention, who for some reason best known to him reached the conclusion that God does not hear the prayers of Jews.)

Evangelical Christians and the Holocaust

Is Christianity *necessarily* Antisemitic? Certainly not — or not, at least, if it can be agreed that it is not necessarily Antisemitic just to disagree with Jews. Few Jews will agree that Jesus is the messiah and Son of God, and that it is God's will that all people believe in him. But belief in these claims hardly commits one to Antisemitism. However, in her book *Faith and Fratricide*, Rosemary Ruether pointedly asks: "Is it possible to say 'Jesus is Messiah' without, implicitly or explicitly, saying at the same time 'and the Jews be damned'?" She goes on to argue that the real root of Christian Antisemitism is Christology; the higher the view of Christ, she says, the more the Antisemitism. "The anti-Judaic root of Christianity cannot be torn out until the church's Christology is rid of its negation of the ongoing validity of the Jewish faith."[6] "Anti-Judaism," Ruether says, "developed theologically in Christianity as the left hand of Christology. That is to say, anti-Judaism was the negative side of the Christian claim that Jesus was the Christ."[7]

But surely Ruether's argument is not to be taken seriously — not, at least, at face value. There just is no necessary connection between holding a high Christology and being an Antisemite, i.e. someone who is actively prejudiced against Jews as Jews. Surely there are far too many counterexamples to that notion for it to be at all believable. And if such a connection did exist we are entitled to wonder why an even worse holocaust than the 1938-1945 event did not occur during the medieval period or some other period of virtually universal Christological orthodoxy. What is true, probably, is that Antisemites used Christology as an ideological buttress for Antisemitism. But there appears to be no good reason to believe that Christians can only avoid Antisemitism by abandoning orthodox views of Christ.

In general, it is difficult to show that historical events have hidden theological causes. Despite this, I am far from denying that Christian Antisemitism helped make the Holocaust possible. Nevertheless, let me propose a hypothesis which like Ruether's is extremely difficult to prove but which seems to me more plausible. I shall state the point radically: the genocide of the Holocaust was not merely the result of Christian Antisemitism but of nineteenth-century liberal criticism of the Old Testament. The Christian church was severed from its Jewish roots and the door was opened to the extermination of the Jews because biblical criticism convinced people that it was no longer possible to believe in the divine authority of the Old Testament, the absolute nature of the Old Testament law, and the uniqueness of Jews as God's chosen people. Jews became merely a dispensable residue.

It is sometimes suggested that in a curious way, Christianity *depends* on the existence of Judaism and even on Antisemitism, as if Christianity somehow cannot survive without Jews around as enemies or at least "existing others." What an absurd idea! Antisemitism is not only not essential to proper Christian beliefs and practice, it is contrary to them. There are doubtless many Christians who have no idea who Jews are or even that there is any connection between the people of the Bible and the Jews of today. Notice too that Christianity thrives in many parts of the world, e.g. Africa, where there are few if any Jews. Perhaps the argument that Christians need Antisemitism is more subtle than this, but it is not clear to me how the argument could be presented in such a way as to turn out at all plausible.

Christians and the Holocaust

Were Christians responsible for the horrors of the Holocaust? Well, the question is ill-formed and cannot be answered precisely till a distinction is made. The word "Christian" can mean many things, as we all know. I believe Jews often use the term as a synonym or near-synonym for the term "Gentile," or, better, Western (i.e. non-African and non-Asian) Gentile. Here virtually any non-Jewish Caucasian citizen of Europe or the Americas is a "Christian." This is a perfectly good usage of the word, and it is not my intention to discourage it. But in this sense of the word, to speak paradoxically, not all Christians are Christian. A second way of using the word "Christian," then, is: "an active and serious follower of Jesus Christ," or something of the sort.

Were Christians responsible for the Holocaust? In the first sense of the word "Christian" — what we might call a "cultural Christian" as opposed to a "committed Christian" — the answer is obviously yes. Does Christianity have anything to do with the fact that certain cultural Christians committed acts of murder and genocide? This is a complex question. The Hitler regime, as we all know, was a pagan regime, strongly opposed to Christianity, and its leaders were not committed Christians. A good many Christians died in the Holocaust. The Nazis in fact, seemed bent on destroying all who confessed an absolute moral alternative to Hitler — God for Jews, Christians, and Jehovah's Witnesses; history for Marxists.

Nevertheless, the main victims of the Holocaust were Jews, and it seems fair to conclude that historic attitudes towards Jews fostered in the church did play a role in the success of the Nazis in achieving their ends. Here, I believe, the church must plead guilty. These attitudes distort true Christian teachings, to be sure, but they were there, nonetheless. The culturally Christian Antisemites who did Hitler's work were able to do so with relative ease and impunity in part because of (1) Antisemitic attitudes sanctioned by the church, (2) idolatrous nationalism sanctioned by virtually all Western Christians, cultural and committed, and (3) the silence of many committed Christians in the face of genocide.

Were committed Christians responsible for the Holocaust? For the Antisemitic attitudes many of them had, yes. For the silence of many of the others, yes. But were any active and serious followers of Jesus Christ murderers? Here I must say no (although, as I shall later admit, my argument for this conclusion is somewhat circular). It is impossible for any sane person to reconcile Christianity with genocide. Here I recall a statement sometimes made by contemporary Germans — that there were no intelligent and moral Nazis. There were intelligent Nazis, it is said, but they were not moral. There were moral Nazis, but they were not intelligent. People who both had a strong sense of right and wrong and who were intelligent enough to grasp the implications of Nazism did not become Nazis.

I have no idea whether this statement is true — perhaps it is merely an exercise in self-justification by post-war Germans. But I do not believe any intelligent committed Christians were murderers. Naturally, a great many people bear some responsibility for the Holocaust, including some committed Christians. And I confess it will take me a very long time to understand how a committed Christian can be an Antisemite. It is depressing indeed for an evangelical to contemplate the case of Poland, the most Christian nation in Europe. By all accounts, it was also the most Antisemitic, and if we can judge by recent events, is still Antisemitic despite the virtual absence of Jews. Again, there are points where Christians must plead guilty of sin against Jews.

In *A Jew Today*, Elie Wiesel says: "In Auschwitz all the Jews were victims, all the killers were Christian." He goes on to say: "As surely as the victims are a problem for the Jews, the killers are a problem for the Christians."[8] There is a sense in which Wiesel is profoundly correct here. But again there is a problem with the word "Christian." Wiesel's statements, and the sensitive and pointed questions he addresses toward "Christians" in many of his works, could much better be made on the basis of some clear thinking about the meaning of the word "Christian."'

In the First Epistle of John we find the following words: "If anyone says 'I love God' and hates his brother, he is a liar; for he who does not love his brother whom he has seen, cannot love God whom he has not seen" (4:20). And: "Any one who hates his brother is a murderer, and you know that no murderer has eternal life abiding in him" (3:15). My own view, then, is that anybody who claims to be a committed Christian and commits murder has shown he is not a committed Christian. I recognize there is a certain circularity in my argument — "Were any committed Christians murderers? No, because no committed Christian can be a murderer" — but nevertheless I shall stand by it.

Evangelism

One area of tension between Jews and Christians is undoubtedly evangelism. Throughout much of its existence, Christianity has been a missionary faith; its adherents believed strongly in trying to convince others to become Christians. Recently, at least in the main-line denominations in Europe and America, Christianity has lost some of its missionary fervor, but this would not be true of evangelical circles. Evangelical Christians (along with many non-evangelicals, of course) still believe in and practice evangelism.

It is easy for evangelicals and all Christians to understand Jewish sensitivities at this point. In the first place, many Jews are for understandable reasons quite hostile to Christianity. And in the second place, evangelism directed at Jews represents a threat to the continued existence of the Jewish community. Naturally, many Jews are suspicious of and strongly opposed to anything — genocide, mixed marriages, or evangelism — that tends to reduce the number of Jews in the world. Accordingly, some theologians, including Reinhold Niebuhr, have proposed that Christians abandon any attempt to convert Jews.

But such a proposal will not be acceptable to evangelicals, who consider themselves still under the biblical mandate to "Go and make disciples of *all* nations, baptizing them in the name of the Father and of the Son and of the Holy Spirit" (Matthew 28:19; emphasis added). Evangelicals should not favor singling out Jews as a special target group more important than other non-Christians, nor should they favor deceptive or coercive or discourteous methods of evangelism. But evangelicals will insist that they be free to preach their gospel to Jews as well as other people, and will doubtless continue to do so. Christianity, they believe, loses its essence and vital force when Christians cease to feel the need to evangelize.

Conclusion

The picture that emerges thus far is quite clearly that there are points where evangelical Christians are less willing than most Holocaust theologians to accommodate Jews. Will the position I have outlined here be acceptable to Jews? I do not know. Very possibly not. While evangelicals are sensitive to the evils of Antisemitism and determined to do their part in preventing future holocausts, they are not willing to make theological decisions on the basis of Jewish approval or disapproval. Most evangelicals will continue to believe in some form of successionism and in the messiahship of Jesus whether Jews like it or not, and Jews ought to recognize the fact. (Most do in fact recognize it, I believe — better than many Holocaust theologians do.)

Let me close, however, on a more positive note — or at least a note of agreement between Jews and Christians, *viz.* their opposition to a common enemy. Following Jacob Bronowski, let us call this enemy "push-button philosophy." In a chapter near the end of *The Ascent of Man,* Bronowski introduces a discussion of Auschwitz and the Holocaust in the following way:[9]

> There are two parts to the human dilemma. One is the belief that the end justifies the means. That push-button philosophy, that deliberate deafness to suffering, has become the monster in the war machine. The other is the betrayal of the human spirit: the assertion of dogma that closes the mind, and turns a nation, a civilization, into a regiment of ghosts — obedient ghosts, or tortured ghosts.

Evangelical Christians and the Holocaust

Standing beside a pond at Auschwitz into which the ashes of its victims were flushed, Bronowski says:

> I owe it as a scientist to my friend Leo Szilard, I owe it as a human being to the many members of my family who died at Auschwitz, to stand here by the pond as a survivor and witness. We have to cure ourselves of the itch for absolute knowledge and power. We have to close the distance between the push-button order and the human act. We have to touch people.

I am not sure that I understand all that Bronowski is saying here, nor do I wish to suggest he would agree with the interpretation I shall place on "push-button philosophy." Nevertheless, I believe he sees something that is utterly crucial in a discussion of the Holocaust and of relations between Jews and Christians. Let us define push-button philosophy as the point of view which says: (1) the end always justifies the means, and (2) decisions about human affairs are to be made solely on the basis of considerations of power and cost-efficiency. Concepts like human rights, justice, the will of God, morality are excluded as irrelevant.

Unless all signs mislead, push-button philosophy, like an insidious cancer, is growing in influence. I believe it was push-button philosophy, and not Christian values, that led to the Holocaust. Whether or not Jews will agree with me on that point, two things are clear: first, both religious traditions oppose push-button philosophy, and second, members of both traditions are potential victims of push-button philosophy. Here Jews and Christians alike are outsiders. On this issue, which is perhaps the most important moral issue of our time, we ought to stand together.[10]

1)   See, for example, A. Roy Eckardt, "Contemporary Christian Theology and a Protestant Witness for the Shoah," Shoah, Vol. 2, No. 1 (Spring/Summer, 1980), p. 12.

2)   See, for example, John K. Roth's contributions to Encountering Evil: Live Option in Theodicy, *edited by Stephen T. Davis (Atlanta: John Knox Press, 1981).*

3)   See, among others, Paul M. van Buren, "Affirmation of the Jewish People: A Condition of Theological Coherence," Journal of the American Academy of Religion *(September, 1977).*

4)   Franklin H. Littell, The Crucifixion of the Jews *(New York: Harper and Row, 1975), pp. 2, 5.*

5)   Except, according to evangelical Christians, in the theological sense that all human beings because of their sinfulness are responsibile for the crucifixion. All people – including Jews – are Christ-killers, but Jews no more than any other group of people.

6)   Rosemary Ruether, Faith and Fratricide: The Christian Theological Roots of Antisemitism *(New York: Seabury Press, 1974). p. 246.*

7)   Ruether, "Antisemitism and Christian Tehology," in Auschwitz: Beginning of a New Era?. *edited by Eva Fleischner (New York: Ktav, 1977) p. 79.*

8)   Elie Wiesel, A Jew Today *(New York: Vintage Books, 1979), pp. 13, 14.*

9)   Jacob Bronowski, The Ascent of Man *(Boston: Little, Brown, and Company, 1973), pp. 370, 374.*

10)   I would like to thank my colleagues John Roth and Don Williams for helpful comments on earlier drafts of this paper.

The Impact of the
Christian - Jewish Dialogue
on Biblical Studies

BY

BY DR. EUGENE J. FISHER

Introduction:

To approach a topic as multi-faceted as that of the impact on biblical studies of the contemporary dialogue between the Church and the Jewish people is, of necessity, to engage in a rather sweeping survey. Likewise, it is to raise up areas of inquiry in which the scholarly enterprise has not yet reached consensus. Given its many challenges, exegetical as well as hermeneutical, it is often enough the case that the implications of fruitful lines of inquiry have not yet been drawn for other lines where one might expect them to have been applied.

So if there is an episodic and even tentative tone to what follows, with the proverbial forest not as clearly delineated as certain trees within it, I would offer this as at least an honest reflection of the state of the art as it stands today. This state is natural enough. While the past few decades have seen the

Dr. Eugene J. Fisher is the Executive Secretary of the Secretariat for Catholic-Jewish Relations within the American Catholic Bishops' Committee for Ecumenical and Interreligious Affairs. He is the first layman to hold this position and is very active in meetings and discussions between Jews and Christians. This essay was originally prepared for presentation at both the meeting of the Catholic Biblical Association in Baltimore and the meeting of the American Academy of Religion in New York, both held in December '82. It is published here for the first time.

rise of an increasing literature in the field, ranging from G. F. Moore's three-volume *Judaism in the First Centuries of the Christian Era* (Harvard University, 1927-1930) to E. P. Sanders' *Paul and Palestinian Judaism* (Fortress, 1977), the Christian-Jewish dialogue in a formal sense can only be dated to the Second Vatican Council's declaration, *Nostra Aetate*.

It must be stated at the outset of this study that the initial impact to be recorded is not that of the dialogue upon biblical studies but rather of biblical studies in making possible the dialogue in the first place. This is a point recently made by Catholic biblical scholar Richard Lux in an official exchange between representatives of the Synagogue Council of America and the National Conference of Catholic Bishops:

> What is well known is that the dramatic reversal in the relationship between Catholics and Jews has principally come about because of the intensive study, critical reflection and painful examination of our mutual histories and relationship in the years after the Holocaust. Equally of importance in bringing about our changed relationship (and not as well.known) is the dramatic shift in methodology which has grown in the Catholic approach to the Hebrew and Christian Scriptures since 1943 . . . The importance of (Pius XII's focus in *Divino Affante Spirtu* on) understanding the Hebrew Scriptures according to the mind of the author and on its own terms cannot be overestimated. Throughout most of Christian tradition the Hebrew Scriptures were seen through the eyes of New Testament exegetes who were imbued with the supercessionist theologies which positioned Christianity over Judaism and bludgeoned Judaism as well with messianic claims concerning Jesus. Even the 'plain sense' meaning of the Hebrew Scriptures was often subordinated to the allegorical and spiritual interpretation wherein only, it was alleged, lay the true meaning of the Word of God.[1]

Divino Afflante Spiritu, in affirming for Catholics the value of a biblical-critical approach to the Scriptures, not only opened the way for what Pius XII called a "fresh investigation" of old patterns of interpretation, but also established a methodology and a "neutral" interpretative language the use of which has enabled Jews and Christians, for the first time in almost two millenia, to approach the sacred texts together in a mutual rather than disputational search for their original meaning. The use of the historico-critical method of biblical studies has, as Lawrence Boadt, CSP, notes in his introduction to *Biblical Studies: Meeting Ground of Jews and Christians* (Paulist Stimulus, 1980; pp. 4-7), enabled Jewish scholars of the New Testament as well as of the Hebrew Scriptures to participate actively in such traditionally Christian enclaves of scholarship as the Society of Biblical Literature and the Catholic Biblical Association. The resulting cross-fertilization of perspectives within the framework of a shared scholarly

The Impact on Biblical Studies

language, it is safe to say, has deeply enriched both Jewish and Christian biblical awareness.

A. Exegetical Enrichments

It is, then, in the area of exegesis that the most obvious contributions of and to the Christian-Jewish dialogue have been made by contemporary biblical studies. Text criticism has been greatly advanced by Christian scholars with the necessary tools to take advantage of rabbinic sources and of spectacular finds such as the Dead Sea Scrolls and the Cairo Geniza.[3] These very Jewish sources have opened fresh debates concerning both the Septuagint and the Massoretic texts, to the mutual enrichment of both, as Moshe Goshen-Gottstein's "Bible Project" for the Hebrew University in Jerusalem exemplifies.

Gone in the main, if not wholly, from modern biblical translations are such essentially apologetical renderings as the *almah/*"virgin" translation and some of the more tortured "exegetical" footnotes and inserted "chapter titles" which filtered the lay reader's approach to the text along strictly confessional lines. The old Confraternity-Douay version, for example, entitled Genesis 3:14-20 "Punishment; the Promise of a Redeemer" and flatly declared in its note that the section "refers principally to Jesus Christ, the Conqueror of Satan" and that "the Hebrew words include also all the faithful children of God in every age who share in Christ's Victory." The NAB notes, however, more modestly point out that "later theology saw in this passage more than unending hostility between snakes and men," referring to New Testament references for the source of the understanding the passage "as the first promise of a Redeemer for fallen mankind." Thus, while the specifically Christian insight is carefully (and wisely) preserved, the Hebrew text is freed to address the reader on its own terms.

Exegetically as well, the use of Jewish sources such as the Tannaim[4] and the Targumuim,[5] while great caution has had to be exercised because of the difficulties of dating much of the material, has begun to work a quiet revolution in New Testament studies. E. P. Sanders' thorough *Paul and Palestinian Judaism* (Fortress, 1977), for example, has shown definitively that many, indeed most of the assumptions concerning first century Judaism held by Christian scholars up to and including Butlmann and his disciples are simply unsupportable on the basis of the Jewish sources themselves. In the light of these investigations it is no longer possible to maintain the older, highly apologetic view of sharp dichotomies between Jesus' teaching and the developing, highly creative complex of Jewish movements of his time. While still to some extent useful for those who have the skills in Hebrew and Aramaic to pursue each and every entry, such previously "standard" works as Kittell's *Theological Dictionary of the New Testament* (Eerdmans: 8 Vol's, 1964); E. Schurer's *History of the Jewish People in the Time of Jesus;* and Strack-Billerbeck's compendium of misinformation, *Kommentar zum Neuen Testament aus Talmud und Midrash* (Munich: 6 Vol's,

"Christianity and Judaism"

1922-61), are revealed today as both dated and in need of serious revision if they are to serve as a help rather than a block to understanding the New Testament.[6] Fortunately, newer works, such as Daniel Harrington's *God's People in Christ* (Fortress, 1980) and Sean Freyne's *The World of the New Testament* (Wilmington, Delaware: Michael Glazier, Inc., 1980) have begun to make available in popular form some of the newer, more objective research into the history of the period and to lead the way to a more balanced presentation.

Still needing radical overhaul, particularly on the text book level, is the abysmal portrait of the Pharisees, seemingly based on accepting as factual the nastier sayings collected in Matthew's Gospel to the exclusion of all other gospel and contemporary evidence. Here, the works of Jacob Nuesner and Ellis Rivkin[7] as well as several Christian authors, such as Clemens Thoma and John Pawlikowski,[8] have been of help.[9]

Another major misunderstanding of the New Testament texts which has had great negative impact on Christian-Jewish relations over the centuries is the so-called "deicide" charge of collective Jewish responsibility for the death of Jesus. Little need be said here concerning this. My own views on the subject are contained in my *Faith Without Prejudice* (Paulist, 1977, pp. 76-88) and updated in my forthcoming book, *Seminary Education and Christian-Jewish Relations* (National Catholic Education Association, 1983). Excellent updates of the scholarly literature have been prepared by Gerard Sloyan and Joseph Fitzmyer.[10]

Finally, a word, if inadequate, needs to be said concerning the growing body of Christian exegetical works on the New Testament which, based on a more thorough and objective understanding of Jewish sources and of insights taken from the dialogue, have already begun to bring fresh insights to bear on the New Testament texts. We have already mentioned the contributions of Jewish scholars, such as Sandmel, Vermes, Flusser, Lapide and now Michael Cooke, who have made significant contributions. Among Christians, the first of the present generation to be mentioned must be Franz Müssner, whose major work, *Traktat uber die Juden* (Munich, 1979) is being translated by Leonard Swidler for publication in this country, and which gives, along with Clemens Thoma's *A Christian Theology of Judaism* (tr. by H. Croner, Paulist Stimulus, 1980) perhaps the best overview of the field as a whole.

Regarding Pauline studies (to approach the question at least somewhat chronologically), it can be said that taking Judaism and Jewish sources seriously has doubtlessly begun to clear away a large number of misconceptions concerning the Pharisaic/Rabbinic understanding of "Law" that Jesus and Paul supposedly opposed. Such corrective works as these by G. F. Moore and W. D. Davies remain classics, if themselves today in need of further refinement. More recent works, such as those by Krister Stendahl, E. P. Sanders, Gerard Sloyan, John Townsend, Samuel Sandmel, John Koenig and Lloyd Gastin[11] have thus been able to engage the ancient question of

The Impact on Biblical Studies

Paul's view of the Law on new, more objective grounds.

These studies have shed new light on the central issues, but they have to some extent equally opened up new still unanswered questions. Surveying the field on the question of both Jesus' and Paul's attitudes toward the Law in a recent article, for example, Gerard Sloyan concludes that the attitude of both (and consequently of the early Church until increasing Gentilization "resolved" the problem by introducing an unbiblical distinction between ethical and ceremonial/dietary commands) was ambiguous. On the one hand, there was by no means the direct assault on the Law later generations of Christians projected back into the text. On the other, immanent eschatology and Pauline soteriology did combine to "relativize" (though not denigrate or abrogate) the Law for the early Church as it developed.

Likewise, Synoptic and Johannine studies, by concentrating on the developing nature of various strata and traditions within the gospel texts, have both clarified and complexified our understanding of the relationship between Jesus and his people, and between the developing Church and developing rabbinic Judaism. Most of the old simplicities of Jesus' teaching *versus* Jewish teaching, and New Testament *versus* Old Testament must be abandoned as wholly inadequate today, especially as the essential Jewishness of Jesus and the earliest Jesus movement is progressively uncovered. Replacing the "still portraits" of the first century Church and Synagogue are two rather more complex motion pictures of growth and interaction, sometimes mutually enriching, sometimes openly hostile. But the difficulties of dating of the rabbinic and the Christian sources render (if I may be allowed to play out the analogy a bit) the synchronization of the two unfolding dramas more than a little difficult, indeed impossible for key frames at present. It is clear only that a bi-focal or "multi-media" approach, as it were, will ultimately enable a convincing overall presentation sic realities to emerge, i.e. a "dialogical methodology" for which I shall argue in the next section of this paper.

B. Excursus: The Necessary Dialogical Nature of the Biblical Critical Enterprise

The rise of a more source-oriented and ecumenically open style of seeking to understand the biblical texts within their own, proper historical context has given made possible progressively freeing of biblical scholarship from the apologetical filters of the past, whether these were of the Protestant/Catholic variety, as in much of 19th Century European studies, or Christian/Jewish, which has characterized the Christian approach to the Hebrew Scriptures from the New Testament period itself. This more ecumenically and interreligiously oriented character of the field has proven in itself to be a useful check and balance on some of the more obvious abuses of biblical scholarship of past generations.

Today, by contrast, major commentaries, from bible dictionaries to the Anchor Bible and most recent translations, are collaborative efforts involving Jewish and Catholic as well as Protestant scholars. Simply put, when one is academically accountable not only to one's co-religionists but also to those of other traditions which have an equal "stake" in the biblical passage at hand, it becomes less easy to ignore the insights of these traditions and, conversely, less easy to make use of the biblical texts for apolgetical purposes. A classic example of this "check and balance" phenomenon in action, of course, was the 1961 Presidential Address, "Parallelomania," delivered by Jewish New Testament scholar Samuel Sandmel at the annual meeting of the Society of Biblical Literature.[12] And despite his normally irenic approach, Sandmel was capable of effectively rebutting fellow-contributor Matthew Black's essay on the Pharisees in *The Interpreter's Dictionary of the Bible* (Vol. 3, pp. 774-81). Black's essay had castigated Pharisaic/Rabbinic Judaism as "a sterile religion of codified tradition, regulating every part of life by a *halachah*, observing a strict *apartheid.*" Sandmel responded in the following terms:

> I am personally a descendant of the Rabbinic tradition, the sterility of which was not so complete as to prevent my being born. Black's article is not only unreliable. It is disgraceful that it should have appeared in the same dictionary to which I and some dozen other Jews contributed.[13]

The intricacy of the polemical uses of stereotypical views of Pharisaic/Rabbinic Judaism can also serve to illustrate the interrelatedness of the contemporary ecumenical and Jewish-Christian dialogues. In commenting on the persistence of misinformation about New Testament Judaism among European scholars, for example, E. P. Sanders surfaces the underlying theological apologetic:

> The supposed legalistic Judaism of scholars from Weber to Thyen (and doubtless later) serves a very obvious function. It acts as the foil against which superior forms of religion are described. It permits, as Neusner has said, the writing of theology as if it were history. One must note in particular the projection on to Judaism of the view which Protestants find most objectionable in Roman Catholicism: the existence of a treasury of merits established by works of supererogation. We have here the retrojection of the Protestant-Catholic debate into ancient history, with Judaism taking the role of Catholicism and Christianity the role of Lutheranism.[14]

One antidote against such apologetic and anachromistic abuses of Sacred Scripture, of course, is found in the increasing practice of collaborative or even dialogical scholarships. The Lutheran/Roman Catholic ecumenical bilaterals, for example, are producing an increasing list of common studies of key points between the traditions. These studies in turn, it is hoped, will increasingly obviate the need for our respective communities to use the Scriptures as a battlefield for our differences of theological emphasis.[15] The literature of direct Christian-Jewish dialogue on biblical texts and themes, such as creation, covenant and redemption, is today reaching major proportions. It deserves, I believe, much more careful attention than it has received to date by biblical scholars in our respective communities. The very setting of such dialogues fosters a self discipline in the participants that might not be forthcoming in writing for their own denominational journals. Further, the interchange context appears to increase geometrically the points of view available to the engaged scholars, so that the final result of such efforts if often greater than the sum of its parts, with a resulting richness of perspective on the text not often found in individual efforts, however meticulous.[16]

Catholic biblical scholar Joseph Blenkinsopp, to whom we shall turn in more detail below, has been joined by Jewish scholar Nancy Fuchs-Kreimer in a call for joint efforts between Jewish and Christian scholars in the area of developing a more adequate biblical theology. "Is it," Blenkinsopp asks, "inconceivable that such mutual testing be carried out in dialogue and cooperation?" To which Fuchs-Kreimer replies:

> It *is* conceivable; indeed, it is imperative. Biblical scholarship today has returned to the theologically neutral issues, in part because of the recognized dead ends reached by the Biblical Theology movement. I have argued that, in light of recent advances in Jewish-Christian relations and the scholarly achievements of Sanders, Childs, van Buren, and others, a renewed effort at biblical theology is called for. Building on the solid insights of the past, but transending the limitations born of Jewish-Christian estrangement, Jews and Christians — separately and in dialogue — could begin to build theologies appropriate to a pluralistic time.[17]

Such calls, it might be noted parenthetically, have also been issued on a regular basis in official Church statements ranging from *Nostra Aetate* (1965) and the Vatican Guidelines (1975) to utterances of local episcopates (U.S., France, Germany) and the World Council of Churches.

C. Hermeneutical Questions: Is the New Testament Anti-Semitic?

An initial problem that needs to be taken up in this category is that of the alleged "antisemitism" of the New Testament. I have placed this question under hermeneutics rather than exegesis because I believe that a rather clear concensus on the latter question is already beginning to emerge. While earlier studies of the issue, such as Gregory Baum's *Is the New Testament Anti-Semitic?* (Paulist, 1965) and Bruce Vawter's "Are the Gospels Anti-Semitic?" *Journal of Ecumenical* Studies (1968, pp. 473-487) attempted to "defend" the Gospels against the charge, with only relative success, more recent studies have tended to admit with admirable frankness that there are, indeed polemical, anti-Judaic strata embedded in the New Testament traditions.

Indeed, Baum himself announced his change of mind on the matter in his trenchant introduction to Rosemary Radford Reuther's book *Faith and*

"Christianity and Judaism"

Fratricide: The Theological Roots of Anti-Semitism (Seabury Crossroad, 1974.[18] Reuther, however, went on to develop a rather straight line from the New Testament polemics to the acknowledged antisemitism of many of the Church Fathers and, by implication, up to the modern ideology of race hatred as preached by the Nazis against the Jews. For her, antisemitism as we know it in this century was the all but *inevitable* consequence of New Testament anti-Juadism.

However, as the theory has been worked out more recently, significant modifications in the Reutherian thesis have both strengthened our awareness of the polemical content of various strata of the New Testament[19] and our awareness of the non-polemical, continuity rather than discontinuity — oriented approach to Judaism of other strata as well.[20]

This refinement of the biblical data corresponds to a growing refinement of the historical question. Regarding the latter Yosef Hayim Yerushalmi, in direct response to Reuther, has pointed out that if the seeds of modern, ideological and genocidal antisemitism were to be found directly in the New Testament, these would have preforce come to fruition at some point during the Middle Ages when the Church held full physical power over the Jews in its midst. "The climactic anti-Jewish measure of which the medieval Christian state was capable," Yerushalmi writes, "was always expulsion and, on rare occasions, forced conversion. The Holocaust was the work of a thoroughly modern, neopagan state."[21] In this view, Christian anti-Jewish and anti-Judaic polemic remains a *sine qua non* for the Holocaust, and a matter in need of urgent reform today. But it is not a sufficient cause of genocide. The question is one of Christian responsibility for its own teachings, not guilt for Nazi atrocities.

Within the New Testament one can find alongside the Matthean polemic against the Pharisees a relatively positive portrait in the Lukan materials, where Pharisees attempt to save the life of Jesus by warning him of the plot against him and do succeed, in Acts, in saving the lives of the Apostles.

New Testament scholar John Townsend, writing in an excellent collection of essays in response to Reuther edited by Alan T. Davies, sees in the Gospel of John distinct strata of development with quite distinct views toward Jews and Judaism: the earlier strata being as positive ("salvation is from the Jews") as the latter is negative.[22] The question, then, has shifted from the original, overly simple "is the N.T. antisemitic?" to the more subtle one posed by Joseph Grassi in his essay "Are the Roots of Anti-Semitism in the Gospels?"[23] The latter question takes into better account the diversity of N.T. views on judaism.

In this latter question, the issue becomes properly hermeneutical. And it is here, in the Catholic conception of the interpretative endeavor, that the teaching authority of the Church has its role to play. As the 1975 Statement on Catholic-Jewish Relations of the National Conference of Catholic Bishops put it with regard to the Pauline corpus:

Admittedly, Paul's theology of Judaism has its more negative aspects; they have been adequately emphasized over the centuries in Catholic teaching. It would be well today to explore and emphasize the positive elements of Paul's thought that have received inadequate attention.[24]

Alan T. Davies, summarizing the conclusions of the dozen essays in the previously-mentioned *Antisemitism and the Foundations of Christianity* (Paulist, 1979) points to a similarly positive conclusion.

> The question of anti-Judaism is more than a question of a few notorious Matthean, Pauline and Johannine passages, but deals with the basic structure of New Testament theology itself ... If a common motif in these essays can be described, it is the Conviction that Christians need not choose between an ideological defense of their scriptures that wards off damaging criticism and the sad conclusion that the New Testament is so wholly contaminated by anti-Jewish prejudice as to lose all moral authority. Instead, Christians can through careful study isolate what genuine forms of anti-Judaism really color the major writings and, by examining their historic genesis, neutralize their potential for harm (p. XV).

D. Hermeneutical Theological Challenges: New Testament Christology and the Relationship Between the Scriptures

The second major area of hermeneutical challenge posted to biblical scholars by the contemporary Christian-Jewish dialogue lies in the area of "Old Testament theology" or, to put the same question another way, the mystery of the relationship between the Scriptures. These two interrelated questions, hinted at already in the quotation from Lux with which we began this paper, have recently been discussed at some length by Catholic scholar Joseph Blenkinsopp and Protestant Andre Lacocque in the *Biblical Studies* volume edited principally by Lawrence Boadt of the Catholic Biblical Association.[25] It is of interest that Pope John Paul II, in listing what he feels are the three central "dimensions" of the dialogue (the biblical, the present encounter with "today's people of the covenant established with Moses," and joint witness and service to the world in the Name of the One God for the sake of the Kingdom of God), begins with this issue:

> The first dimension of this dialogue, that is the meeting between the people of God of the old Covenant never revoked by God (Rom 11:29), on the one hand, and the people of the new covenant on the other is at the same time a dialogue within our own Church, so to speak, a dialogue between the first and second part of its Bible (Nov. 17, 1980, Mainz, Germany).

The Pope's deceptively simple phrasing here, I believe, goes to the heart of the hermeneutical question and addresses itself to both of the key sets of question and addresses itself to both of the key sets of questions which

Blenkinsopp points to as lying behind the list of failure, from Wellhausen to von Rad, to write an adequate Old Testament theology. These failures, as I have written [26] elsewhere, and as Blenkinsopp's careful survey of efforts in the field appears to support,[27] can on one level be described as a failure to balance properly, or at least to appreciate the delicate balance between continuity and discontinuity either on the level of the texts (canon criticism) or on the historical level. Blenkinsopp writes:

> It [the way of doing Old Testament theology ... which has dominated the field over the last two centuries] seems to imply in the first place that post-biblical Judaism (which logically includes present-day Judaism) is a different entity from the Old Testament and represents in effect a disintegration of the theological unity which it is the purpose of an Old Testament theology to display and interpret. Coming as it does between the Old Testament and early Christianity, it can providentially serve to illustrate the problem to which the New Testament provides the answer or, alternatively, the failure of a way of life (works, osbervances) which highlights by contrast the Christian dispensation (grace).[28]

Blenkinsopp then illustrates how this *a priori* theological thesis can lay the religious history of Israel on "the procrustean bed of Hegelian dialectics"[29] and become transposed into chronological terms, in which the original spiritual loftiness of the Old Testament (thesis) gives way to the revelation of sin and failure of early Judaism's leglistic morbidity (antithesis) to which Christ provides the answer (synthesis). As Blenkinsopp shows, this radical sense of discontinuity itself represents little more than a new version of the ancient Heilsgeschichte of Irenaeus in which "a continuous providential history ... reaches its climax or goal in Christ and the Church."[30]

Unfortunately, the procrustean bed aspect of Heilsgeschichte, to be maintained, forces the Old Testament theologian to ignore the theological pluralism of both the Hebrew Scriptures and early Christianity on the one hand, and the fact that early Christianity must itself be viewed as part of the developing history of Second Temple Judaism on the other.[31] This type of Old Testament theology, Blenkinsopp notes, experiences "remarkable difficulty in integrating the so-called wisdom writings." At its extreme, if one takes seriously the idea, however articulated, that Judaism exhausted itself in the early writings and only in its failures provides a *preaeparatio evangelica* one is left with little defense against Marcion's extrapolation of the promise/fulfillment theme to its logical conclusion that one can dispense altogether with the Hebrew Scriptures, a conclusion closely approximated in Bultmann's reduction of *Tanakh* to a mere propadeutic.

Thus, Schleiermacher and Harnack could espouse the view that "it was merely a historical accident that Christianity arose out of Judaism," and Frederick Delitzsch could close the circle by speaking of an "Aryan" Jesus,

The Impact on Biblical Studies

both rather logical conclusions from Wellhausen's a-historical view that "Judaism is a mere empty chasm over which one springs from the Old Testament to the New."[32] By asserting the continuity of ongoing Jewish history with its biblical past and a dialogic rather than exhaustive or supercessionist continuity between the Scriptures (and hence between the Church and the Jewish people) Church teaching today, I believe, is working toward a hermeneutic which will enable Christian scholarships to extricate itself from what Blenkinsopp and others see as "the impasse in which Old Testament theology now finds itself."

Andre LaCocque's essay on the humeneutical problem in Protestant tradition, like Blenkinsopp's, begins with the question of canon and aims at taking what he calls the "Prime Testament" seriously as history. LaCocque especially the weaknesses involved in utilizing the ancient methods of allegory and typology, both of which evacuate the scriptures of their historical specificity and are open to the problem of arbitrariness (*eisegesis*). The "promise/fulfillment" theme, which has been a major hermeneutical key (not least in Catholic liturgical tradition) he finds in serious need of revision. On the one hand, "promise" as a summary of Tanakh (cf. Rom 1:2; 4:14ff; Gal. 3:17 ff., etc.), if taken in isolation, will surely empty the Hebrew Scriptures of any immediacy as Word of God addressed to us today. The biblical particularism, which is to say its own meaning on its own Jewish terms, is soon lost in a maze of "hidden meanings" and "fuller senses." All in Scripture that cannot be somehow fitted into the retrospective procustean led of "realized eschatology" loses its force and majesty.

Embedded in the traditional promise/fullfillment scheme, especially as applied catechetically and liturgically, is an implicit supercessionist view. Equally left dangling, of course, is what we do theologically with our own time, our own "sacred history" if all came to absolute fruition two millenia ago. As LaCocque puts it, what many biblical theologians today

> ... are saying is that God's revelation in each instance is always complete, so that the schema 'promise-fulfillment' ... must be revised, and that anything relativizing our 'C.E.' time (cf. O. Cullmann) is wrong. Even when Jesus Christ is seen as the paradigm *par excellence* of history, he cannot fill so much of the horizon as to swallow history, so that we 'of the generations after' come 'too late.' There is no cumulative science of God finding its fullness in Jesus Christ (Wellhausen and Protestant Liberalism). Jesus Christ is not the chronological result of the Old Testament, but its 'axiological meaning' ... Fulfillment does not mean that the promise comes to an end and is replaced by the very thing that was promised, but it means that now the promise itself becomes unambiguous and consequently effective.[33]

Obviously, this insight, while challenging, does not answer all of our questions nor provide fully adequate theological terminology by which we can, as we must, affirm what is authentic in the promise-fullfillment schema while avoiding the pitfalls which history teaches that the schema can lead us into. One attempt, while perhaps not fully satisfactory, at least serves to point a sound direction for further reflection. The 1975 Vatican Guildelines for Implementing *Nostra Aetate*, in its section on the Liturgy, note:

> When commenting on Biblical texts, emphasis will be laid on the continuity of our faith with that of the earlier covenant, in the perspective of the promises, without minimizing those elements of Christianity which are original. We believe that those promises were fulfilled with the first coming of Christ. But it is nonetheless true that we still await their perfect fulfillment in His glorious return at the end of time.[34]

While the distinction between fulfillment and perfect fulfillment may be a thin one, it has the very necessary virtue of acknowledging, in this context, the "unfulfilled" or "not yet" aspects of the Christ event that anyone, looking at the realities of the two thousand years since that event, would have to concede: The Messianic Age clearly is not yet fully here. War, famine, and corruption continue unabated. Two World Wars, the Holocaust, and the prospect of nuclear annihilation of the human race all testify to the aptness of the Jewish people's age-old "no" concerning the more triumphalist (and a-historical) elements of certain Christian claims on the Kingdom.

In recent Christian scholarship, I believe, there is a growing consensus concerning the validity of the critique of the traditionally "simple fulfill-ment" theory. This consensus, interestingly, appears to be emerging among systematic and biblical scholars as well as among those who have been active in the Jewish-Christian dialogue to date.[35] It emerges in one way in liberation theology and for distinct, but compatible reasons in major continental, "political" theologians as well. Surveying such European thinkers as Pannenburg, Moltmann, Kung, and Schillebeckx, and such Latin Americans as Gutierrez, Bonino, Sobrino and Boff, John T. Pawlikowski concludes that these systematicians concur with those more directly involved in the dialogue (e.g. Littell, the Eckardts, Paul van Buren Rylaarsdam, Parkes, Hruby, Fleischner. Hellwig, Rijk, M. Barth) that "the Kingdom of God must be seen as a future rather a present reality" and that Jesus can no longer be explained simply as the one who fulfilled the Messianic prophecies of the Hebrew Scriptures." The latter scholars, Pawlikowski's survey shows, simply make explicit the implications of this overall consensus for Christian-Jewish relations. Their consensus, which it must be pointed out is given a certain support in official Catholic and Protestant statements,[36] Pawlikowski sums up in the following dictum:

> The Christ event did not invalidate the Jewish faith perspective . . . Christianity is not superior to Judaism, nor is it the fulfillment of Judaism as previously maintained.[37]

Among Catholic biblical scholars as well, a more careful framing of the relationship is also emerging, one with numerous implications for "doing" biblical theology, New Testament as well as Old Testament. Blenkinsopp

The Impact on Biblical Studies

cites John L. McKenzie's *A Theology of the Old Testament* (Doubleday, 1974) as the only one he knows of "which as attempted (to) take Tanakh seriously on its own terms" (pp. 113 & 119) along with Clemens Thoma's *A Christian Theology of Judaism* (Paulist, 1980) as breaking new ground by "taking Judaism with absolute theological seriousness" (p. 114). McKenzie's position is a trenchant one. Noting the complex nature of messianic thought in the Hebrew Scriptures, and the fact that no particular version of it leads directly or inexorably to Jesus as its fulfillment, McKenzie affirms:

> This writer has said elsewhere that Jesus is the Messiah of Judaism. I stand by this observation, but I do not believe that it obliges me to find faith in Jesus Messiah in the Old Testament, nor to base faith in Jesus Messiah in the Old Testament. Jesus transformed the idea of Messiah when he fulfilled it. The total reality of Jesus Messiah is found nowhere in the Old Testament, not even in its totality. Jesus would have emerged from nothing except Israel and the Old Testament; but the study of the Old Testament does not demand that Jesus Messiah emerge from it.[38]

Here, McKenzie disassociates the enterprise of Old Testament theology — from the Wellhausen — type school which would see the Testaments related only accidentally or peripherally (because essentially negatively). He frees Tanakh to speak to us directly, without New Testament "filtering" but also without in any way diminishing the validity of the New Testament's insight into the Christ-event on *its* own proper terms. The two Testaments remain spiritually linked, in concrete historical terms and in the full sense of theological mystery. Both can, in the words of *Dei Verbum*, serve to "illumine each other." But the covenant link between them is one of dialogue, not absorption or supercession, just as is the "spiritual bond" (to use the Conciliar phrase constantly re-iterated by Pope John Paul II) linking the Church and the Jewish people "at the very level of their respective identities." To "do" biblical theology, in short, is to become involved, like it or not, in dialogue with "today's people of the covenant established with Moses," i.e. the Jewish people.

Further, an interesting consensus of terminology and approach seems to be emerging among those Catholic scholars who have addressed the dialogue most directly. This has perhaps best been expressed recently in Catholic theologian David Tracy's seminal article "Religious Values After the Holocaust: A Catholic View." Tracy, who considers the Holocaust "theologically the *tremendum* of our age," argues for the develop of a hermeneutical methodology more suited to our time.

On the one hand, Tracy seeks to develop a "hermeneutics of suspicion." This would cast suspicion on "all nonworldly, non political forms of spirituality," and equally "upon the this-wordly and anti-privatizing spiritualities which accord too optimistic a portrait of the world," as well as upon the "pessimistic spiritualities of retreat from our historical and political responsibility."

> The Catholic 'return to history and the world' initiated by Vatican II has received its proper corrective from (the) political and liberation theologians. For these theologians have developed profound theological hermeneutics of suspicion upon the world and an equally profound hermeneutics of the this-worldly reality of Christian salvation. They have retrieved half-forgotten (and, it should be noted, almost always Jewish rather than Greek) resources of the tradition.[39]

A hermeneutics of suspicion, applied to the New Testament issues outlined above, enables Tracy to acknowledge the anti-Jewish polemics of the N.T. While at the same time relativizing them as historically conditioned and as standing condemned as false before the essence of the gospel message:

> The painful, repressed memories of Christian anti-Semitism have also been aided by the anti-Judaic statements of the New Testament, especially but not solely in the Gospel of John. If those scriptural statements cannot be excised, then minimally they should always be commented upon whenever used in liturgical settings and noted critically in every Christian commentary on the Scriptures . . . Those anti-Judaic statements of the New Testament bear *no* authoritative status for Christianity . . . The heart of the New Testament message — the love who is God — should release the demythologizing power of its own prophetic meaning to rid the New Testament and Christianity once and for all of these statements.[40]

Similar statements, and a similar hermeneutic of posing the essence of the biblical tradition, authentically understood, over against the anti-Jewish material as the latter's critique and judge, can be seen in the works of other Catholic theologians grappling with the same issue.[41]

Regarding the positive, or "retrieval" pole of Tracy's hermeneutic, here again a certain consensus seems to be emerging that the key issue involves taking seriously the dynamic tension that characterizes New Testament eschatology. The issue that both unites and divides Jews and Christians is Christology. In approaching it, one must be clear that the question is not one of "accommodating" Christian to Jewish claims, but rather allowing the New Testament to speak for itself and in so doing taking both it and the ongoing validity of the Jewish witness to us with fundamental theological serious. Monica Hellwig in this context cautions wisely:

> The contempt for post-Christian Judaism is not really grounded in the divinity claim that is so central in Christian attention . . . Rather, what appears to be at the root of the issue is the understanding of redemption which is packed into the messianic claim.[42]

The Impact on Biblical Studies

Tracy's attempt is thus to "retrieve" a more authentic (but no less "high") Christology as it emerges out of the New Testament. He offers the model of a "proleptic" Christology as an "appropriate route to take."

> For to affirm the belief in Jesus Christ is, for the Christian, to affirm the faith that in the ministry, death and resurrection of Jesus the decisive token, manifestation, prolepsis of the future reign of God and, thereby of Messianic times) is both already here in proleptic form (indeed, for myself has been manifested as always already here) and just as really, not yet here . . . Christology thus reformulated as proleptic reaffirms on inner Christian grounds the status of the Jews as God's chosen, covenanted people . . . The always/ready/not yet structure of belief pervading Israel's expectancy of Messianic times remains the fundamental structure of Christian belief as well.[43]

In this, more dynamic perspective, true dialogue between Christians and Jews is possible. Both have glimpsed, decisively and proleptically, the future, end time. Neither claims to encapulate the eschaton fully within itself. The Church, as Daniel Harrington, S.J., reminds us, should is not itself identified with the Kingdom, though open to it and experiencing, specially sacramentally, a foretaste of its "perfect fulfillment."

Rosemary Reuther, in a careful summation of her present position, which manages to avoid the rhetorical excesses of *Faith and Fratricide,* states very much the same thing as Tracy. For her, the problem has been the uncritical (and essentially triumphalist) claims of "realized eschatology" and "fulfilled Messianism."

> Christians must formulate the faith in Jesus as the Christ in terms which are proleptic and anticipatory rather than final and fulfilled. Jesus should not be said to fulfill all the Jewish hopes for the coming Messiah, which indeed he did not . . . The proleptic understanding of Jesus' Messianic identity is familiar to Christian exegetes. It has been particularly renewed in liberation theologies. It is the exegesis that best translates the New Testament experience. Jesus' message is falsified when it is translated into a final fulfillment that is spiritualized and institutionally lodged in the past.[44]

In other words, a major impact of the dialogue on biblical studies has been to allow us, within a devloping hermeneutical methodology, to recover today a clearer sense of Jesus' own message of the Kingdom "at hand," helping thereby to clarify, without diminishing the early Church's teachings *about* Jesus.[45]

In conclusion, I would recommend highly Lawrence Boadt's introduction to the volume, *Biblical Studies,* which has featured prominently in this survey. There he lists, in concise fashion, both areas where a *mutual* re-examination of Scripture by Jews and Christians together can enrich the biblical appreciation of both traditions and areas within Christian biblical studies where challenges remain to be met. Contemporary Christian biblical scholarship, I hope I have shown, has been vastly enriched and profoundly challenged by the dialogical encounter with a living Judaism, an encounter that it itself in large measure helped to make possible. That it has proven itself capable of acknowledging the Jewish roots of that enrichment and of rising to meet its challenge in a no less profoundly positive way I hope I have also shown. While, as yet, many more questions have emerged than clear answers, exegetically as well as hermeneutically, I would perceive a healthy sense of progress at least in clarifying the questions that need to be addressed. This, in the light of two millenia in which Jews and Christians have used Tanakh disputationally as a battleground for "disproving" each other's claims rather than allowing it to speak to us in humility and openness, is no small miracle — and no small witness to the ongoing nature of revelation as the Spirit hovers protectively over our troubled waters.

Footnotes

1) *Richard C. Lux, "What Do We Mean When We Say that Life is Sacred," unpublished paper (Nov. 8, 1982) pp. 2-3. This and the other papers from the Synagogue Council/Bishops' Conference Colloquium are being edited for publication by the university of Notre Dame in their "Social Policy in the Catholic and Jewish Traditions" series.*

2) *E. g. Samuel Sandmel,* We Jews and Jesus *(Oxford University, 1965); David Flusser, Jesus (Herder & Herder, 1969); Geza Vermes,* Jesus the Jew *(Collins, 1973); Pinchas Lapide,* Juden und Christen *(Benzinger, 1976).*

3) *A useful survey of the more important finds, Boadt notes (cit., p. 14), that affect biblical studies appears in Edwin Yamauchi, "Documents from Old Testament Times: A Survey of Recent Discoveries,"* Westminster Journal of Theology *41 (1978) 1-32. Cf. L. Boadt el al., ed's,* Biblical Studies *(Paulist 1980).*

4) *E g. Morton Smith,* Tannaitic Parallels to the Gospels *(Journal of Biblical Literature Monograph Series, Vol. 6, 1951).*

5) *E. g., among others, R. LeDeaut,* The Message of the N.T. and the Aramaic Bible *(Targum) Rome: Biblical Institute Press, revised 1982); M. McNamara,* Targum and Testament *(Grand Rapids, Wm B. Eerdmans, 1972); and S.H. Levey,* The Messiah: An Aramaic Interpretation: The Messianic Exegesis of the Targum *(Hebrew Union College, 1974).*

6) *Eugene Fisher, "From Polemic to Objectivity? A Short History of the Use and Abuse of Hebrew Sources by Recent Christian New Testament Scholarship," (National Association of Professors of Hebrew:* Hebrew Studies *journal, Vol. XX-XXI, 1980) 199-208. Cf. L. Boadt's trenchant comment on Kittell and Strack-Billerbeck (cit. 7) as well. E. P. Sanders'* Paul and Palestinian Judaism *(Fortress, 1977) devotes considerable attention to detailing and de-bunking the biased*

information of these and other major Christian commentators on the nature of first Century Judaism. The first half of Sanders' volume (pp. 33-426), I believe, should be required reading for all beginning biblical students.

7)   J. Nuesner, The Rabbinic Traditions of the Pharisees Before 70 *(3 Vol's. Leiden: Brill, 1971) and E. Rivkin,* The Hidden Revolution *(Nashville: Abingden, 1978). Michael Cook surveys the* status questions *in his "Jesus and the Pharisees: The Problem As It Stands Today,"* Journal of Ecumenical Studies *(Vol. 15, no. 3, Summer 1978) 441-460.*

8)   *Cf. C. Thoma,* A Christian Theology of Judaism *(Paulist Stimulus, 1980); and J. Pawlikowski,* What Are They Saying About Christian-Jewish Relations? *(Paulist, 1980) 93-108; and* Christ in the Light of the Christian-Jewish Dialogue *(Paulist Stimulus, 1982).*

9)   *For a recent example of how uniformed stereotypy and ignorance of the sources can still mar otherwise serious studies, see John Riches,* Jesus and the Transformation of Judaism *(Seabury, 1982). My review of this work will appear in the next issue of* Catholic Biblical Quarterly.

10)   *G. Sloyan,* Jesus on Trial *(Fortress, 1973), updated in "Recent Literature on the Trial Narratives" in T. Ryan, ed.,* Critical History and Biblical Faith *(Villanova U., 1979) 136-and J. Fitzmyer, "Antisemitism and the Cry of all the People (Matt. 27:25),"* Theological Studies *(Vol. 26, 1965) 667-671, and "Jesus the Lord,"* Chicago Studies *17 (1978) 87-90. For a summary of Jewish as well as Christian views, see the special issue of* Judaism *(Winter, 1971), "The Trial of Jesus in the Light of History."*

11)   *On Pauline studies, as well as the broader question of the Law, see especially Gerard Sloyan,* Is Christ the End of the Law? *(Westminster, 1978); E. P. Sanders,* Paul and Palestinian Judaism *(Fortress, 1977); Lloyd Gastin, "Paul and the Torah," in A.T. Davies, Ed.,* Antisemitism and the Foundations of Christianity *(Paulist, 1979); J. T. Townsend, "I Cor 3:15 and the School of Shammai,* "HTR 61 (1968) 500-504; J. Koenig, *Jews and Christians in Dialogue: New Testament Foundations (Westminster, 1979) 37-59; Krister Stendahl,* Paul among the Jews and Gentiles *Fortress, 1976).*

12)   *December 27, 1961 at Concordia Theological Seminary, St. Louis, Missouri,* Journal of Biblical Literature *31 (1962) 1-13. The text was reprinted in Sandmel's* Two Living Traditions: Essays on Religion And the Bible *(Detroit: Wayne State University Press, 1972) 291-304. Many of Sandmel's essays here collected, such as "Jewish and Catholic Biblical Scholarship" and "Understanding and Misunderstanding: Prepossession versus Malice" remain basic to an appreciation of the contemporary dialogue between Jewish and Christian biblical scholars. Sandmel's open style should not mask the pain and frustration often felt by Jews in this process. In his treatment of "the persistence of the view of rabbinic religion as one of legalistic works-righteousness," E. P. Sanders (cit., 35) cites Sandmel's revealing lament: "It can be set down as something destined to endure*

eternally that the usual Christian commentators will disparage Judasim and its supposed legalism, and Jewish scholars will reply, usually fruitlessly... The issue is not to bring these interpreters to love Judaism, but only to bring them to a responsible, elementary comprehension of it." S. Sandmel, The First Century in Judaism and Christianity *(N.Y., 1969)* 66.

13)   Ibid.. *101f.*

14)   *Sanders, cit., 57.*

15)   *E.g. R. E. Brown, K. Danfried, J. Fitzmyer, J. Reumann, ed's.,* Mary in the New Testament *(Fortress/Paulist, 1978)* and Peter in the New Testament *(Augsburg/Paulist, 1973).*

16)   *Several excellent examples of this phenomenon can be found in various special issues of journals such as* SIDIC *(Rome),* Immanuel *(Jerusalem),* Journal of Ecumenical Studies *(Philadelphia)* Christian-Jewish Relations *(London),* and Freiburger Rundbrief *(Germany), which regularly publish the results of such scholarly symposia from around the world. An excellent recent example of this process in action can be found in the summer, 1982 issue of* Face to Face: An Interreligious Bulletin, *published by the Anti-Defamation League of B'nai B'rith. This issue records the brilliant and provocative exchange between Israeli scholar Pinchas Lapide and Catholic scholar Gerard Sloyan on the Johannine and Lucan materials.*

17)   *Nancy Fuchs-Kreimer, "Christian Old Testament Theology: A Time for New Beginnings,"* Journal of Ecumenical Studies *(18:1, Winter 1981) 91-92. In the same context, Fuchs-Kreimer pinpoints both the central problem and the obvious solution to the "impasse" in the biblical theological enterprise today: "If Christianity has tended theologically to write itself out of Israelite history as early as Second Isaiah, thus having no motivation to see the subsequent history in a positive light, Judaism has done nothing to discourage this view. When Jews claim the Hebrew Bible as their exclusive heritage, Christianity does become the inexplicable offspring gone astray. After insisting that Ezra is ours alone, Jews should not be surprised if Christians proceed to count him out of their spiritual history. When Jews no longer feel a need to respond in kind to Christian polemics, they may be able to evaluate such key issues as legalism and particularism with new eyes. When we each begin to grant the claims of the other to full[biblical] ancestry, we may find both our faiths growing in their effort to absorb their newly widened inheritance." Fuchs-Kreimer is on exactly the right track, in my opinion, in viewing the entire Hebrew Bible as the spiritual antedent of both Rabbinic Judaism and Christianity ("the two contemporary offspring" (ibid., 90). Put another way, as Catholic scholar Joseph Fitzmyer has done, this is to see both rabbinic Judaism and early Christianity as creative, ongoing developments of the one biblical Judaism which both can claim as their proper heritage, though not exclusively. Put negatively, it is not that either movement can lay claim to sole continuity with the other relegated to being a "divergence" from the biblical vision (itself highly pluralistic). Both*

The Impact on Biblical Studies

stand in dynamic continuity (and discontinuity) with biblical Judaism, with major differnces between them being the Jewish continuity of peoplehood on the one hand and that of faith in the Jew, Jesus, as the Christ on the other.

18)   Baum writes: "When in the late fifties I tried to give a partial response to Jules Isaac in a book entitled The Jews and the Gospel, I readily acknowledged the anit-Jewish trends present in Christian preaching, but I then thought that it was my religious duty as a Christian theologian to defend the New Testament itself from the accusation of prejudice and falsification. At that time I thought that the anti-Jewish trends were later developments in Christian history ... While I was bound to acknowledge that already the New Testament proclaimed the Christian message with a polemical edge against the religion of Israel, I refused to draw the consequences from this. I was still convinced that the anti-Jewish trends in Christianity were peripheral and accidental, not grounded in the N.T. itself but due to later developments, and that it would consequently be fairly easy to purify the preaching of the Church from anti-Jewish bias. Since then ... I have had to change my mind. (Introduction to Faith and Fratricide, Seabury, 1974, pp. 2-4).

19)   E. g. Samuel Sandmel's Anti-Semitism in the New Testament? (Fortress, 1978). Sandmel notes, however, that, strictly speaking, "anti-Semitism" is the wrong term. His caveat, I think, is crucial: "Accordingly, the nineteenth and twentieth century word anti-Semitism is a completely wrong term when transferred to the first and second Christian centuries. Yet wrong as it is, it has been and continued to be used in connection with Christian hostility to Jews. Scholars have proposed other terms: anti-Jewish or anti-Judaism. These terms are better because they are correct; they simply have not caught on. In this book we use 'anti-Semitism' consciously, aware of how wrong the term is" (p. xxi).

20)   My own treatment of the subject in Faith Without Prejudice (Paulist, 1977, pp. 54-75) attempts just this sort of synthesis.

21)   Y. H. Yerushalmi, "Response to Rosemary Reuther," in E. Fleischner, ed., Auschwitz: Beginning of a New Era? (KTAV/ADL/ Cuthedral Church of St. John Divine, 1977) 103.

22)   A. T. Davies, Ed., Antisemitism and the Foundations of Christianity (Paulist, 1979). This volume remains basic to the field today.

23)   J. Grassi, "Are The Roots of Anti-Semitism in the Gospels?" in M. Zeik and M. Siegel, ed's., Root and Branch (Roth Publ., 1973) 71-88.

24)   Cited in E. Fisher, Faith Without Prejudice (cit.) 164-165. This, I believe, is the careful point being made, albeit in strong language, by Msgr. Jorge Mejia of the Vatican Commission for Religious Relations with the Jews when he states:

"Here (in Dei Verbum) we have then a set of humeneutical rules which go well beyond the boundaries of scientific exegesis."

Mejia offers the example of the Conciliar Declaration Nostra Aetate *that "what happened in his (Jesus') passion cannot be charged against all the Jews, without distinction, then alive, nor against the Jews of today" (no. 4). "This," Mejia states, "is founded on sound exegesis as has by now been made quite clear. But once the affirmation is thus made by an official organ of the Church's magisterium, it becomes normative and gives the right clue for the interpretation of difficult passages like 1 Thes 2:14-16 and others." Mejia notes that "the same applies" to the affirmation, in the Guidelines that "the Jews should not be presented as rejected or accused by God, as if this followed from the Holy Scriptures." J. Mejia, "A Christian View of Bible Interpretation"* in L. Boadt, et. al., Ed's., Biblical Studies *(Paulist, 1980) 60, 71.*

25)   *J. Blenkinsopp, "Tanakh and New Testament: A Christian Perspective" (96-119) and A. LaCocque, "The 'Old Testament' in Protestant Tradition" (120-146) in L. Boadt, et. al., ed's.,* Biblical Studies, cit. *For a Jewish response to Blenkinsopp's article, cf. footnote no. 17, above.*

26)   *Eugene J. Fisher, "Continuity and Discontinuity in the Scriptural Readings,"* Liturgy *(May 1978) 30-37.*

27)   *Blenkinsopp writes, for example, that "what... is significant about von Rad's* Theology *for our present purpose is the fact of discontinuity which led him, quite logically, to a typological linking of Old and New Testament and a virtual bracketing of post-biblical Judaism." (cit., 113).*

28)   Ibid., *110.*

29)   *As in the works of Wilhelm Vathe and Wellhausen. Blenkinsopp, cit., 103.*

30)   Ibid., *100.*

31)   Ibid., *101.*

32)   *Wellhausen,* Prolegomena to the History of Ancient Israel *(1878; Meridian Books, 1957) P. I. Wellhausen, with the same logic, can conclude (p. 512) that "the Church is not his (Christ's) work, but an inheritance from Judaism to Christianity." He thus manages to see in the gospels not only a repudiation of Judaism but, for the same ideological reasons, of the Church (especially the Roman Catholic Church) itself.*

33)   *LaCocque, cit., 138.*

34)   *Cited in E. Fisher,* Faith Without Prejudice *(cit.) 154-155.*

35)   *For an analysis of recent developments in the dialogue, see E. Fisher, "Jews and Christians: The Next Step for Theology,"* Commonweal *(Nov. 5, 1982) 588-591.*

36)   *For English texts of these official Church documents up to 1977, see Helga Croner, ed.,* Stepping Stones to Further Jewish-Christian Relations *(Stimulus/ADL, 1977). Commentary on these documents and on the theological opinion as well can be found in Michael B. McGarry, C.S.P.,* Christology After Auschwitz *(Paulist, 1977). More recent papal statements, a number of them quite remarkable such as that given in Mainz, Nov. 1980, cited above, can be found in John B. Sheerin, C.S.P., and John F. Hotchkin, ed's.,* John Paul II: Addresses

The Impact on Biblical Studies

and Homilies on Ecumenism 1978-1980. *(U.S. Catholic Conference, 1980.*

37)   *J. T. Pawlikowski,* Christ in the Light of the Christian-Jewish Dialogue *(Paulist, 1982).*

38)   *J. L. McKenzie,* A Theology of the Old Testament *(Doubleday Image, 1976) 31-32.*

39)   David Tracy, "Religious Values After the Holocaust: A Catholic View," *in A. Peck, ed.,* Jews and Christians After the Holocaust *(Fortress, 1982) 96-97. Daniel Harrington's chapters on the Kingdom and Jewish Apocalyptic, in his* God's People in Christ *(Fortress, 1980).*

40)   *Tracy, cit., 94.*

41)   *E. g. Gregory Baum's "Catholic Dogma After Auschwitz," and Monika Hellwig's "From The Jesus of Story to the Christ of Dogma" in A. T. Davies,* Antisemitism and the Foundations of Christianity *(Paulist 1979) 118-150. In this volume, Baum writes: "Since, in the history of the West, the spiritual negation of Jewish existence has led to contempt, injustices, and, however, indirectly, physical extermination, the traditional teaching stood condemned by a superior principle, namely the redemption of human life, which constitutes the spirit and substance of the Bible. Divine revelation is* propter nos et proper nostram salutem ... *the pure and uncontaminated source of new life. Because of this supreme biblical teaching, it is possible to correct certain positions of scripture and tradition when they serve the destruction of life and the enslavement of human beings"* (Ibid., 140-141). *So too Raymond Brown, who states flatly:*

> *"Here I must beg the reader's indulgence for an aside. One cannot disguise a hostility toward 'the Jews' in the Johannine passion narrative, neither by softening the translation to 'Judeans' or 'Judaists,' nor by explaining that John speaks of the 'Jews' when the context implies that the authorities (i.e. the chief priests) alone were involved. By deliberately speaking of 'the Jews' the fourth evangelist is spreading to the Synagogue of his own time the blames that an earlier tradition placed on the authorities. He is not the first to do this, for the oldest extant Christian writing speaks of 'the Jews who killed both the Lord Jesus and the prophets' (I Thessalonians 2:14-15). But John is the most insistent New Testament writer in this usage ...*
>
> *"This context of mutual hostility between the Johannine community and the Synagogue must be taken into account when reflecting on the Johannine passion narrative. Today Christians are embarrassed by such hostility (and some Jews have begun to question the wisdom of excommunicating believers in Jesus from the Synagogue). An initial response is one of 'Speak no evil; see no evil, hear no evil.' namely, to omit the anti-Jewish sections from the public reading of the passion narrative. In my opinion, a truer response is to continue to read the*

"Christianity and Judaism"

whole passion; not subjecting it to excisions that seem wise to us; but once having read it, then to preach forcefully that such hostility between Christian and Jew cannot be continued today and is against our fundamental understanding of Christianity. Sooner or later Christian believers must wrestle with the limitations imposed on the Scriptures by the circumstances in which they were written. They must be brought to see that some attitudes found in the Scriptures, however explicable in the times in which they originated, may be wrong attitudes if repeated today. They must reckon with the implications inherent in the fact that the word of God has come to us in the words of men. To excise dubious attitudes from the readings of Scripture is to perpetuate the fallacy that what one hears in the Bible is always to be imitated because it is 'revealed' by God, the fallacy that every position by an author of scripture is inerrant." (Worship).

42)   Hellwig, cit., 122.
43)   Tracy, cit., 100.
44)   Reuther, in A. Peck, ed., cit., 37.
45)   *In my* Commonweal *piece (cf. footnote no. 28, above), I list several areas, based on Pawlikowski's survey, where Christian scholars have tended in the past to pose dichotomies between Jesus' teaching and that of the pluriform, developing Jewish spiritual malice of his time. In each of these cases, I argue, the perceived "antithesis" fail to be sustained on the basis of the evidence itself. They are only sustainable to the extent that one stereotypes and trunates the Second Temple and rabbinic evidence (as does Strack/Billerbeck) to fit the apologetic a priori one wishes to erect. These categories, to whet the reader's critical appetite, are: the Abba experience (made prominent by Joachim Jeremias); the notion that Jesus upholds that dignity of the human person over above the law in a way that would break radiacally with Jewish tradition (Jesus' teaching on key points of the Law is actually quite Pharisaic in spirit and interpretation); the notion of a "presumed antipathy between the Pharisees and the* am haaretz; *the nature of evil and the "evil inclination;" and love of enemy (the only one of the Matthean antitheses to have any validity, but a matter of degree, I argue, more than actual discontinuity with Pharisaic spirituality). Only in the teachings about Jesus, I conclude, does a distinction emerge between early Christianity and developing rabbinic Judaism which can explain the ultimate "schism" between the two, otherwise closely parallel Jewish movements of the time.*

X

Anti-Semitism and
The Christologies of Barth,
Berkouwer and Pannenberg

BY EUGENE B. BOROWITZ*

Rosemary Ruether has called anti-Semitism "the left hand of Christology," described christology as "the other side of anti-
Judaism" and said that "Christology and anti-Judaism in-
tertwine."[1] While Ruether's study is a strong and thorough-going polemic
against Christian theological anti-Semitism, it never charges any contemporary Christian thinker with such views. Rather her book deals with
documents and doctrines of Christianity's classic periods, and mentions
modern thinkers only as interpreters of history. Ruether makes no claim, for
all her insistence that christology is linked with anti-Semitism that contemporary theologians in their doctrines of the Christ carry forward the pernicious corollaries of a previous age. That matter is surely worth investigating.

A preliminary typological hypothesis may help sensitize us to the pos-
sibilities. Liberal Christian thinkers, being deeply concerned with the bonds
which unite all human beings despite cultural differences, are likely to
consider it a high moral responsibility to disavow anti-Semitism and create
christologies which accomplish that end. Traditionally minded theologians,

---

*Eugene B. Borowitz is a professor at the Hebrew Union College -
Jewish Institute of Religion. This essay is taken from Dialog. Vol. 16,
1977, pp. 38-41. It was itself excerpted from a larger manuscript entitled
"Contemporary Christologies: A Jewish Response." Copyright 1977 by
Eugene Borowitz. It is reprinted here by permission of the publishers.*

being deeply reverent of New Testament teachings, might carry forward the anti-Jewish tendencies found there despite the liberal ethical concerns of modern times. Let us then examine the implications for the Jews and Judaism of the christologies of three contemporary theologians of a relatively traditional bent, Karl Barth, G. C. Gerkouwer and Wolfhart Pannenberg.

Karl Barth has treated the question of the Jews and Judaism in several places in the *Church Dogmatics*. Barth's doctrine of the Jews is dialetical. He not only affirms that God once chose the Jewish people but insists, with some passion and typical repetitiousness, that they are still God's chosen people, indeed they are close to God in a way that no Christian, because not born to covenant, can ever hope to be. The Barth completely negates the classic root of Christian theological anti-Semitism, the abrogation or nullification of the people of Israel's relationship with God once the Christ has come and been rejected. But Israel is now chosen "to reflect the judgment from which God has rescued man and which He wills to endure Himself in the person of Jesus of Nazareth ... It will express the awareness of the human basis of the divine suffering and therefore the recognition of man's incapacity, unwillingness and unworthiness with regard to the divine mercy purposed in Jesus Christ." (II/2, 206) "Over against the witness of the church it can set forth only the sheer, stark judgment of God, only the obduracy and consequent misery of man ... This is how Israel punishes itself for its sectarian self-assertion ... (One can see this) even in the spectral form of the Synagogue." (II/2, 209) I forebear from multiplying references to this, the negative side of the Barthian dialectic toward the Jews, though there is much worthy of citation. The tension may be summarised this way. The church "will thus regard itself as united and bound to all Israel—in spite of the very different form of its membership in the community of God. Even more, it will reckon it as a special honour to have in its midst living witnesses to the election of all Israel in the persons of Christian Israelites." (II/2, 213)

Since the negative side of the Barthian evaluation of the Jews and Judaism might easily be snatched from its context for political or social exploitation these theological views should be balanced by what Barth sees as an appropriate consequence of his teaching. Speaking specifically of Germany, he said in Bonn in 1946, "Anti-Semitism is the form of godlessness besides which, what is usually called atheism (as confessed say in Russia) is quite innocuous. For in anti-Semitic godlessness realities are invoked irrespective of whether those who invented and worked this business were aware of them or not. Here what is involved is conflict with Christ."[3]

This dialectical attitude toward the Jews is clearly illustrated in Barth's discussion of a Christian mission to the Jews. Positively there can be no "mission" as such for here "there can be no question of the (Christian) community proclaiming the true faith in place of a false ... What have we to teach him that he does not already know ...?" Negatively, however, "Israel denied its election and calling ... the Synagogue became and was and still is the organization ... which hastens toward a future that is empty .. Necessarily, therefore, the Jew ... is dreadfully empty of grace and blessing." (IV/3/2, 877) Yet when it comes to what the church should do Barth largely gives up direct action for indirect influence. Since the Jews have repudiated the gospel "not just accidentally or incidentally, but in principle, a *priori*" there is "therefore no prospect of revision from the human standpoint." While one "can and should hold talks with the Jews for the purpose of information" there is "needed the direct intervention of God Himself." The Christian responsibility to the Jew is to "make the Synagogue jealous" by "the life of the community as a whole authentically lived before the Jews." In this task Christianity has failed. "It has debated with him, tolerated him, persecuted him, or abandoned him to persecution without protest. What is worse, it has made baptism an entrance card into the best European society ... This failure, which is often unconscious, or perhaps concealed by all kinds of justifiable or unjustifiable counter charges against the Jews, is one of the darkest chapters in the whole history of Christianity and one of the most serious of all wounds in the body of Christ." (IV/3/2, 878)

On one level, that of action, hence the most important level, Barth is clearly against anti-Semitism. As a matter of theory, however, is not Ruether's proposition here proved correct, that in rejecting the Christ, Jews draw upon them the repressed ambivalence Christians feel in exalting the Jew Jesus to Divinity? Or, to put it more directly, if prejudice means judging out of one's own inner concerns and needs as against an evaluation based on an effort to confront the external reality, the Karl Barth must be called prejudiced against Jews. He does not care what, in fact, is the religious reality of life in the Synagogue or what Jewish practice might say about God and God's promises to those who know its living spirit. Israel is assigned a role in Barth's system by the system, for faith determines reality for him and in terms of it he will evaluate what passes for reality in the Jewish community. Here Ruether's association of christology with anti-Semitism holds true on a theoretical level though fortunately Barth has insisted that no socio-political degradation of the Jews may be based on the negative side of his teaching about the Jews.

G. C. Berkouwer

Because of G. C. Berkouwer's biblicism we might expect him to be the most explicit anti-Semite of the group studied here. In fact, however, Berkouwer seems almost devoid of anti-Jewish sentiment. Rather he systematically applies a universalizing hermeneutic to passages which speak of the Jews as opponents of the Christ or the church. He regularly applies them to humanity as a whole, omitting significant reference to the Jews of Jesus' time or since. See for example his discussion of the responsibility for the trial and crucifixion of Jesus[4], the guilt of Pilate and the crowd he speaks to[5], and the exegesis of Romans 9.[6] A particularly striking example of his sensitivity is his treatment of Hos. 13.9 which was employed by the Formula of Concord in speaking about the "wicked will of Satan and man.' The verse reads, "It is thy destruction, O Israel, that thou art against me, thy helper." Berkouwer deals here only with humanity as a whole, commenting in passing that he is "leaving aside the correctness of the (Formula's) exegesis" of the verse.[7]

Berkouwer has no hesitation in discussing the radical differences between Judaism and Christianity;[8] yet it is clear that he does not wish to carry forward the anti-Semitism once so closely associated with New Testament teaching. This emerges most clearly in the one extended passage where he discussed Judaism.[9] Here I find his discussion of the prophetic passages tendentious and eisegetic. I think his reading of Israel's interpretation of its election is unfair and probably prejudiced. But it is also clear that in this crucial statement he makes a shift from the Israel of the Bible to the Pharisees to what is then termed "historical Pharisaism"and thence to the tendencies he has seen in these terms, wherever they are to be found. His focus is not "the Jews." Thus while I detect remnants of prejudice against the Jews in Berkouwer, he is far more revealing of what a thoughtful, humanly responsive exegete can still do in interpreting Christianity from a scriptural base so as to transcend the old anti-Semitic Christian traditions.

Wolfhart Pannenberg

Since Wolfhart Pannenberg seeks to speak in rational terms about the resurrection, one might expect him to be rational about the post-Christian status of Jews and Judaism. Instead, he writes, with "the message of the resurrection ... the foundations of the Jewish religion collapsed. This point must be held fast even today in the discussion with Judaism. One may not be taken in by benevolent subsequent statements of liberal Jews about Jesus as a prophet or allow that the conspiracy for Jesus' death was merely a failure of the Jewish authorities. There may be some truth in such explanations. But the conflict with the law in the background of Jesus' collision with the authorities must remain apparent in all its sharpness: either Jesus had been a blasphemer or the law of the Jews—and with it Judaism itself as a religion— is done away with."[10]

While I have seen a certain amount of writing about Pannenberg, I recall only one Christian who has objected to Pannenberg's attitude toward the Jews. Richard John Neuhaus in his introduction to Pannenberg's *Theology and the Kingdom of God* calls this passage "highly objectionable and thoroughly disappointing."[11] It is worse than that. To say Judaism ended 2000 years ago is to make the Jews dispensible if not satanic and therefore reempowers prejudice and persecution. To make christology again the source of anti-semitism is to be blind to Christian teaching as the preparation for Hitler and the Holocaust. To make this a pillar of a religion of love is contemptible. But to be a contemporary German and say such things is intolerable. So much suffering, so many deaths and the old Jew-hate reasserts itself! Such grand theorizing about history and eschatology and no sense that the thinker stands on bloody ground and lends the devil a hand.

I hasten to add that, perhaps as a result of his first visit to the United States, Pannenberg awakened to his sinfulness. In the foreword to his 1972 work *The Apostle's Creed in the Light of Today's Questions* he wrote, "The expert reader will notice that I have modified my views at certain points. I should like expressly to draw attention to one alteration, which goes deeper than the others. In my book *Jesus–God and Man,* I represented the rejection of Jesus by the Jewish leaders of his day as being the result of his criticism of the Law; and I went on to remark that the raising of Jesus, therefore, conversely put the Law in the wrong and to that extent meant (in principle) the end of the Jewish religion. Today I regret this conclusion, which seemed to me inescapable at the time. It involved the resupposition of a view widespread in German Protestantism, that the religion of the law and the Jewish religion are identical. I have meanwhile learnt to distinguish between the two. I think that I can see how for the Jewish faith, too, the God of Jewish history can stand above the Law. For it is only in this way that the earthly activity of Jesus can be also understood as a Jewish phenomenon. It is obvious that this recognition makes possible greater open-mindednes towards dialogue between Christians and Jews, since it takes account of the broad common basis which spans the Christian-Jewish contrasts."

That is quite a shift of views indeed. Unfortunately it is buried in this relatively unimportant work while his 1968 book on the Christ remains one of his classics. In 1974 when the American Theological Society discussed this topic none of its members apparently knew of Pannenberg's change of heart. Had not Dr. Paul Meacham of the Westminister Press kindly called it to my attention I should probably not have come across it.

Dr. Meacham was also good enough to provide me with a copy of the "Afterword" which Pannenberg has prepared for the re-issue of "Jesus—God and Man" (scheduled for 1977). The original text is to be retained for the following reasons given by Pannenberg: "More than a decade has passed since the first publication of this book. During that time work in systematic theology has turned to Christology with increasing intensity. In the process the methodoligical procedure and these of this book have been extended and made the object of critical discussion. It would seem obvious to incorporate into this presentation the points of view that have emerged as well as new exegetical studies. However, that would take such a thorough reworking of the text, especially since my own understanding of Christology has advanced considerably during this decade, that for the present I must defer the task. On the other hand, the alterations that appear to be necessary still do not mean any departure from the path engaged by this book, but rather a continuation of it. This seems to justify allowing the book to continue to appear in its present form." Thus the Jewishly offensive material of pages

254-5 will appear without comment in the reissue. Considering the strong language Pannenberg used in 1972 to discuss his change of mind concerning Judaism one searches the ''Afterword'' for a statement of Pannenberg's current assessment of Judaism. In vain. In twenty five full typewritten pages there is not a word indicating the author has any different view of Judaism than that given in the old text.

What are we to make of this? Has Pannenberg changed his mind again since 1972? Or, to extend Jewish charity, is this matter not important enough to him to merit attention in his few new additional pages? Yet what does it mean when a Christian theologian in our time is relatively unconcerned that his teaching might again fuel religious anti-Semitism? And how shall we judge a German theologian who does not feel a special sensitivity that his words might be used to provide a Christian backdrop for Nazi-like bestiality? If Pannenberg simply overlooked this matter then one must say that he has something of a block in this area, which is to say that he is emotionally blocked with regard to the Jews. This is commonly called prejudice and its name is anti-Semitism. I should think that Christians interested in Pannenberg's theology would find it important to dissociate themselves from his early explicit christological anti-Semitism and his later disturbing failure to give his recantation of it the exposure it morally required. Christians speaking of their faith to Jews should recognize that Pannenberg is an excellent example of the possibility that leading figures in the church today have learned little or nothing about the way in which they teach hatred of the Jews.

Based on the three thinkers studied above, Ruether's assertion about the inter-locking of christology and anti-Semitism bears some revision. While classic christology was closely associated with anti-Semitism and thus contemporary traditionalist theologians are still led in that direction (Pannenberg), others have found ways to mitigate its effects (Barth), or even virtually to eliminate it from their teaching (Berkouwer).

1) *Faith and Fratricide: the Theological Roots of Anti-Semitism.*
2) *II/2, 195-305; III/3, 176-183, 210-227; IV/3/2, 876-878.*
3) *Dogmatics in Outline. 77.*
4) *The Work of Christ, 138-141.*
5) *Ibid, 158-159.*
6) *Divine Election, 68ff.*
7) *Ibid, 185. See also 208-9, 214, 244.*
8) *The Person of Christ, 141-2, 173.*
9) *Divine Election, 312ff.*
10) *Jesus, God and Man, 254-255.*
11) *Page 35.*

XI

Christ Against the Jews:
A Review of Jon Sobrino's Christology

BY CLARK M. WILLIAMSON

O ne of the most important movements in contemporary Christian theology is surely that which comprises the liberation theologies. Arising, as they do, from the lived experience of third-world peoples, an experience of oppression, suffering and, at the same time, hope, these theologies command our attention. Because they take as central the criterion of *praxis*, they challenge us to examine once again the meaning of "doing the truth."

Central to the theological effort of these liberation theologies is the endeavor so to restate traditional Christological formulations as to bring Christology itself under the criterion of *praxis*. One important effort to do just this is Jon Sobrino's book *Christology at the Crossroads* (Maryknoll, New York: Orbis Books, 1978). Precisely because Sobrino's Christological effort is likely to have a significant impact on the consciousness of Christians, it is important to bring it under critical scrutiny.

Some are likely to conclude that to criticize liberation theology is to fail to serve the cause of liberation and to lend support to the very oppressive

Clark M. Williamson is Professor of Theology at Christian Theological Seminary in Indianapolis. He has taught Philosophy of Religion, been an Interim Minister and Assistant Dean at the Disciples Divinity House. He worked closely with Paul Tillich for two years

powers that would themselves delight in seeing such criticism occur. I know no ready answer to this response. However, another issue is also at stake: the nature of theology. The question should not be *whether* theology serves the cause of human liberation, but *how* it does so. I make some suggestions on this point at the end of this review. Meanwhile, theology is a self-critical discipline, as the very concept of *praxis* itself implies. To engage in the criticism of theology is to do the very thing which the liberation theologians demand that we do.

This is not a full-scale review of all aspects of Sobrino's Christology. Instead, it tries to get at the basis of his Christology, i.e., the use he makes of the figure of Jesus as historically reconstructed. Some theses which have arisen from a careful reading of the text will guide this discussion. (1) In his effort to replace the "dead Christ" of Latin American piety with the "historical Jesus," Sobrino unwittingly repeats the standard anti-Judaism of Christian theology. (2) He ignores the effect this anti-Judiasm has had, since the Council of Elvira, on Christian practice. (3) This anti-Judaism violates the criterion of *praxis*. It is an inherited theory that is not brought under critical review by the pressing concern for liberation. It undermines the concern for liberation, which has been at the heart of Judaism since the Exodus. (4) This anti-Judaism derives from Sobrino's German scholarly sources and in no way reflects the situation in El Salvador from which he writes.

Prior to a look at Sobrino's text, some background information is necessary to establish the point of view of this analysis. The first point has to do with the role of anti-Judaism in Christian theology. Anti-Judaism has long played a structural role in shaping the very articulation of the meaning of the gospel. Anti-Judaism is not merely one theme that can be found in Christian theology, lying alongside other themes. Instead, it is a model of Christianity itself. This anti-Judaic model comes to clear expression, historically, in the theology of Tertullian. [For extensive documentation of this analysis of Tertullian, see David Patrick Efroymson, *Tertullian's Anti-Judaism and its Role in His Theology* (Ph.D. Dissertation, Temple University, 1976). See also my article, "The *Adversus Judaeos* Tradition in Christian Theology," *Encounter*, 39, 3, 273-296.]

All the major doctrines of Tertullian's theology are constructed under the

---

and served as special editor and advisor for the 3rd volume of his Systematic Theology. He has published numerous articles and critical reviews and is the Editor of the journal Encounter. His books are: "God is Never Absent" and, "Has God Rejected His People?" In 1972-73 he was a Senior Member of Westminster College, Cambridge University and for a while served on the faculty of the Graduate School of the Ecumenical Institute of the World Council of Churches in Bossey, Switzerland.

impact of his anti-Jewish theology. (1) *God*, for Tertullian, is one, but not as exclusively one as Jews believe, being also three; father, but unacknowledged by Jews; merciful, forgiving even Jews; just, punishing especially Jews; wise, even in dealing with sinful Jews; consistent, despite the Jews; humble enough to accept death from Jews; patient despite impatient Jews; revealed, but Jews fail to understand; lord of history, and proves it against Jews; limitless, except that God cannot now ask anything Jewish.

(2) *Jesus* is the second focal point of Tertullian's theological anti-Judaism, and an effective means for giving it striking expression. There are several patterns of discourse on this theme in Tertullian, and in each either the image or the function of Tertullian's Christ has a fundamental anti-Jewish resonance. There is first of all a kind of Christological scheme, in which Jesus is a divine object of faith. What is typically Jewish in this series of assertions is the rejection of the more-than-human. Then there is the emphasis on Jesus' life and death, frequently described as spent or happening in conflict with the Jews. Third, Tertullian writes of the teaching of Jesus as a teaching against Jews and Judaism. Tertullian uses Jews and Judaism as a foil against which his conception of who Jesus is and what he does is expressed. The tension or conflict between Judaism and Tertullian's Christ is as strong, as bitter, and as profound as is the opposition between Judaism and his God. Christ is the "dividing line" between Christianity and Judaism, but he is also clearly and directly on "our" side of the line, and is the sign of the annihilation of the other side.

With regard to (3) the *Law* (what Jews call *Torah*, "teaching"), Tertullian's most frequent assertion is that the old law has been transformed or renewed. This axiom has its variations: less is expected of Christians, or more is expected, but always better is expected. The theme of transformation for the better makes constant reference to the unrenewed, old, Jewish Law as unthinkable for Christians. Finally, the "spiritual meaning" of the old law is an attempt to salvage something of value from what is deemed old, Jewish, and therefore valueless.

One theological implication of this kind of framework becomes apparent by asking the ethical/disciplinary question: "What does God demand of Christians?" The inevitable answer, within this framework, is "Not what Jews did. More—or better—is required." God becomes the One who demands that Christians be different from, better than, Jews. Judaism becomes that which Christianity must "transcend" in some way. Christianity itself becomes that which is not Jewish, that which, by definition, is precisely everything new and good that Judaism could never be.

One last construct needs to be noted: Tertullian's conception of (4) *the Church* and the heavily anti-Jewish ideas and emphasis which characterize much of it. Like law, the Church tends to be a logical product of God and Christ: it is that with which God has replaced Israel, and that whose newness and superiority is expressed in and through Christ. Tertullian's Church seems to be the "payoff" symbol, the point at which the "cash value" of the anti-Judaism of the other symbols is redeemed. With Tertulllian's conception of his Church, his people, we are dealing with his understanding of himself and his community. God, Christ, and law contribute to that sense of identity, precisely through their contribution to the conception of the Church as its symbol.

The Church is here fundamentally a community, a new people which in God's design has *replaced* the old. It is further a *gentile* people, *universal*, and therefore *superior* to the old ethnocentric Jews. The emphasis is throughout on differentiation from and superiority to Judaism.

Tertullian's work is not simply academic theology. It is preaching, pastoral care, and community organizing for the Christian community at Carthage. More than an attitude, his anti-Judaism is a kind of model: both a model of and a model for.

It is a model of Judaism: of a system, of a people rejected by God, unfaithful to God, rejecting Christ, opposed to Christianity, and caught up in a trail of crimes which culminates in deicide. It is a model of sterility, disobedience, and the past. On the contrary, Christianity, on the same model, becomes a people of newness, of fidelity, of spirituality, of moral vigor, and of universality.

But Tertullian's anti-Judaism is also a model for: a model (5) for reading the Bible correctly (*exegesis*), for (6) *praying* or worshipping spiritually (as opposed to carnally)—all in clear opposition to the Jewish way of reading the Bible, of praying, and of acting.

Each aspect of this anti-Judaic model is to be found in Sobrino's *Christology at the Crossroads*. Each theme can be documented in his text.

However, much water has gone under the bridge since Tertullian's day, as is evidenced by the fact that Sobrino's methodology for inquiring into the historical Jesus claims to be historical-critical. Nothing could have been further from Tertullian's mind. A look, then, at how the anti-Judaic model appears in its historical-critical form, particularly in German biblical scholarship, helpful, especially in light of Sobrino's dependence on this very scholarship. [An exhaustive analysis of the presence of this anti-Judaic model in German biblical scholarship can be found in Charlotte Klein, *Anti-Judaism in Christian Theology* (Philadelphia: Fortress Press, 1978.)]

(7) What is called *late Judaism*, the Judaism from the period of the Babylonian exile to the revolt of bar Kokhba, is characterized as inauthentic Judaism, as a Judaism that turned its back on Yahwism and the message of the prophets. Henceforth, Judaism is on the wrong track and has abandoned its true faith. This Judaism is said by Georg Fohrer to have failed in its "divine task by constantly falling away from the way of life imposed on [it] . . . by constantly falling away from the way of life imposed on them and wanting to use God merely as metaphysical security for their own life" (cited in Klein). Late Judaism is an absurd result of a decadent, "blind" rabbinic scholarship that is exaggeratedly preoccupied with the letter of the law. As such it is preparatory for and inferior to Christianity. Jesus rejects this "old" Judaism and,, with his words and work, no longer forms a part of the history of Israel. In him the history of Israel has come, rather, to its end.

Christ Against the Jews: A Review

What belongs to the history of Israel is the process of his rejection and condemnation by the Jerusalem religious community. Late Judaism was in a state of decadence, of orthodoxy and legalism. Its faith was externalized and rigid, God had become a distant God and the prophetic message was forgotten. Jesus is to be understood as the decisive rejection of this old, dead Judaism. Unfortunately, this so-called "late" Judaism is a figment of non-scholarship, a scholarship ignorant alike of Jewish piety, mysticism, prayer and of Jewish sources, such as Mishnah and Talmud.

(8) *Law and legalistic piety*, characteristic of "late" Judaism, are condemned. That Torah means more than "law" is not acknowledged. Legalistic piety, says Jeremias, is the "cancer" of Judaism, "the piety that separates us from God (*New Testament Theology*, 147). It is self-assured, self-righteous, and loveless. Consequently, legalistic exegesis of the Old Testament is "blind."Only the Church can read the scriptures. Jews, says Jeremias, were "deaf to the gospel." Such views are shared by many German scholars; Klein shows it in scores of them.

(9) *Pharisees and Scribes*–these hapless creatures are mostly represented in the gospels as *the* enemies of Jesus' teaching. The picture of the Pharisees and scribes given in other historical sources and in the work of other scholars, e.g., Neusner, Zeitlin, Sandmel, Baeck, does not correspond to that of the gospels. Briefly, the reasons for this contrast are that Jewry, after the destruction of the Temple in the year 70, recognized the Pharisees and their rabbis as its natural religious leaders and the organization of the Jewish religion after the disasters of 70 and 135 as their work. The more the early church came up against the opposition of the Jewish communities (or vice-versa or both), the more urgent it became to portray them as the enemies of Jesus himself, since they were undoubtedly the opponents of the Christian mission and it was largely their opposition which led to the failure of that mission as a whole in the synagogue. As an example we may refer to Matthew 23, where Jesus accuses the Pharisees of every possible transgression. A close reading of this passage shows that it originated after the destruction of the Temple and after the controversy between church and synagogue, i.e., after the "desolation" of Jerusalem to which Jesus allegedly refers (Matt. 23:38). Nonetheless, searchers after the historical Jesus still continue to judge the scribes and Pharisees as though the gospels provided an objective, non-polemical account of their mentality and views. Sobrino is an excellent case of this approach.

(10) Jewish guilt in the death of Jesus is also still affirmed, even after Vatican II, by Catholic and Protestant theologians. Rahner, in his "Meditations on St. Ignatius' Exercises," repeats: "The crucified Lord is betrayed and abandoned by his friends, rejected by his people, repudiated by the Church of the Old Testament" (cited by Klein). Sobrino utilizes this document. Jeremias, in *Jerusalem in the Time of Jesus*, states: "It was an act of unparalleled risk which Jesus performed when, from the full power of his consciousness of sovereignty, he openly and fearlessly called these men [the Pharisees] to repentance, and this act brought him to the cross" (cited by Klein). Sobrino depends heavily on Jeremias.

This constitutes the two-fold schema or model of anti-Judaism which has shaped much Christian theology from the time of the gospels, all redacted finally after the year 70, until the present. How much of it do we find in the Christology of Sobrino? The following is my answer to the question.

(1) *God*. The poor, lowly people whom Jesus addresses "must believe," says Sobrino, "that God is infinitely greater than the God preached by priests and rabbis" (p. 57; parenthetical references are to Sobrino).

"The transcendence of God, his holy and unmanipulable mysteriousness, is the underlying presupposition of Jesus' preaching, of his reverent attitude, and of his polemical debates with those who thought they had God neatly boxed in their traditions" (p. 165).

(2) *Jesus*. Though he comes as "a religious reformer preaching the best traditions of Israel" (p. 43); Jesus is apparently the only Jew of his time who understood these traditions. He proclaims a kingdom that is unavailable on the terms of the Pharisees (p. 46) and finds himself in opposition to the oppression wrought by Jewish society against the sick, lepers, women, Roman centurions, sinners, and those possessed by demons (p. 47). The good news he proclaims "can only be understood as being in total discontinuity" with the situations of these people in a Jewish context. Jesus forgives all sinners, *except* "the Pharisees, who put their trust in the works prescribed by the Mosaic law" (p. 49). These "are not pardoned by Jesus," Hence, "the real sinner is typified by the Pharisee and the person with power" (p. 52). Jesus "hurls anathemas at the Pharisees because they pay no attention to justice; at the legal experts because they impose intolerable burdens on people and have expropriated the keys to knowledge for their own use"; he also lets the rich and powerful have it (p. 53).

(3) *Law*. Pharisees are committed to "strict fulfillment of the law," to which Jesus must be opposed in his affirmation of the grace of God's inbreaking kingdom (p. 46). Such an attitude is the kind of works-righteousness that sees "liberation as lying in continuity with" the present situation. Pharisaic clinging to the law is obviously a way of saying "no" to the kingdom of God. Emphasis on law is one form of a sinful self-affirmation of one's own powers (p. 51). "People close their hearts to the future of this coming God by concentrating on the present and relying on works that are regarded as just by the law" (p. 52).

(4) *Church*. Although Sobrino does not develop a doctrine of the church, glimmerings of that may perhaps be attained by noting the few passages on the meaning of discipleship. The discipleship demanded by Jesus must be understood primarily as an exigency of the kingdom of God. So far, so good. This means, however, that "Rather than following something pretty much in line with Jewish orthodoxy (*sic*), they must follow something which will call that very orthodoxy into question" (p. 58). Here discipleship contrasts with the attitudes of late Judaism. Sobrino repeats the falsehood that Judaism "was a religion of orthodoxy" (p. 59, 60). In fact, Judaism was and is a behavioral system, having no creed. It was and is an *orthopraxy*—the very thing Jesus is said to have demanded. The question should be the opposite: how Christianity began in the context of praxis and became an orthodoxy. Judaism, says Sobrino, "had its creeds and its orthodox hopes of various sorts concerning the coming of God's kingdom" (p. 59). This fact of creeds remains unknown to rabbis of my acquaintance.

Christ Against the Jews: A Review

(5) *Jewish exegesis*. Sobrino hardly breathes a word on this topic, usually treated as the "blindness" of the scribes and Pharisees. It is clear enough, from his general statements about these two groups, that they were, indeed, blind to the new reality proclaimed by Jesus, in Sobrino's view of the matter. He does say, twice, that the "legal experts" are oppressive "because they . . . have expropriated the keys to knowledge for their own use" (pp. 53, 54). What, in fact, according to Neusner, the scribes and Pharisees were trying to do was just the opposite—to spread the knowledge of Torah among the people as widely as possible, so that the whole people could be a people of God.

(6) *Prayer*. Significantly, Sobrino commences his discussion of Jesus' approach to prayer under the rubric of "Jesus' Criticism of Contemporary Prayer" (p. 146). He starts with the parable of the Pharisee and the publican, in its Lukan version. For Sobrino, however, this story is no longer a parable. It is not aimed, as Luke has it, "at those who were sure of their own goodness and looked down on everyone else (Luke 18:9). No. According to Sobrino, "Jesus condemns the prayer of the Pharisees [note the plural] because it is the self-assertion of an egotistical 'I' and hence vitiated at its very core" (p. 147). The Pharisee's "pole of reference" is not to God but to himself. Also, the Pharisee is "even less oriented toward other human beings. He holds them in contempt . . . , and he thanks God that he is not like them . . ." (p. 147). The prayer of the Pharisees is a mechanical ceremony in self-deception. Although Sobrino is willing to grant the fact of Jesus' participation in the prayer life of Judaism, this participation "does not show what is most typical of Jesus' own prayer" (p. 152).

In his discussion of prayer, Sobrino basically follows Jeremias' *New Testament Theology*. Jeremias finds the Pharisees in the parable under discussion to be "separated from God by their theology and their piety. For a piety that leads men astray to pride and self-assurance is an almost hopeless thing" (Jeremias, *New Testament Theology*, p. 151). The best that can be said for such a view of Jesus' attitude toward prayer is that it is historically *un*critical or uncritically historical, simply taking a parable as an actual instance of a generalized attitude *or* simply taking a parable as an event *or*, in any case, taking the parable out of context of its situation in the *Redaktionsgeschichte* of the gospels. The latter comment, however, is applicable to Sobrino's entire approach to the historical Jesus and is a basic structural flaw, methodologically, in *everything* he says about Jesus.

Furthermore, unless I missed it, Sobrino never talks about Jesus' most well-known prayer: the Lord's prayer. The Lord's Prayer is *the* Christian prayer *par excellence*. Yet every phrase and sentence in it evoke in Jewish hearts echoes of their own liturgical heritage and fundamental religious affirmations. Perhaps Sobrino's neglect of the Lord's Prayer is necesary to his outlook on the Pharisees, the synagogue, and popular Judaism. These three constitute the only proper setting within which to come to a full appreciation of the Lord's Prayer and of the fact that Christianity and

Judaism are at one in the affirmations and aspirations voiced in the Lord's Prayer. Things are more perplexing than this, however. It is more than passing strange that the Lord's Prayer, with its focus on the transcendence of God and its petition that God's kingdom may come on earth, God's will be done on earth, would be overlooked when prayer is discussed from the perspective of liberation theology. What prayer could be more authentic from the criterion of liberating praxis? Yet what prayer is more Jewish? Perhaps that is the problem—it doesn't fit Sobrino's anti-Jewish model.

(7) *Late Judaism* (8), *Legalistic piety* (9), *the Pharisees*. By now enough has surely been said to convey Sobrino's attitude toward these three topics. The attitude toward Sabbath worship is also taken by Sobrino as an instance of what Braun calls "a terrifying reversal" of the whole assumption that man is made for the Sabbath (p. 168). Sobrino concurs in Braun's claim that Jesus makes this terrifying reversal. A bit of reading in Jewish scholarship will show that this so-called "terrifying reversal" was actually made by the liberal Pharisees, the followers of Hillel and Hillel himself, in their practice of "oral Torah." Jesus and Hillel might well have both been quoting a third, earlier, practitioner of the oral Torah in their mutual claim that "the Sabbath was made for man, not man for the Sabbath." Rabbi Jonathan ben Joseph put it pointedly: "Scripture says, 'The Sabbath is holy for *you* (Exodus 31:14).' This means it is given to *you* (man) not you to the Sabbath (Yoma 85b)." Unfortunately, Sobrino has allowed an anti-Jewish polemic against Jewish worship, a polemic at least as old as the *Epistle of Barnabas*, to pass for what he considers to be the "historical Jesus."

(10) *Jewish guilt for the death of Jesus*. One might think that a text in liberation theology, published eleven years after the closing of the Second Vatican Council, would adhere to that Council's proscription against the deicide charge. Sad to say, such is not the case. Opposed to the unpardonable Pharisees, in total discontinuity with his Jewish context, Jesus' opposition to the religious oppression imposed on the people by the Pharises spells his doom. As Sobrino puts it, "his liberalism and nonconformism really did bring him to the cross" (p. 75, n. 4). Though Jesus was not a prophet, he "was a prophet among other things, and he was crucified for that reason" (202). His seventh thesis on the death of Jesus states: "Jesus is condemned to death for blasphemy" (204). Mark's account is taken as straightforward history, explained by the comment that "it was his particular conception of God that underlay his ongoing conflict with the Jewish religious authorities" (205). Opposed to the "blind leaders of the blind," Jesus "was a liberal on religious matters and that led him to the cross" (206). "Here, I think, we come to the crux of the matter. In the last analysis Jesus is hostile to the religious leaders of his day and is eventually condemned because of his conception of God" (206). "It is the radical difference in their two viewpoints," those of Jesus and the Pharisees, "that explains the tragic end of Jesus" (208). As best I can understand Sobrino, Jesus is legitimately called "the Christ" because of the historical way of faith that he actually followed,

although he can only be so named by those who also follow in that way with him (107-108). It is precisely Sobrino's claim that following this way is what brought about his intentional crucifixion at the hands of the Pharisees, legal experts, and high priests. This is a fairly clear claim of deicide, still made in the fourth decade after the "final solution."

Sobrino's discussion of responsibility for the death of Jesus ignores the fact that there were theological, apologetic, and polemical considerations at work throughout the composition of each gospel. I do not pretend any ability to shed any historical light on the crucifixion of Jesus and responsibility for Jesus' crucifixion, "wie es eigentlich gewesen ist." What I do know is that while the gospels were receiving the form they now have, the church was extending to the Jewish people an invitation to depart from almost two millenia of history as a people. This invitation was declined, by and large, and the gospels reflect this Pharisaic "no" to Jesus. What is strange, is to find a liberation theologian who fails to appreciate that this "no" comes just at a time when solidarity in peoplehood and against oppression was being given fresh impetus by the siege of the Romans. The deep division that resulted yielded for the evangelist new enemies and animosities, ones largely missing from Paul. For a time, these divisions and animosities toward "scribes and Pharisees" and "the Jews" may have made some sense though this concession is highly questionable. Many Psalms identify the author's enemies with the enemies of God. But now, after all the Jewish blood that has been shed by so-called Christians from the fourth through the twentieth centuries, it hardly does any longer. Now, such talk is moral rubbish.

More fundamentally, Sobrino's whole project of a Christology for liberation theology is jeopardized critically by his way of approaching the historical Jesus. A liberation Christology that cuts itself off from *the* liberating event of the Bible, the Exodus of a people from oppression, from real slavery to real freedom, is self-defeating. A liberation Christology not based on Easter rather than the life of Jesus fails to note what Easter and the Exodus have in common. What was proclaimed in the days of Moses has been also said to us gentiles: namely, that evil, oppression, torture and death are real, all too real, but they are not the last reality. The last reality is always God's new beginning, God's new initiative, the freedom, life, liberation, and righteousness that come from the gentle workings of a good not our own, a good redemptive of all people, even of those who resist God's new beginnings. Christianity will become a force for liberation when it rediscovers the connection between Easter and Exodus, when it replaces the "dead Christ" with the living Christ.

A Decade of Catholic-Jewish Relations – A Reassessment

BY HENRY SIEGMAN

During the past decade, relations between the Roman Catholic Church and the Jewish people have changed in a fundamental way. Our theologies and historically-conditioned reflexes will have to catch up with a new reality: we perceive one another and we are able to talk to one another in ways that were utterly inconceivable only a generation ago. Moreover, it seems reasonably clear that the process is an irreversible one. The capacity to hurt one another is still there, and — more likely than not — will not remain unexercised. The areas of misunderstanding still remain vast. But the traditional Christian triumphalistic notion of the Jewish people as role-players in someone else's passion play is a thing of the past, and that is a far-reaching change indeed. It is a change that also frees Jews to shed their own peculiar kind of triumphalism, the defensive triumphalism of the persecuted and the abused, and to relate in a more open and creative way to the world about it.

This new reality in which we find ourselves as Jews and Christians is not

---

This article is based on a paper presented at the March, 1976, meeting of the Liaison Committee of the Vatican Sacretariat on Religious Relations with the Jews and the International Jewish Committee on Interreligious Consultations in Jerusalem, Israel. The views expressed in this paper are personal ones and do not necessarily represent the views of any particular organization or segment of the Jewish community.

so much the result of fundamental changes in theology as it is the consequence of history — the common predicament which brings into question the very survival of our planet, and the dizzying pace of technological and scientific change — "future shock," if you will — which, on the one hand, has made us aware as never before of the incredible variety of religious experience in different cultures all over the world, while on the other hand we are left stunned by the assault of these changes on traditional perceptions and values, looking to each other for some reassurance and support.

The first and most important question that needs to be asked in this kind of retrospective is precisely what kind of dialogue is possible between Jews and Christians. What impels us to dialogue, and what does each of us seek to get out of it? Ten years of all kinds of interreligious activity, including the formal dialogue between the Vatican Committee on Religious Relations with the Jews and the Intenational Jewish Committee on Interreligious Consultations,[1] should yield some clarification of this important question.

Ellen Flesseman-van Leer, a Dutch Protestant ecumenist, in an article surveying Jewish-Christian dialogue, comes to the disappointing conclusion that "we still live in the time of the pre-dialogue, in which we do not advance beyond a better mutual understanding and an increasing collaboration in the theological and socio-political field . . . The question of truth is excluded."[2]

There is, I believe, a certain inevitability to the disappointment Christians will experience in the expectations they entertain for the dialogue with the Jews. There are two reasons for that inevitability, and both result from the same consideration: the fundamental disparity, or asymmetry, in the situation of Jews and Christians. To put the matter simply — if not altogether

Henry Siegman has been the executive vice president of the Synagogue Council of America since 1965, prior to which he was director of international affairs for the National Community Relations Adv. Council, executive secretary of the American Association of Middle East Studies, and national director of community activities for the Union of Orthodox Jewish Congregations in America. He was editor of Middle East Studies *from 1959 to 1964. He has lectured at the University of Illinois, Columbia, and Williams College. Ordained a rabbi in 1951, he received a B.A. from the New School of Social Research in 1961, where he did graduate work, 1961-1964. His articles have been published in* Judaism, Worldview, *and* Moment. *He has travelled widely in the Middle East, and participated in many consultations at the White House, Congress, the United Nations, and national and international church organizations concerning civil rights, anti-war, Soviet Jewry, and Jewish-Christian concerns. Founder of the International Jewish Committee on Interreligious Consultations, he chaired the first formal encounter between World Jewry and the Vatican in 1970. This essay is taken from the Journal of Ecumenical studies Spring 78, 15. pp. 244-260 and is reprinted with permission of the publisher.*

elegantly — Christianity chose to validate itself within Judaism, seeing itself the logical and necessary fulfillment of the earlier dispensation. Judaism should have fallen away like the spent first stage of a multi-staged missile heading into space (or, perhaps more appropriately, toward heaven). It did not do so. Given his or her own self-understanding, the Christian cannot avoid being confronted by the persistence of a living, thriving Judaism. That living, reality poses for the Christian the question of ultimate truth, and that is what makes the dialogue necessary and compelling. A dialogue that avoids the question of truth is, in the words of Flesseman-van Leer, nothing more than a "pre-dialogical conversation."[3]

In this respect, the situation of Judaism is quite different. There is nothing immanent in its nature or structure which requires a confrontation with Christianity. The existence of a thriving Christianity does not pose for the Jew the question of "truth."

What impels the Jew to the dialogue with Christianity are not theological but historical considerations. For the Jew, the problematic of Christian-Jewish relations is determined by a history of Christian attitudes and actions toward the Jews which diminished their humanity and inflicted on them suffering and martyrdom. It may be argued that I am begging the question, since this kind of Christian behavior (or behavior of Christians) was the inevitable consequence of doctrine — whether normative or aberrant. However, from a Jewish perspective, it is not the fact that Christian doctrine diverges from Jewish doctrine, but that it resulted in pernicious consequences in the way Christians dealt with Jews, that causes the problem in our relationship.

It is important to add, however, that if the Jew is motivated to seek dialogue with Christians because of an obsession with history, and a concern for present and future survival, this does not mean that the Jew fails to appreciate the potential the dialogue holds for Jewish theological enrichment, for mutual religious support, and for the contribution that can be made jointly with Christians — and with persons of other faiths — in resisting the forces in society that threaten to empty life of transcendent meaning and to rob the individual of his or her *tzelem elokim* (divine image). Furthermore, Judaism cannot remain uninterested in Christianity for theological reasons as well, for if Israel's election has a purpose, that purpose is "through you shall be blessed all the families of the earth."[4] In a mysterious way, the Jewish people are to be the instrument for the redemption of the entire human family. The Jew cannot help, therefore, but be vitally concerned with the spiritual life of the nations, with whom Israel is jointly embarked on the path to redemption, and most particularly with Christianity, which has mediated the vocabulary and message of Israel to the ends of the earth.[5] But these considerations are secondary; they are not what makes the dialogue a compelling Jewish enterprise, and it would be dishonest to pretend otherwise.

History is not what brings most Christians to the dialogue with Jews — at least not in the Jewish perception. True, for some it is a sense of guilt for the role the church played in the persecution of the Jew, and a desire to correct Christian causes that contributed to that sordid history. But for the church as a whole, what impels it to dialogue with Judaism is precisely the mystery of Jewish, rejection of Christianity.

If the past ten years have taught us anything, therefore, it is that we come to each other with different "agendas."That need not be a disastrous circumstance, however, as long as we are aware of it, and as long as we are open to each other's concerns. All too often, however, we have been so intent on our own agendas that we pass each other like ships in the night.

There is yet a second reason, also resulting from this fundamental asymmetry, why Christians are likely to experience some disappointment in their expectations for the dialogue with the Jews. As I have indicated, the Jew's obsession with history does not preclude serious consideration within the dialogue of issues of a spiritual and theological character. But that does not embrace for the Jew the question of "ultimate truth," the one that stands between the Jew and the Christian. There is a common misconception which ascribes the refusal to subject this question of "truth" to dialogue to the "obscurantism" of Orthodox Jewish theologians. In fact, even the most avid Jewish advocates of dialogue substantially share this position. Thus, Abraham Joshua Heschel declared that religious authenticity is not fostered by exposure of one's inner life of faith. "The community of Israel must always be mindful of the mystery of the aloneness and uniqueness of its own being," he declared in his famous essay, "No Religion Is an Island."[6] Heschel insisted that the supreme issue that we need to be in dialogue about is not "truth" but "the terms underlying both religions, namely, whether there is pathos, a divine reality concerned with the destiny of man which mysteriously impinges upon history; the supreme issue is whether we are alive or dead to the challenge and expectation of the living God." It is our awareness that despite the "no" we say to each other on ultimate questions of faith, we both remain accountable to God; we both remain objects of God's concern, precious in God's eyes. It is that which makes possible, and indeed requires, that we engage in dialogue.[7]

Few people have made a more thoughtful contribution to the advancement of Christian-Jewish dialogue in the United States than has Jacob B. Agus, who belongs to the liberal camp. But Agus also opposes the exposure of "the inner life of faith" to interreligious dialogue. Indeed, he sees it as an act of folly. "Each Faith creates its terms within the fullness of its own experience in its own unique way . . . the corresponding terms of the faiths are incommensurate . . . in the private realm of religious feelings and symbols . . . it would be easier to move geometric figures into a non-Euclidean world" than to communicate about such matters.[8]

It must be conceded, however, that the reluctance of Jews to place theological issues at the top of the interreligious agenda applies not only to questions of ultimate truth — to the profoundly personal and intimate experience of faith — but to the more formal and objective questions of theology as well. That reluctance is determined only in part by a certain defensiveness, by a residual fear that despite all assurances, such discussions will be seized by Christians as an occasion for mission. Far more determining is the fact that Jewish religious life has always been marked by a certain theological reticence, by a reluctance to concretize in theological formulations the Jew's encounter with the divine. This Jewish sensibility is expressed in the rabbinic understanding of the story in Exodus in which Moses beseeches God to permit him to behold God's glory. He is informed that this is a human impossibility; only after God has passed by, can God's presence be discerned. In pursuance of this metaphor, rabbinic Judaism did not invest its most creative energies in the theological enteprise, in those areas which reveal the ''face'' of God. Instead, it directed its religious imagination to the traces left by the Divine presence as it passes through human history. For that task, the *halachah* was seen as a more certain guide than theology.

Indeed, it has been argued that the Jewish preoccupation with the ways God's immanence enters history is of the essence of Judaism,and defines its point of divergence from Christianity. For the Jewish rejection of Jesus — of an incarnated mediation between humans and God — inheres ''in the structural-cognitive form of Torah hermaneutics.'' According to the Torah, ''God and his manifestations cannot be mediated, only intepreted.''

> Not a Messiah but the *Torah* with its all embracing earthliness, with its roots in timelessness and its revelation in history interprets the unity of God and Being, of the infinite Absolute and its finite creatures. Therefore while God is beyond any description, location or limitation, his creative power resides in the finite universe. While God is hidden, his mighty actions are transparent, not through a mediator but, according to Rabbi Ishmael, whose hermeneutics prevailed throughout Jewish history, in the *Torah*, because it ''. . .speaks in the language of men,'' and thereby maintains the unmediated presence of God amidst his Creation, on earth rather than in heaven.[9]

Be that as it may, the different strategies chosen by the two faiths constitute another Impediment to the dialogue. It is an impediment that places Judaism at a disadvantage, for dialogue, by its very nature, is most congenial to the tradition that has developed an elaborate theology.

If I am correct in identifying the *Jewish* interest in dialogue (i.e., the historical rather than the theological), and if there is a readiness on the Christian side to deal with the Jewish ''agenda,'' then of course we must be prepared to encounter our common history. That would seem to be elementary. In practice, it turns out not to be a simple matter at all. While there are notable exceptions, I think it is not unfair to say that, by and large, the history of the church's persecution of Judaism and the Jewish people is even today not part of the consciousness of the church. That is the case not only for early history, but for our most recent past as well. For Jews, the Holocaust remains a haunting presence hovering in the background of all our encounters. The dialogue takes place over a massive graveyard in which lie buried one third of our people. We cannot pretend it is not there, and if we choose to do so, then the dialogue is surely doomed to failure and frustration. If it is faced honestly — not for the sake of recrimination, for who can lay claim to virtue and self-righteousness after Auschwitz — but in order finally to be able together to say "Kaddish" for the martyrs, then our enterprise might yet assume a sacred dimension.

In my view, we are still far from that point. Recent statements from official Catholic sources, based on newly-released archival materials, are painful, above all, in what they revealed about the continuing inability of the Roman Catholic Church to deal meaningfully with this problem. While there has taken place a lively and unresolved debate about the role that the Catholic Church, in general, and the Vatican, in particular, played during the Holocaust, that debate is actually beside the point. For even if the role of the Catholic Church during this difficult period had been exemplary, the real point is that the Nazis were able to go as far as they did because western culture had been steeped thoroughly in Christian dogmatic and theological hostilities toward the Jew that had long been regnant in the Christian world. The matter is therefore hardly resolved by citing this or that conversation between a Nuncio and an Ambassador. Of course, Nazism was a reversion to paganism, and at heart as anti-Christian as it was anti-Jewish. But it is equally clear that its poison would not have found so fertile a seedbed if the church of Jesus Christ had not been a knowing and willing participant in the centuries-long demonry of antisemitism.

A genuine confrontation with history, and most particularly with Auschwitz, demands of Christians the submission of their tradition to a searching critique. In this respect, *Nostra Aetate,* and, to a lesser, although not entirely negligible extend, the 1975 Guidelines, are seriously flawed. George Higgins and others have patiently and repeatedly urged Jews not to see *Nostra Aetate* as a document that was addressed to them.[10] Had it been that kind of document, "absolving" Jews from responsibility for the Crucifixion, then its contents should indeed have been seen as condescending and entirely inadequate, Higgins writes. But that was not its purpose. Rather, "it was meant to be a sincere examination of the Christian conscience — which has so much to answer for in this area."

While I do not doubt for a moment where George Higgins' heart lies, his own generosity cannot alter the objective reality that is *Nostra Aetate.* Whatever else one may discover in it, the one thing even the closest examination fails to yield is "a sincere examination of the Christian conscience" on the subject of antisemitism. Even the Guidelines, in their passing reference to the "memory of the persecution and massacre of Jews which took place in Europe" falls considerably short of the kind of "examination of conscience" Higgins talks about.

The two documents do not face up to the simple inescapable truth that whatever secondary causes may have come into the picture — and so many of them clearly did — antisemitism from the first century to the twentieth century is a Christian creation and a Christian responsibility. Instead, we find what amounts virtually to a pretense that antisemitism is one of many forms of intolerance and inhumanity which, it should go without saying, the church clearly rejects. From the Jewish perspective, this is so grievous a distortion of the historical truth which brings us together in dialogue as to compromise the enterprise before it ever gets off the ground.

I say all of this with diffidence, not only because, even now, sensitivities are still raw on both sides, and candor can be misconstrued as malice, but primarily because I do not wish to encourage the notion that the Holocaust be exploited as a device to generate Christian guilt and thereby manipulate the relationship in ways that give the Jewish side an advantage. Such manipulations must be seen as a desecration of the memory of the victims and utterly destructive of the real hope which the dialogue holds.

The State of Israel

Another "historical" issue is the State of Israel. I admit that many well-intentioned Jewish efforts at enlightenment on this subject have more often served to confuse our Christian friends than to enlighten them. This has been so, at least in part, because Jews have hardly sorted out for themselves the meaning of the return of Jewish political sovereignty to the Land of Israel and the ways this miraculous phenomenon affects their lives and religious sensibilities. The development is too recent and too overwhelming for things to be otherwise.

Christians, on their part, would be happier if they were allowed to deal with Israel as a strictly political phenomenon, if Jews were not to insist on its religious meaning. But even if the State of Israel were to be seen as a political phenomenon that is devoid of religious meaning, it must be conceded that the warmest theological friendships would be meaningless and utterly without human content if they could contemplate the collapse of Israel with equanimity. In the words of Jacques Maritain, "to wish to reject into nothingness this return which finally was accorded to the Jewish people, and which permits it to have a shelter of its own in the world . . . is to wish that misfortune hound again this people, and that once more it be the victim of iniquitous aggression. Anti-Israelism is not better than antisemitism."[11]

However, the State of Israel not only presents a political issue but also has the profoundest theological implications, and these go to the very heart of the Christian-Jewish problematic. Ironically, the theological connection was perceived far more clearly by a Catholic pope than by the founder of Zionism himself. When Herzl went to see Pope Pius X in 1904, he said to Herzl, "We cannot prevent the Jews from going to Jerusalem but we can never favor it.' "We are not asking for Jerusalem, but Palestine," Herzl replied, "only the profane part of the country." Of course, Herzl was wrong and the pope was right; it is not only Jews returning to Palestine but the inescapable symbolism óf Judaism returning to Jerusalem that defines the issue for both Jews and Christians.

Contrary to Herzl's and Zionism's assumptions, the creation of the Jewish State has not resolved the Jewish predicament. The situation has not been "normalized" and the State has not solved the problem of Jewish isolation. Indeed, in some ways, it has intensified it. The Jew "continues in his national character to be the object of the same hatreds, the same unnatural fears and fantasies; and he continues to harbor within himself the same intensities and obsessions."[12] The reason for this is that Zionism is really not just another national liberation movement. The State of Israel is the result not only of the modern forces of nationalism, or even of the persecution of the Jew. It is that, to be sure, but it is above all the consequence of "an inner need, a positive impulse working within Jewish life and history."[13] It is the actualization of a quest for authenticity, the incarnation of the Jewish burden of otherness. The Jew is driven by a force as old as the Bible to reunite with the land.

The importance of this "internal" significance of Israel is one which Christians (and Jews) often fail to grasp. To insist that Zionism deserves Christian support because it is the stepchild of Christian prejudice is to deny, however unintentionally, its integrity and legitimacy. In a sense, it is to insist on continued Christian parentage. To be sure, the persecution of Jews throughout their diaspora existence, both in Christian Europe *and* in the Muslim world (there are in Israel today more Jewish refugees from Arab oppression than from Europe) gives the State of Israel a pragmatic, non-ideological urgency. But this should not be permitted to detract from its ideological content. There is a vitality to Jewish peoplehood and to its attachment to its historical homeland that is not dependent on persecution and external pressures. Ultimately, Israel must be understood as the result not of outside rejection but of an inner Jewish affirmation.

In light of the above, the failure of the Vatican Guidelines to deal with the theological dimension of the Jewish relationship to the land of Israel constitutes a grievous omission. Within the context of the document's own declared desire to understand Jews as they understand themselves, it must be faulted for failing to spell out to Catholics that in the year 1975 it is impossible to understand Jews, nor can anyone communicate meaningfully with them about their deepest fears or aspirations, without an appreciation of the role of the State of Israel in Jewish consciousness.

This brings us to a point which I believe to be absolutely crucial to a proper understanding of how one deals with so complex a phenomenon as Israel in the arena of secular politics. To insist that the return of Jews to their historical homeland raises theological issues is not to say that the assertion of secular Jewish sovereignty in modern times can be validated — particularly over against competing political claims — on purely theological grounds and by simple reference to biblical verses. And a recognition that Judaism — unlike Christianity — is a faith uniquely dependent on the national existence of a particular people does not translate itself automatically into an argument for present-day Jewish political rights in Palestine. This confusion has been responsible for more painful misunderstanding between Jews and Christians, and among Jews themselves, than any other single consideration I can think of. Let me therefore state certain propositions whose obviousness, under different circumstances, might be a source of acute embarrassment:

> 1. The fact that the Hebrew Bible records the divine promise of the Land of Israel to Abraham and his descendants is *in itself* no absolute warrant for Jewish claims in our day. If that were the *only* basis for the Jewish claim, then Muslims and Christians could maintain with considerable justice that it is unreasonable to expect them to conform to Jewish religious expectations, particularly when these do not accord with their own religious convictions. The fact is that no contemporary political rights to the Land of Israel necessarily flow from a Christian understanding of the Hebrew Scriptures, or from a religious supersedence — to a greater or lesser degree — which negate such claims.
>
> 2. The Jewish *political* claim to the Land of Israel is based, *in the first instance*, on secular rather than theological considerations, i.e., the fact that there has been no separate Palestinian sovereignty since the destruction of the last Jewish kingdom nearly 2,000 years ago; a virtually unbroken Jewish presence in Palestine since the first exile; the existence of a Jewish majority in Jerusalem since 1896; and international sanction by the League of Nations (which assigned the Mandate to Britain and confirmed the terms of the Balfour Declaration) and by the United Nations (which partitioned Palestine into Jewish and Arab States).

The unbroken attachment of Jews at all times and in all the lands of their dispersion to the Land of Israel is a datum not of theology but of history; it is a hard, uncontested "secular" fact. The biblical promise and the centrality of land in Jewish theology explain this stubborn and heroic tenacity, but they do not diminish either its historical reality or its implications for secular politics. If nothing else, the biblical record substantiates the antiquity of Jewish nationalism; few, if any, nationalisms have such deep roots.

Ironically, it is those who deny the possibility of Jewish nationalism who introduce unsupportable and irrelevant theological considerations. It is a phenomenon that brings the Christian Right and the Christian Left into strange fellowship. Opposition to Israel from the Christian Right has the advantage of familiarity. Opposition from the Left is a more recent phenomenon; their hostility is a peculiar blend of an uncritical celebration of the Third World and a theological antisemitism that is nourished by a Christian universalism which cannot abide the earthiness of Jewish particularism. They love Jews who are disincarnated, who are suffering servants, who are ghostly emissaries and symbols of an obscure mission. They cannot abide Jews who are flesh-and-blood people, who are men and women like other men and women in all their angularities and specificities, who need to occupy physical space in a real world before they fulfill whatever loftier aspirations they may have. They are distressed by the notion that Jews should want a flesh-and-blood existence as a people in the real geography of this world.[14]

From a Jewish perspective, at least, we continually run the danger of dividing the world around us into separate spheres and of marking off the "spiritual" realm as the special domain of God's activity. The Jewish case against that kind of separation could not have been better stated than in the study *Israel en de Kerk* (Netherlands Reformed Church, 1961): "The election of Israel . . . has to do with life in all its dimensions, the profane as well as the sacred. Accordingly, the chosen people is a nation involved in a certain land and a set of occupations, varied joys and pains, marriages and births, sorrows and fears, and a history and political life completely bound up in world events and entangled in the international politics of its time."

In this connection, it is interesting to note Bernhard Olsen's discovery (in his *Faith and Prejudice*) that the most "liberal" religious school curriculum was also the most antisemitic — for the same reason, interestingly enough, that it was also anti-Catholic: it is marked by a predisposition toward a universalism which is not hospitable to particularity and repudiates the peculiar history of any religious groups. It is a liberalism that resents the earthiness of human history, the finitude of all human experience, the particularity of all discrete events. In its search for "timeless truths and high spirituality," it is offended by the paradoxes and concreteness of the Hebrew Bible, which deals with real human beings. It is an attitude that cannot manage the biblical dialectic of particularism and universalism.

Not surprisingly, we Jews have managed to contribute our share to a confusion of the issues. We have been less than meticulous in making those necessary distinctions that need to be made when invoking religious tradition and biblical texts. Also, we have not been as forthright as we might have been in dealing with a form of Jewish religious zealotry that invests political institutions and geographic boundaries with an absolute religious sanctity that becomes impervious to the normal give-and-take of the political process in secular history. Given our own experience with the consequences of ideological and mythological nationalisms in Christian Europe, we should have more reason than most to be concerned about the implications for politics of all ideological absolutes.

To raise this concern is not to bring into question the fundamental Jewish unity of faith, land, and people. This unity remains at the core of our identity and existence. What it does is emphasize the danger of blurring the crucial distinction between the religious meaning that Jews appropriate — individually and collectively — from political events (a biblically-conditioned

A Decade of Jewish-Christian Relations

Jewish reflex), and imbuing these events with an absolute sacredness that removed them from the realm of history. The latter is Jewishly uncharacteristic and can lead to a chauvinism that is oblivious to the rights and aspirations of others. In theological terms, it risks becoming *avodah zarah* — idolatry.

The Jewish View of Christianity

I noted earlier that the disparity of our agendas need not present an insurmountable impediment to the dialogue, provided we are genuinely prepared to attend to each other's concerns. This cuts two ways, of course, and an important question is to what extent Jews are able to attend to the Christian agenda — short of addressing the question of the ultimate truth that separates them. Taking full advantage of the perquisites of the injured party, Jews have successfully managed the dialogue so that it has focused entirely on what we consider to be Christian failings; we have not been compelled to examine ourselves and the problematic of our own theology and traditions — at least not within the context of the dialogue.

I suppose that Christian forbearance with this one-sided situation is compounded of a sense of guilt and of *nobless oblige*. However, it is a situation which cannot persist for long, not only because our Christian partners are not likely to continue the dialogue on these terms, but more importantly because there is an inner Jewish need to come to terms with the implications of our own traditions for a meaningful pluralism. We have been forthright in calling Christianity to account, but we have been somewhat less than daring in initiating a process of self-examination.

There is a two-fold task that thus far has gone largely unattended. The first is a reexamination of the Jewish stance toward a pluralistic world. It is refreshing to note that this challenge was taken up in the pages of *Tradition*, the journal of the Orthodox Rabbinical Council of America. Gerald Blidstein, an Orthodox scholar, dismisses the cliches of traditional Jewish apologetics on this subject as "barren and misleading." It is no longer enough, he writes, "to cite the Me'iri for his broadmindedness, or to scurry about in the self-satisfaction of saving a Gentile's life on the Sabbath." Furthermore, Blidstein urges a reexamination of the image of Christianity in traditional Jewish pedagogy and folk culture, which still tends to be defensive and hostile, "all the pieties about *b'nai Noach* notwithstanding."[15]

No doubt, the memory of Jewish suffering at the hands of the church makes it difficult for Jews to take as seriously as they should their own classical affirmations of the religious worth of Christianity. But Jews need not compromise their religious integrity by recognizing — as did our classical authorities — that Christians who are good and decent human beings are so not despite, but because, they profess Christianity. Thus, Jehuda Halevy writes (Kusari IV) that "these religions (Christianity and Islam) are the preparation and preface to the Messiah we expect." Maimonides, in his Code, writes, "All these matters relating to Jesus of

Nazareth and the Ishmaelite (Mohammed) who came after him served to clear the way for the King Messiah, to prepare the whole world to worship God with one accord . . . thus (because of Christianity and Islam), the Messianic hope, the Torah and the commandments have become familiar topics (among the inhabitants) of the Far Isles and many peoples . . ."

According to a more recent Jewish thinker, Rabbi Jacob Emden (1693-1776), unlike Jewish sects such as the Karaites and the Sabbatians, Christianity and Islam will "endure" because they constitute "a community that is for the sake of heaven." They are seen by him as acknowledging the fundamentals of Judaism. They "make known God among the nations . . . proclaim there is a Master in heaven and earth, divine providence, reward and punishment . . . who bestows the gift of prophecy. This is why their community endures. . . . Since their intention is for the sake of heaven, reward will not be withheld from them."[16] This attitude also characterized the views of Nachman Krochmal (1784-1840) and Abraham Isaac Kook (1865-1935).

What these authorities had in common was a genuine, unapologetic rootedness in classic Jewish sources. It is interesting to note that post-Emancipation Jews, who by and large were alienated from the primary sources of Jewish tradition and uncertain about their own Jewish identity, were far more disparaging in their views of Christianity than were their classical predecessors. For them, the Christian neighbor became a putative point of reference, for by determining who the Christian was, they at least knew who they were not. For this reason we find in the modern era, beginning with Moses Mendelssohn, a continuing dialectic between Judaism and Christianity in which the one is defined negatively in terms of the other.[17] I believe that a more authentic Jewish response to Christianity is in the process of development and will become more fully realized when the Jewish people will have regained a measure of self-confidence, a process that a secure and flourishing State of Israel will undoubtedly accelerate.

Christian Mission[18]

Many Jewish critics saw the section of the 1975 Vatican Guidelines dealing with "witness" as a most problematic one, for in this section the Catholic Church reasserts its inescapable mission "to preach Jesus Christ to the world." Among Jews who favor Christian-Jewish relations, there exist two fundamentally divergent attitudes toward the dialogue. There are those — primarily the more traditional ones, and particularly the Orthodox — whose starting point is the ultimate "incommensurability" of the two faiths, but who maintain that this incommensurability does not preclude a recognition of the other's salvific status in the divine economy. Then there are those, primarily in the liberal camp, who insist on the need for new theological formulations which allow for the legitimacy and compatibility of the two covenants — what has been described as the "theology of equality." It is the latter who find difficulty with the Catholic Church's insistence on the retention of its mission to the Jews. The reassertion of the missionary imperative in the new Guidelines and in other Catholic documents is seen by them as religiously offensive and destructive of the dialogue itself.

While I do not share this latter view, I would suggest that the Guidelines — while admittedly stopping short of a renunciation of the Catholic Church's mission to the Jews — do break new ground. For the qualifications they impose on witness are significant and represent a sharp departure from the Church's earlier traditions. Specifically, the Guidelines declare that "Dialogue demands respect for the other as he is, above all, respect for his faith and his religious conviction." Furthermore, the Church's witness must be compatible with "the strictest respect for religious liberty." Finally, the Guidelines express an understanding of Jewish rejection of the proffered witness that is striking in its contrast to the Church's earlier attitude. Until modern times, the Catholic Church explained Jewish refusal to accept the Christian in demonological terms: it was seen as a result of a perfidious and malevolently stubborn streak in the Jew. How startlingly different the words of the Guidelines, which admonish Catholics to "strive to understand the difficulties which arise for the Jewish soul — rightly imbued with an extremely high, pure notion of the divine transcendence . . . when faced with the mystery of the incarnate Word."

The more traditional Jewish view rejects the notion that the only Christian posture acceptable to Jews is one that grants the "equality" of Christianity and Judaism, if for no other reason than that it is an equality that Judaism itself is not prepared to grant to Christianity. Traditional Jews affirm that Judaism is the "truest" religion. That affirmation is part of what makes them Traditional Jews, and they do not expect Christians to be offended by it. Conversely, Jews cannot be offended by parallel affirmations of faith made by Christians — or by Muslims, for that matter. Furthermore, a Jewish "demand" that Christian theology recognize the validity of Judaism for Jews is problematical in that it implicitly grants a Jewish legitimacy to Christian theology. Judaism constitutes a denial of the central Christian mystery and its notion of salvation; it cannot at the same time demand that Christianity be reformulated to accommodate the "equality" of Judaism.[19]

Judaism is very much in need of a respectful understanding by people of other faiths. It can gain much, spiritually and intellectually, from an open and honest dialogue across faith lines. What Judaism does *not* need from others, and what no other faith can give it, is a validation of its own central faith commitments. That can only come from within Jewish life and thought, not from outside it. It is no denigration of Christianity to state that a Christian acknowledgment that the Sinaitic covenant was not abrogated can have no weight in Jewish theology.

A distinction needs to be made between an active campaign of mission directed at the Jewish community, which precludes meaningful dialogue, and an insistence that Christians abandon their eschatological hopes concerning Judaism. The latter is not only unnecessary but theologically imprudent. Equally unnecessary and imprudent are Jewish suggestions concerning the special rootedness of Christian faith in Judaism. A genuine Christian self-understanding which emphasizes this essential relationship to Judaism can emerge only from within Christianity.

We need to develop approaches that are capable of greater distinctions, that welcome the "de-demonologization" of Judaism in Christian thought, but stop short of theological advocacy. It is entirely proper for Jews to suggest to Christians that they find ways of defining their Christian identity in terms that will not involve the dehumanization of Jews; the price that we have paid for such theology in history gives us a certain "standing" to advance such suggestions. But that is essentially a request to be left alone. It is quite another matter for Jews to suggest to Christians that they cannot understand themselves without reference to their Jewish roots. This may or may not be the case, but that is a determination Christians will have to make.

Only recently, I came across a particularly telling example of the potentially pernicious effects of Jewish involvement in the internal Christian theological debate concerning its own confrontation with Judaism. In a publication issued by Seton Hall's Institute for Judaeo-Christian Studies, one of the leading institutions committed to the furtherance of the dialogue with Judaism, the Director of the Institute castigates a rabbi for having lent his endorsement and support to Rosemary Ruether's new book, *Faith and Fratricide*. This Catholic theologian, who has been unstinting in his support of Jewish causes and of the interreligious dialogue, warns the rabbi in question that if he does not wish to destroy the new encounter between Christians and Jews, he should not, as a Jew, "assist attempts to drain the Christian message of its true significance, to rob it of its heart."[20] The propriety of this reaction is not as important a question as its inevitability. It argues, in my opinion, for the wisdom of a certain restraint in the way Christians and Jews seek to help along and further each other's theological development.

I have said that an active Christian mission to the Jews precludes serious dialogue. That is fairly obvious. Christianity's understanding of Judaism is inevitably inhibited and distorted at the point where its essential missionary impulse becomes dominant. What is not at all obvious, it seems to me, is that the very notion of mission is itself inadmissible from a Jewish perspective, and that we have the right to suggest that it be abandoned by Christians. Jews have insisted — correctly, of course — that Christians must finally come to terms with the Jew's own self-understanding. The fact is that a fundamental dimension of the Christian's self-understanding is the mandate to "go forth" and spread the truth of Christianity. Deny Christians that mandate, and you have robbed them of their identity and religious purpose, as they understand it. I would maintain that there exist no moral or religious grounds on which to base such a demand. If Judaism has not engaged in missionary activity, it is not because it found the very concept of mission unacceptable.

Witness is a legitimate religious enterprise, as long as it respects fully the freedom of conscience of people of other faiths, and as long as that enterprise is insulated from considerations of political and other forms of coercion. There is a sense in which every Jew is obliged in Jewish tradition to live constantly a life of "witness," a life that will lead Gentiles to a recognition and acceptance of the God of Abraham. The principle of witness — Christian or Jewish — need not be offensive to religious sensibilities nor pose a barrier to Christian-Jewish relations.

Be that as it may, the Guidelines represent substantial progress over *Nostra Aetate*. For the one message that comes through the Guidelines — despite all of its acknowledged shortcomings — is that the Catholic Church does not aim at the disappearance of the Jewish community but seeks a living link with it. *Nostra Aetate* had left fundamentally unchanged the universal and perennial Catholic view that Judaism's vitality and religious worth are to be found in its pre-Christian incarnation. If God finds the Jewish people "most dear," it is for the sake of the pre-Christian patriarchs. And the climactic words of that part of the "Declaration on the Relationship of the Church to Non-Christian Religions" that is concerned with Judaism and the Jewish people are that the Cross of Christ has become the "fountain from which *every* grace flows." (Emphasis added.)

In contrast to these sentiments, the Guidelines are the first Catholic document on the highest level of authority that views Judaism as a rich and vital religious movement in the period following the rise of Christianity as well. That is perhaps the document's most significant contribution, a contribution for which it is undoubtedly indebted to such precursors as the American Guidelines, and particularly the French Orientations. It is a sentiment that also found significant expression in the remarks of Pope Paul when he met with Jewish and Catholic delegations in January, 1975. In his address during that unusual encounter, Pope Paul described how leading medieval Jewish and Catholic theologians influenced the development of each other's religious thought.

The Guidelines state categorically that "the history of Judaism did not end with the destruction of Jerusalem," but went on to develop a religious tradition. Of course, the Catholic Church has not given up on the notion that "the importance and meaning of that tradition were deeply affected by the coming of Christ," but this affirmation now accommodates a perception of Judaism that remains "rich in religious values." Compare this nuanced text of the Guidelines with the pronouncement of Cardinal Bea, the moving spirit beyond *Nostra Aetate*, in the aftermath of Vatican II: The Jewish people "is no longer the people of God in the sense of an institution for the salvation of mankind.... Its function in preparing the Kingdom of God finished with the advent of Christ and the founding of the Church."[21]

The Guidelines call on Catholics to study Judaism in all of its aspects and to end the ignorance that has been at the root of past hostility and rancor. They encourage the establishment of formal studies of Judaism within Catholic educational structures, including the creation of special chairs in

Jewish studies. Equally significant is a passage in the Guidelines that says that the "Old Testament" and Jewish tradition founded upon it must not be juxtaposed to the New Testament in such a way as to make the Old Testament appear as a religion of justice and legalism as opposed to a New Testament emphasis on love of God and neighbor. The passage cites specific biblical sources that stress the centrality of love. Catholics are urged to exercise care in the selection of liturgical readings, in homilies based upon them, and in translations of liturgical texts, particularly those passages "which Christians, if not well informed, might misunderstand because of prejudice."

Perhaps most important, the document proposes that Christians seek to "learn by what essential traits the Jews define themselves in the light of their own religious experience." A genuine openness to Jewish religious categories and self-definition would, for the first time, make possible an honest and faithful dialogue between the Catholic Church and the Synagogue.

It may be true, as some critics have argued, that as far as the United States and France are concerned, the Guidelines offer little that is new. But this criticism ignores the reality in most other Catholic countries throughout the world, where the Guidelines, for all their sobriety, represent a revolution in traditional attitudes. And even in the most progressive countries, one cannot begin to compare the weight of a Vatican document of the highest level of authority with statements issued by episcopal offices on Catholic-Jewish relations. It is doubtful that the American and French statements have made much of an impact on the attitudes of the bishops in those countries, not to speak of the rank and file.

If the Guidelines were the culmination of a process that had run its course, if they represented the Catholic Church's new theology of Judaism, then they would indeed be disappointing. However, the Guidelines were not intended to *end* but to *initiate* a process. What the Catholic Church has done is create the tools that make possible a reexamination of the entire range of its own internal life — in education, in training for the priesthood, in its understanding of the Bible, in its catechism — insofar as these relate to an understanding of Judaism. These tools did not exist before, and that is why nothing much came of the Vatican II declaration of the Jews.

The big question, therefore, is to what use the Catholic Church will put these new tools. An ever larger question is whether the Church can, in fact, successfully exorcise its Jewish problem. For reasons I have indicated earlier, I — as a Jew — do not wish to enter the debate that was opened by Rosemary Ruether in her *Faith and Fratricide.* I hope she is mistaken in her conclusion that "anti-semitism is the left hand of Christology," and that the New Testament and its anti-Judaism are inseparable. But even if Ruether is wrong, it remains clear that the Catholic Church still has a formidable task ahead of it, for its mythological life to this day is inextricably linked to knowledge of a people who rejected and continues to reject Jesus. And twist and turn as one may, the Gospels remain a significant source of antisemitism.

Despite these difficulties — indeed, because of them — the Guidelines constitute a hopeful first step. In their efforts to realize the promise inherent in the Guidelines, those dedicated Catholic Church officials and theologians whose untiring efforts have brought the Church to this new state will find, I am persuaded, openness, appreciation, and, where appropriate, support and reciprocity in the Jewish community.

1)   *The International Jewish Committee on Interreligious Consultations is a coalition of the following organizations: World Jewish Congress, Synagogue Council of America, American Jewish Committee.*
5)   *Michael Wyschogrod, "Footnotes to a Theology,"* The Karl Barth Colloquium of 1972, *ed. Martin Thumscheidt, SR Supplements.*
      Union Seminary Quarterly Review, *January, 1966, p. 119.*
      Ibid., p. 118.
8)   *"Response to Father Danielou's* Dialogue with Israel." *in Jacob B. Agus*, Diaglogue and Tradition
9)   *Uriel Tal, "The Future of Christian-Jewish Dialogue,"* Concilium, *September/October, 1974, p. 180.*
11)   De l'Eglise due Christ-Le personne de l'eglise et son personnel *(Paris: Desclee de Brouwer, 1970), as cited by Frank Talmadge, "Christianity and the Jewish People"* Commentary, *February, 1975, p. 62.*
12)   *Harold Fisch, "The Meaning of Jewish Existence,"* Mizpeh *(Jerusalem), Vol. 1, No. 1 (Spring, 1974).*
14)   *Arthur Hertzberg, "Daniel Berrigan on 'Settler Regime': A Response"* Congress Monthly, *Vol. 40, No. 13 (November 23, 1973).*
15)   *Gerald Blidstein, "Jews and the Ecumenical Dialogue,"* Tradition, *Vol. XI, No. 2 (Summer, 1970), pp. 103-113.*
16)   *Quoted by Heschel, "No Religion Is An Island."*
17)   *Frank Talmadge, "Christian Theology and the Holocaust,"* Commentary, *October, 1975.*
18)   *This section does not take into account the paper on Catholic mission presented by Professor Tomasso Federici in March, 1977, at the sixth meeting of the International Catholic-Jewish Liaison Committee in Venice. In his paper, Federici denounced proselytism and "organizations of any sort" that aim at conversion of Jews. His paper was commissioned by the Vatican Secretariat on Religious Relations with the Jews in response to the issues raised by the author in this article.*
19)   *A Jewish rejection of traditional Christology does not preclude recognition that Christianity has a salvific status in the divine economy. In the Jewish view, that status derives not from its Christology, but from considerations cited by Jehuda Halevy, Maimonides, and Emden (see previous section). Modern thinkers, such as Rosenzweig and Buber, who allowed for the possibility of two*

171

"truths" mysteriously standing side by side before God, nevertheless maintained that the gulf separating the two truths is unbridgeable and, as Jews, rejected the "truth" of Christianity.

20) John M. Oesterreicher, *"Anatomy of Contempt," (South Orange, NJ: Seton Hall University, 1975), p. 38.*

21) *Augustin Cardinal Bea*, The Church and the Jewish People *(New York: Harper and Row, 1966), p. 11.*

XIII

Response to Henry Siegman

By Edward H. Flannery

abbi Henry Siegman's "A Decade of Catholic-Jewish Relations: A Reassessment"[1] is an admirable statement but not one without problems for this respondent. Endowed with a keen perspicacity, and a generosity of spirit rare even among seasoned ecumenists, it presents perspectives and critiques of the Jewish-Christian dialogue that have, to my knowledge, not been enunciated before. It is dilemmatic, on the other hand, to find his concept of that dialogue inadequate. His chief contributions are found in his penetrating psychological insights into both Christian and Jewish participation and his advocacy of forthright loyalty to one's own tradition in the dialogical encounter. The benefits we gain from these must,

Edward H. Flannery was ordained in 1937, after attending St. Charles College, Catonsville, MD; Seminaire St. Sulpice, Paris; and the Theological College at Catholic University, Washington, DC. Following thirteen years in Rhode Island parishes, he was associate director of The Christophers for five years in New York, then editor of The Providence Visitor *(1955-65). From 1965-70, he was associate director of the Institute of Judaeo-Christian Studies and on the faculty of Seton Hall University, and from 1967-76 was Executive Secretary of the Secretariat for Catholic-Jewish Relations of the National Conference of Catholic Bishops, Washington, DC. He is presently director of the Office of Continuing Education of the Clergy for the Dio-*

however, be balanced against certain limitations he places on the boundaries of the conversation between Christians and Jews.

He broaches the question of "what kind of dialogue is possible between Jews and Christians" early in his paper. Countering Ellen Flesseman Van Leer's assessment of the Jewish-Christian encounter, as practiced until now, as "pre-dialogue" because therein "the question of truth is excluded," he claims that "what impels the Jew to the dialogue with Christianity are not theological but historical considerations." As he sees it, what motivates Jews to seek dialogue with Christians in the way they do stems in part from the asymmetrical theological relations between Judaism and Christianity and a Jewish "obsession with history and concern with survival" resulting from age-long Christian oppression of Jews.

The asymmetry of the Christian-Jewish relationship is well recognized, but should not, in my view, be overdrawn or made an impediment to a symmetrical conversation. Judaism, it is true, needs no reference to Christianity for validation, whereas Christianity cannot dispense with reference to Judaism for its own — though a Marcionist tendency in Christianity has long attempted to do so. But symmetry or asymmetry of theological requirements need have no necessary determing effect on dialogical discussions. If the symmetry principle is accepted as a norm of dialogue, one may wonder what would be the fate of other dialogues than the Jewish-Christian one, e.g., the Christian- or Jewish-Islamic, the Christian- or Jewish-Buddhist, or the Christian- or Jewish-Atheist dialogues? Could they exist at all and if so, under what prohibitions to full discussion? The simpler and normal solution to the problem of dialogue, I should think, is an openness of both parties in the dialogue to discuss fully whatever either of the parties wishes to discuss. Any restriction should be accepted by mutual, unpressed agreement. Siegman practically concedes this when discussing the "different agendas" of Jews and Christians in dialogue. These agendas are not harmful, he holds, "as long as we are open to each other's concerns." The principle is a good one. Why not make this openness an intrinsic quality of dialogical relationship? If the Christian concern includes comparative theology and the "ques-

cese of Providence. His publications include numerous articles and translations, and collaboration for writings in English in M. Blondel's Bibliographie Analytique et Critique *(Louvain, 1975). His* Anguish of the Jews *(Macmillan, 1956) has won six awards and been translated into three languages. A consultor to the Vatican Secretariat for Catholic-Jewish Relations from 1969-74, Fr. Flannery has received numerous citations, most recently at the 1978 annual convention of the Central Conference of American Rabbis. This essay is from the* Journal of Ecumenical Studies, *78, 15, pp. 503-511 and is reprinted by permission of the publisher.*

A Response to Henry Siegman

tion of truth," should these be discouraged, let alone placed out of bounds?

Siegman may encounter this by disclaiming any intent to discourage or bar full discussion by Christians of whatever interests them or, for that matter, any reactive or *pro forma* Jewish participation in that discussion. But if the Christian discussant is aware of the Jewish reluctance or refusal to take up his or her agenda with full dialogical vigor, an inevitable artificiality will affect his or her presentations, not to mention the Jewish responses. This is *a fortiori* true when the subject under discussion devolves upon what the Christian considers of primary interest or concern. The very dialogical process, thus made asymmetrical in principle, becomes a deterrent to true dialogue. To prefer one's own agenda or area of concern is one thing; to cloud that of the other party can only vitiate the encounter in the long run.

Jewish and Christian concern with history, in turn, is not as asymmetrical as Rabbi Siegman seems to believe. If Judaism is "obsessed" with it, Christians are very much interested in it. Christian universalism and concern with the hereafter have certainly tended to conceal Christianity's particularism; they can never undo its inherently historical character. Its triumphalism mostly behind, Christianity's attention to history will increase and probably center upon new interpretations of the past, further discovery of its Jewish roots, an admission of its historical sins, probings for intimations of the Parousia, and other historical concerns again. Moreover, the histories of Judaism and Christianity are inextricably intertwined, and Siegman can rightly speak of our "common history" — our common post-biblical history. And he is equally right when he reminds us that the "history of the Church's persecution of Judaism and the Jewish people is even today not a part of the consciousness of the Church." This "page torn out of our history books" will be inserted. The crime of Antisemitism is an integral part of Christian history that comprises an important side of church life which, when fully faced and integrated, will probably transform the Christian mind in a revolutionary way. Then, too, the history of positive contacts between Christianity and Judaism, comparatively meager as they are, must be elaborated.

There is hardly a problem in reaching agreement that historical considerations hold first claim on the agenda of the Jewish-Christian interface. Full attention to theology and ultimate questions can wait. The point is, can they wait forever? This question points toward a distinction which is important to make—that between the existential and essential to dialogue. By the first is meant the dialogue as it exists and as it is practiced; by the second, what it is in its proper nature, what it should be. The two are not necessarily identical. The first can fall short of the second. The dialogue, as practiced to date, has failed to attain its essential stature. What "impels" us to dialogue need not determine what the dialogue essentially is or what it must be. To describe its present state as "pre-dialogue" is, to be sure, a severe evaluation that exaggerates its deficiencies; to say that it has realized its true nature or reached its proper boundaries would be another exaggeration. The peculiar theological relationship of Judaism and Christianity and their abnormal historical relations have prevented the normal development of dialogue and thrust historical considerations into the foreground, indeed have made them an integral and important part of the Jewish-Christian dialogue. But should this development be viewed, as Siegman seems to have it, as normative? Should it not be seen rather as a first and tentative stage of the dialogue?

This first stage, moreover, was by no means devoid of theological considerations or matters of "truth." Not only on less advanced levels of dialogue or only at Christian insistence were these areas taken up; often enough on the highest level of encounter they were mutually and fruitfully worked out on the agenda. But by and large theological subjects were usually on the Christian agenda and graciously concurred to by the Jewish party. On the other hand, a Christian reluctance to deal with historical subjects was often discernible, especially when Christian Antisemitism or Israel and Zionism were involved. For a while the subject of Israel became a veritable stumbling block, because of a widespread Christian refusal to accept it as legitimate dialogical fare. It is an evidence of the dialogue's progress that that difficulty is already pretty much a thing of the past. One of the first fruits of the dialogue in this country was for the Christian dialogists no longer to see Israel as "mere politics" for Jews—or for themselves. It is a development that should not be viewed as prejudicial to legitimate Arab concerns.

The failure to engage in theological discussions was not so much due, however, to the reasons given by Rabbi Siegman as to a certain shyness and awkwardness that is typical of first stages of intimate interface. In a newly found amity oversensitivity to the feelings of the other party and an overdesire to locate agreements and affinities and even to please tended to mark off those delicate areas of ultimate commitment where Jew and Christian must, if they remain loyal to their tradition, disagree—if not contradict one another. One may wonder whether this initial reticence and restraint has not been a cover, a "reaction formation" as Freud might call it, masking the old hostilities and alienations so recently put aside, or again a distrust of the other's equanimity that is most likely a projection of one's own unrecognized intolerance and volatility. It is perhaps in this realm of interpersonal feeling more than in methodical or theoretical problems that the main inhibition to complete openness resides. When this initial oversensitivity is surpassed, the dialogue, it may be hoped, will of its own momentum expand its horizons and enter another—the essential—stage to which interreligious dialogue by its nature tends. Siegman himself comes close to this vision and appears to break the bounds of his own restrictions when he writes.

> Judaism cannot remain uninterested in Christianity for theological reasons as well, for if Israel's election has a purpose, that purpose is "through you shall be blessed all the families of the earth." In a mysterious way, the Jewish people of Israel are to be the instrument for the redemption of the entire human family.

A Response to Henry Siegman

The Jew cannot help, therefore, but be vitally concerned with the spiritual life of the nations, with whom Israel is jointly embarked on the path to redemption and most particularly with Christianity, which has mediated the vocabulary and message of Israel to the ends of the earth.

In the wake of these precious observations he is able to rejoin his original thesis only by discounting them as, for Jews, "secondary considerations."

It is difficult to follow Siegman as he elaborates his thesis. Assuring us, for example, that "the Jew's obsession with history does not preclude serious consideration within the dialogue of issues of a spiritual and theological character," he resorts to a distinction between these issues and the question of "ultimate truth," identifying this latter as the really unapproachable area on the Jewish agenda. Then after enlisting two renowned Jewish ecumenists in support of his view that "truth" or the "inner life of faith" cannot be subject to dialogue, he concludes that the Jewish reluctance to discuss theology "applies not only to questions of ultimate faith but to the more formal and objective questions of theology as well."

His allowances for actual discussions of theology in a secondary way and his use of such terms and phrases as "reluctance," "what impels" or "motivates to seek" dialogue, "what makes dialogue compelling," and the like, give the impression that he is merely strongly emphasizing normal preferences in dialogue. Such preferences are part of the baggage every person or group takes into dialogue and need in no way vitiate or depress it provided they are not permitted to prevent or discourage not only what the other party wishes to treat but also, and more importantly, the natural course a dialogue between two related religious traditions normally takes.

Trouble arises again when Siegman takes up the question of "ultimate truth," placing it outside the scope of the dialogue. His entire thesis stands or falls of course with the validity of his stricture against involving this area in dialogical discussion. He is correct, I believe, in finally tying "more formal and objective questions of theology" to that of "ultimate truth," since theology by definition is a rational or discursive explicitation of the experiential life of faith. The question is, whether the "inner life of faith," the "profoundly personal and intimate experience of faith," can or cannot be submitted to dialogue. If this matrix of religious and spiritual life are accessible to dialogue, the theological deductions and conclusions derived from it obviously are.

Is the life of faith, of ultimate truth, the proper concern of conversation between the two faith-traditions? Siegman responds in the negative. In support of his negation he cites a "certain theological reticence" in Judaism that does not encourage one to "concretize in theological formulations the Jewish encounter with the divine." It is a reticence to be respected by Christians certainly. Nonetheless, one may proceed as far as the reticence will allow. Not all Jewish thinkers remain within the limitations Siegman appears to impose. He apparently would prefer to hold his considerations to the Torah and the *halachah,* but even here a wide latitude of "theologizing" is possible. It is not a matter of submitting them to a scholastic or Thomistic ratiocination, to be sure, but rather of educing the simple meaning and significance of these records of sacred events. Other Jewish dialogists, moreover, accept the Tanach, its commentaries, and the philosophical and mystical Jewish traditions as a wider base of their "theologizing." And not only Jews find therein a depth and a latitude of religious revelation and truth of which all of humankind can be the beneficiary. This in no way purports to deny that Judaism and Christianity have adopted "different strategies" in approaching the data of faith; it does submit that these strategies are not as exclusive or dissimilar as generally supposed, and that in any case the differences are not, as Rabbi Siegman has it, "another impediment to the dialogue." The very differences of approach might serve more as an enrichment rather than an impediment. Beneath the differences lie the same God and to a large extent, materially, the same Word of God, the Hebrew Scriptures. The earliest Christian Scriptures were the Tanach; the Christian Founder was an observant Jew out of the Pharisaic tradition. These basic facts must be taken into account in measuring the incommensurability or uncommunicability of Judaism and Christianity and in determining the boundaries of the dialogue between them.

The arguments propounded by Rabbis Heschel and Agus, especially the latter, to the effect that the ultimate truth, the inner life of faith, of anyone is incommensurate and incommunicable with that of someone not of the same tradition only beg the question; they assume what must be proved. There are other voices that speak in an opposite sense. It is fast becoming a truism in the Aquarian Age that all faith-traditions rejoin in esoteric places of their beliefs and experiences. The great mystics of Judaism, Islam, and Christianity as well as of the East are one in speaking of the ineffability of the God-experience and how this experience can be better described by what it is not than by what it is; yet none have more forthrightly attempted to give an account of the experience than they. The beliefs and teachings that have been drawn from these primordial noumenal experiences are already a step away from them toward the communal and institutional and are thus still more amenable to translation into objective theological categories.

Recent witness to this point of view may be found on the Catholic side in Dom Bede Griffith, Benedectine monk in India,[2] and on the Jewish side, Rabbi Zalman Schachter of Temple University.[3] Both look for a closer approach of the great religious and spiritual traditions to one another on the deepest level, from which contact, they believe, both will return to their own tradition strengthened and enriched. Rabbi Schachter's conclusion is of high interest:

I am convinced that learning Torah together is an important prelude to the kind of dialogue we will hold with each other when our escatological expectations will have been fulfilled. I trust we each will find that we were right, though not quite in the way we thought we would be. Only by holding on to our shape and color do we form the mosaic in which we are God's tiles.[4]

From scientific quarters support for the fundamental unity of religious experience at its deepest roots comes from C.G. Jung's investigations, which locate all religious experience, psychologically, on a collective, archetypal level.

Nothing in the foregoing is intended as favoring religious relativism or syncretism. The uniqueness and integrity of Judaism and Christianity is held in this response as an absolute of dialogue. What is intended is a realization of the unity of God and beneath the uniqueness of every human person and religious tradition a unitary humanity. What is also envisaged is an attempt to determine a base for an ultimate interfaith dialogue that includes within its focus ultimate truth, the exposure in proper circumstances of the inner life of faith.

Before the ultimate exchange is reached, however, many truths, beliefs, and tenets derivative of the original experience must be proferred for discussion. In the dialogue in which Jews and Christians engage, what are these? What are the sacred realities or symbols in which Judaism or Christianity are to some degree at one, or in which they find themselves at odds, yet sharing a common interest? No listing would exhaust them. At the summit of these considerations stand those pertaining to the One True God, Transcendent and Immanent, Creator, Revealer, Lawgiver and Judge, Provider and Retributor, and Final End of all things. There are God's operations and embodiment in divine works: God's Covenants with humankind; God's Word, Inspired and Revealed; God's elections; God's Reign on earth, and God's mandates, light and graces, and salvific and redemptive actions. In both faiths these are supreme realities and basic conceptualizations, yet understood in a different way. As they are concretized in teachings about the centrality of Jesus or Torah, grace or halachah, church or synagogue, divergence becomes division, yet division that fructifies and often cross-fertilizes respective understandings. They constitute issues that must be joined by two faith-communities that worship the same God who for both is a God of universal salvation and redemption. And of course there are collaborative biblical studies wherein contrasts can be sharpest, but mutual comprehension most rewarding. In the realm of morality agreements increase; in social action they abound. But here we distance ourselves from what is theologically ultimate and inner.

Let not the lofty listing we have drawn be seen as an invitation to dialogue. It comprises, in my view, the ushering in of the ultimate stage. Priorities must remain respected. Before these sacrosanct issues are broached, many more earthly and practical ones must be sufficiently discussed. Rabbi Siegman is right: history retains the first priority, but here "first" should connote temporal sequence. History holds first importance and first claim on the agenda until its problems have been satisfactorily resolved for both parties to the dialogue. With the historical debt resting as it does so heavily on the Christian side, it is for the Jewish participant to propose an agenda with an historical emphasis if his or her Christian counterpart has not had the insight and sensitivity to anticipate that same agenda.

In the first place Antisemitism has to be explored in all its dimensions—in history, in the present, in the Christian psyche, in the New Testament, in Christian theology. It still remains a fact that the majority of Christians are unaware of their own Antisemitism and of that of their history. When this situation is rectified, and only then, can one intelligently and justly understand and deal with the Holocaust and its full reality, nature, and causes. At this point, and preferably not before, should the subject which most Jews consider to be of overarching importance and central to their self-understanding as a people, culture, or a faith community be taken up—the State of Israel. If this subject is introduced earlier or at the beginnings of the conversation, opposition and misunderstanding will be the likely result. Even in experienced settings this subject can prove a source of dissension, owing doubtless to an unrecognized anti-Zionism on the Christian side.

Rules such as these suggested are certainly not hard-and-fast norms. To dialogues already in an advanced stage they are of little help, but they do apply to the larger number of those yet inadequately practiced in the dialogical experience. On the other hand, purely theological interchanges of the most advanced kind are, and for a long time have been, among the most fruitful and rewarding encounters in the Jewish-Christian relationship. The most gratifying and enriching dialogical experience in which I personally have been privileged to participate was that set up by the Vatican Office for Catholic-Jewish Relations in Nemi, Italy, ten years ago. In its course every vital area of the inner life of Judaism and Christianity was explored, compared, and reverenced by five Christian and five Jewish theologians and scholars over a five-day period. By all accounts this experience was unique in the experience of these seasoned ecumenists and productive of a greater insight and appreciation of their own respective traditions as well as that of the other than had been gained in any other arrangement or setting. Still further back in time those remarkable exchanges, classical as well as pioneering in the history of the dialogue, between Rosenzweig and Rosenstock-Huessy and between Buber and Schmidt stand out. The horizons expanded by these early and gifted explorers must not be allowed to recede. Their goal was to plumb the very core of Judaism and Christianity and their inherent relationship, whether positive or negative.

The full flowering of the Jewish-Christian dialogue, in the vision of this paper, will come to pass in the inner sanctum of Judaism and Christianity, where both touch the living God. Such is the normal destiny of two faith-traditions that have, for better or worse, been fatefully bound together in some basic assumptions and in conflict. Not to reach that final stage would, one may think, bespeak a failed encounter, or an encounter incapable of throwing off the burdens, of exorcizing the demons, of the past. There are many things in Rabbi Siegman's paper, despite the clear exposition of his thesis to the contrary, that invite us to believe that he, too, partakes in the same vision, but in different terms and shadings.

From the many rich reflections in his paper on Israel, Jewish views of Christianity, and Christian mission I should like to single out one perspective for special affirmation. It is a valuable one, if only for its rarity, and one which, coincidentally, helps to achieve what this response seeks—an enlargement of the Jewish-Christian dialogue. The enlargement in this response has to do with its content; in his, with its clientele.

Siegman forthrightly states that "more traditional" Jews reject the "theology of equality" which some Christians have proposed as the basis of dialogue. By "theology of equality" is meant a theological refusal of any claim by one member of the dialogue that his or her faith or tradition is truer or better than that of another member. This "theology of equality" has found a competitor—if it is not actually a spin-off from it—in a relativist posture found in more secularized quarters of the dialogue (including Christians and Jews). This posture would insist on all entrants to the dialogue renouncing all claim to a greater degree of truth for their tradition than for that of other participants in the dialogue, let alone to absolute truth. It is often put in political terms, to the effect that a claim to final truth illegitimately casts all other parties to the dialogue in the role of "second-class" participants. To bar access to those with absolutist claims effectively eliminates of course most traditional Christians, most Orthodox Jews—and in the trialogue, Muslims also—restricting the forum of dialogue to those of a (theologically) more or less relativist stamp. One can ask whether this tightening of the circle of dialogue impoverishes it by reducing its pluralism and removing provocative stimulations.

Siegman states the case clearly when he writes:

> Traditional Jews affirm that Judaism is the "truest" religion. That affirmation is part of what makes them Traditional Jews, and they do not expect Christians to be offended by it. Conversely, Jews cannot be offended by parallel affirmation of faith made by Christians—or by Muslims, for that matter ... Judaism constitutes a denial of the central Christian mystery and its notion of salvation; it cannot at the same time demand that Christianity be reformulated to accommodate the "equality" of Judaism.

The vigor and good sense of these words is refreshing. One need not be an absolutist in belief to recognize that there are many who are such, and for more than one reason. It is easy to distinguish three categories: (1) those who adhere to absolute conceptions of truth or morality from personal conviction;

(2) those who hold this claim not so much from personal conviction as from loyalty to their faith-tradition, which includes a claim to absolute truth among their tenets; and (3) some who, logically, cannot conceive of the possibility of genuinely adhering to a faith without at the same time holding it to be, at least for themselves, truer, better—call it what you will—than other faiths, unless of course one no longer sees one's faith-tradition as an object of personal faith commitment. Here Rabbi Jacob Petuchowski's advice is pertinent.[5] He would have all participants in the Jewish-Christian dialogue identify their precise position with respect to their faith-tradition, letting other participants know to what extent they represent that tradition. Certainly such a procedure would lend toward more open and honest dialogue.

Rabbi Siegman has had the courage to point to this issue affecting membership in the dialogue, one generally eschewed. The relativist ethos has ruled by a tacit assumption that absolutist claims are destructive of dialogue. It is an assumption that should be openly elaborated and evaluated. Is it possible that the refusal to undertake this task accounts in large part for the Jewish-Christian dialogue's failure to progress more rapidly toward its status as a theologically-oriented enterprise? It may be that Siegman's reflections on the nature of the dialogue, the directions they appear to take to the contrary notwithstanding, will accomplish more toward nearing that status than will the efforts of those who press theological agendas unduly or prematurely.

1) *J.E.S., Vol. 15, No. 2 (Spring, 1978), pp. 243-260.*
2) *See* Return to the Center (Springfield, IL: Templegate, 1976).
3) *See "Bases and Boundaries for Jewish, Christian, and Muslim Dialogue"* in Journal of Ecumenical Studies, *Vol. 14, No. 3 (Summer, 1977), pp. 419-432.*
4) *Ibid., p. 418*
5) *See his unpublished paper presented at the Third National Workshop of Christian-Jewish Relations held in Detroit, Michigan, April 19-21, 1977.*

XIV

Judaism and Christianity: A Theology of Co-Existence

By HAROLD H. DITMANSON

J ewish, Catholic, and Protestant observers tend to agree that the recent improvement in Jewish-Christian relations stands out as a bright spot in a century filled with unbelievable violence and suffering. Rabbi Seymour Siegel writes:

We sometimes tend to forget that it was relatively only yesterday that Jews were branded as deicides in most of the Christian churches; that Judaism was seen as a fossilized religion born out of a stubborn reluctance to see the light; and that Jews and Christians hardly ever met to discuss seriously the problems and prospects of their mutual existence. All this has changed. There is a new appreciation of Judaism in Christian circles. The history and theology of Jewish religion is being taught sympathetically in Christian schools and seminaries. The deicide charge has been repudiated in both Catholic and Protestant churches. There are numerous meetings, consultations, and conferences all over the world where individuals professing different religions can discuss their fears and hopes ... Of course, here and there vestiges of the old enmity exist. But clearly the direction is toward mutuality and dialogue.''[1]

Harold H. Ditmanson is a Professor at St. Olaf College in North-field, Minnesota. This essay is taken from Dialog, 16, Winter 1977, pp. 17-24 and is reprinted by permission of the publisher.

"Christianity and Judaism"

Christians who have worked hard to achieve the goals mentioned by Rabbi Seigel can only be gratified that the inter-faith encounter of recent years can be given such a positive evaluation by members of the Jewish community. The Christian search for a new and humane relationship with the Jewish people came very late in history. Christians and Jews have lived side by side for many centuries. During this time Christians have sought to evangelize Jews, and Jews have resisted missionary pressures. The confrontation has often been a violent one, involving persecution and suffering for the Jewish people. Now and then a few voices called for a different understanding of the relationship between Christianity and Judaism. But it was not until Christians acknowledged the full horror of the mass extermination of Jews during the Nazi period, the continuing precariousness of Jewish existence in various parts of the world, the more subtle forms of discrimination against Jews in other parts of the world, and the complicity of "Christendom" in these disasters, that representative bodies of Christians began to express strong and concrete interest in making amends for past wrongs and offering assurances of a better future.

Beginning with the First Assembly of the World Council of Churches in 1948, dozens of ecumenical and denominational statements concerning Jewish-Christian relations have been issued. These declarations focus on certain basic themes. Anti-Semitism is condemned and the guilt of the churches is acknowledged. Christian penitence is expressed. The notion that the Jewish people live under a corporate or inherited divine curse because of the crime of deicide is repudiated. The Jewish roots of Christianity are acknowledged with gratitude. Christians are urged to show respect and love for their Jewish neighbors and to cooperate with them in the struggle to eliminate discrimination and to foster human rights. Churches are asked to examine their publications for possible anti-Semitic references and to remove all false and injurious generalizations about Jews. Dialogue between Christians and Jews is endorsed. A mere listing of such themes does not convey the rich texture of the historical and moral reflection or the sense of struggle characteristic of these Christian declarations.

Acting on these propositions and imperatives, many churches have made substantial progress during the last fifteen years with respect to institutionalizing dialogue and removing misrepresentations and negative attitudes toward Jews and Judaism from their educational materials. There is much, however, that remains to be done in order to give a true and positive picture of Jews and Judaism in Christian manuals of instruction, as Gerald S. Strober has pointed out in his monograph, *Portrait of the Elder Brother*. Strober found that nine years after Bernhard E. Olson's pioneer study, *Faith and Prejudice*, Protestant teaching materials continue to present certain key themes in ways likely to foster hostility against Jews, their religion and experience. Chief among such themes are the nature of Judaism, Jesus' relation to his Jewish contemporaries, the Pharisees, the Jews' rejection of Jesus as the Messiah, and the crucifixion. The handling of these topics by mainstream Protestant denominations is less negative than in the past, but remains largely negative in conservative publications. The content of recent Christian declarations of repentance and reform are rarely reflected in teaching materials.[2]

Jews and Christians are grateful, however, for the progress that has been made. Christians have belatedly moved from indifference or hostility to concern and friendliness. The denunciation of anti-Semitism and the endorsement of conversation and cooperation are to be appreciated. Security and justice are preferable to danger and discrimination. But more is needed. There can be little doubt that the impulse behind the Christian initiatives to make amends to the Jewish people for centuries of defamation and mistreatment, and especially to respond in a spirit of repentance and reform to the calamities of the twentieth century, has been primarily humanitarian. The conscience of Christians could not ignore the fate of the Jewish people during the years 1939-1945. In a confused, inadequate, yet genuine way, Christians have asked to be forgiven for their part in the Holocaust and have pledged themselves to the prevention of such a disaster in the future.

Humanitarian motives have brought us to the stage of peaceful co-existence. Yet there is something unstable and unsatisfactory about a position that aims only at de-fusing anti-Semitism and treating Jewish neighbors with respect and fair-play. For peaceful co-existence may leave the dividing wall between Judaism and Christianity as solid as ever. This means that whenever the social, political, and economic sectors of Christendom suffer a severe setback, the peaceful co-existence can easily turn into hostility and the Jewish people will have reason to fear that at any time they could again become the victims of the "scapegoat" tendency of the majority group. This danger arises from the fact that there is an uneasy tension involved in the policy of treating Jewish people with respect but at the same time regarding Judaism as a rejected or defective religion. There are logical, psychological, sociological, and theological problems present in such a position.

If the humanitarian motives of Christians are sound enough to warrant the actions we have taken, and if the stakes are as high as we say they are, then we ought to rest those motives on a theological base. But more is involved than taking steps to make the humanitarianism secure. For it is doubtful whether the recent improvement in Jewish-Christian relations has led to any real contact or communication between the two faiths. If we are to go beyond the stage of peaceful co-existence to a real meeting between Christianity and Judaism, we must, on the Christian side, clarify in a new and decisive way the theological premises upon which we estimate the significance for the church of present-day Judaism. Unless we clarify the Christian "theology of Israel," little in the way of mutual enrichment will occur.

The Theology of Replacement

The needed clarification can be stated in the form of a thesis: the essential precondition for any fruitful contact between Christianity and Judaism in the future is a recognition by Christians of the reality and autonomy of Judaism. Such a thesis would be considered unsound by many Christians, yet it is being put forward increasingly by Christian students of Judaism and it is implied by the official statements of churches concerning Jewish-Christian relations. The major obstacle to a Christian recognition of the reality of Judaism is the centuries-old theological attitude according to which the "old" Jewish order or covenant has given way to a "new" Christian one. Since God's covenant with Israel was displaced by the new covenant in Christ, it follows that Judaism, as a living community of faith, ceased to exist nearly twenty centuries ago. The synagogue has been expropriated by the church which is alone God's chosen means of revelation and redemption. Since Judaism has been displaced by Christianity, Judaism is without a mission and a message and there is no need for the Jew, in terms of his own vocation and covenant. Therefore Jews should become Christians. This approach can be called the theory of rejection and substitution.

It is a matter of debate whether or not this traditional description of the relationship between Judaism and Christianity can be found in the New Testament. But there can be no doubt that it took shape in the very early centuries of the church. By the end of the third century, the Jew was seen by Christians in general as an unbeliever. The medieval Christian saw the Jew as one who was actually convinced of Christian truth but stubbornly and perversely withheld his belief. Since the church had become the true Israel, the unbelieving Jew was regarded as an object of mission. Compulsory exposure to Christianity continued for centuries. The rapid deterioration of the Jewish image and status during the fourth century was due to an ominous addition to the picture of the Jew as a special type of unbeliever. Justin Martyr was the first to express the idea that Jews are a people punished for the crime of deicide. Hippolytus and Origen soon expanded the theme of deicidal punishment. No early theologian equalled John Chrysostom in his rage against the Jews. At the heart of his denunciations is the thesis that the supreme crime of deicide cannot be forgiven and that all the troubles which come upon Jews are the expression of divine rejection and vengeance. The belief in the deicidal guilt of the Jews and their punishment was taken for granted during the Middle Ages and succeeding centuries. The image of the Jews as Christ-killers was an essential part of the pogroms and forced emigrations of the nineteenth century.

Christian attitudes toward Jews are surely negative if Jews are seen as unbelievers, targets of conversion, Christ-killers, and objects of divine punishment. But even worse was the image of the Jew as a ritual murderer. Jews were first accused by Christians of ritual murder in the twelfth century. The charge has been repeated in every century thereafter and to its account must be laid many of the tortures, imprisonments, expulsions, and massacres of Jews throughout the ages. It is clear that social, political, and economic frustrations led Christians to find in the Jew the scapegoat needed

The Coexistence of Christianity and Judaism

to rationalize their disappointments. Yet the dogmatic tradition of the church furnished a pseudo-theological basis throughout many centuries for an attitude of hostility toward Jews. The element of competition had much to do with the anti-Jewish character of the developing Christian tradition. The church's bid for acceptance in the empire during the first three centuries met a strong challenge in a Judaism that refused to die. The church considered Judaism obsolete, yet its appeal to the public caused strong Judaizing tendencies in the church, its proselytizing continued, and Jews were associated with several of the Christian heresies. Signs of irritation and alarm can be seen in theologians and administrators as they tried to prove that the church was the true Israel and Judaism a mere pretender. The theological offensive against Judaism began with the claim that it had been displaced and moved on to a systematic refutation of its doctrines and practices. As time went by, the offensive took the form of the denigration and debasement of the people the church claimed to have replaced. Anti-Jewish legislative measures taken by both church and state were a translation into statutory form of what the theological tradition seemed to call for.

Christians have now at long last repudiated the falsehoods, negative images, and hostile attitudes of the past. But they have not modified or renounced the theory of rejection and substitution which furnished the theological base or excuse for anti-Jewish attitudes and actions. There is good reason to believe that the attempt to eradicate anti-Semitism, while simultaneously teaching the abrogation or displacement of the covenant of Jewish faith, cannot succeed. So long as the traditional "theology of Israel" remains in force, an uneasy tension will exist between commendable humanitarian impulses and the belief that Jews are unaccountably stubborn and perverse in their refusal to accept Jesus as the promised Messiah.

A new theological rationale that is compatible with the positive moves in recent Jewish-Christian relations has not been developed. Such a rationale has not seemed necessary to Christian theologians who received their education under the influence of the theory of rejection and substitution. This theory has provided a convenient and seemingly adequate explanation of the Jewish phenomenon. Because of the dominance of this tradition, the curricula of Christian seminaries have largely ignored Judaism as a living religion and active spiritual force. The result is that in the press of ecclesiastical business and curricular revision, Judaism is seen as one item among many, and not an important one at that. This also holds true of particular aspects of Jewish existence, such as the state of Israel and the struggle against anti-Semitism. Moreover, when theologians suggest that the traditional perspective be replaced by a new approach, people become afraid that the whole structure of Christian doctrine will collapse if Judaism is recognized as a valid and active form of spirituality in the present.

Rejection of Replacement

What we must ask ourselves is whether the traditional theory of rejection and substitution will stand up to biblical and theological examination, or whether it is in need of reform. Many serious theologians today argue that the classical description of the relationship between Judaism and Christianity has become untenable. It is very interesting to note that the church members to whom such theological arguments are unknown or unconvincing have in fact committed themselves in a series of official declarations to a position which, at least by implication, challenges the traditional "theology of Israel." With respect to themes found in all Christian statements about Jewish-Christian relations, one can say either that certain actions entail further actions consistent with them, or that in certain actions there are implications that have not generally been brought to the surface and acknowledged.

The traditional theory of rejection and substitution has already been undermined by the repudiation of anti-Semitism. At its First Assembly, in 1948, the World Council of Churches denounced anti-Semitism "as absolutely irreconcilable with the profession and practice of the Christian faith." In 1964, the Lutheran World Federation urged its member churches "to examine their publications for possible anti-Semitic references, and to remove and oppose false generalizations about Jews. Especially reprehensible are the notions that Jews, rather than all mankind, are responsible for the death of Jesus the Christ, and that God has for this reason rejected his covenant people." Also in 1964, the House of Bishops of the Protestant Episcopal Church declared: "The charge of deicide against the Jews is a tragic misunderstanding of the inner significance of the crucifixion. To be sure, Jesus was crucified by *some* soldiers at the instigation of *some* Jews. But this cannot be construed as imputing corporate guilt to every Jew in Jesus' day, much less the Jewish people in subsequent generations. Simple justice alone proclaims the charge of a corporate or inherited curse on the Jewish people to be false." The statement issued by the Second Vatican Council in 1965 was equally explicit: "True, the Jewish authorities and those who followed their lead pressed for the death of Christ; still, what happened in His passion cannot be charged against all the Jews, without distinction, then alive, nor against the Jews of today. Although the Church is the new people of God, the Jews should not be presented as rejected or accursed by God, as if this followed from the Holy Scriptures."

The Lutheran Council in the USA forwarded to its member churches, in 1971, a document entitled, "Some Observations and Guidelines for Conversations between Christians and Jews." One of the observations states: "Christians should make it clear that there is no biblical or theological basis for anti-Semitism." The LCUSA document was accepted by the American Lutheran Church and the Jewish Community." In this Convention document, it is said that "whole generations of Christians have looked with contempt upon this people who were condemned to remain wanderers on the earth on the false charge of deicide."

Churches have explicitly disavowed the teaching of the curse and denied that there is a biblical warrant for it. But if we no longer attribute the fact and life of Judaism to a divine curse, how do we account for it? Does not the very logic of the disavowal invalidate all that the church has said in the past about the status of the Jew and the hope of Judaism in the sight of God? For if the deicide charge is rejected because it is false, then it follows that Christians do not think that Jews are the objects of a special form of divine punishment. If there is no curse, there is no reason to believe that satanic forces cause a veil of blindness to come between Jews and the Christian gospel. By disavowing the curse, the church has accepted the necessity of producing a new and different explanation of the continued survival and vitality of Judaism.

Christians who take seriously the disavowal of the curse have already begun to entertain the conviction, at least by implication, that Judaism lives not because of stubbornness or demonic influences, but by God's design. The vitality of Judaism is a sign of faithfulness, not blindness. The millions of Jews who have suffered and died for their faith have paid the price of obedience, not disobedience. If this is true, it follows that Judaism has a witness that God wants it to bear. Thus God does not want a world without Jews. If Jews have such a witness to bear, then Christians need Judaism and can learn from it something about their own faith. Hostility, then, is impossible, as is any imperialism or condescension in approach.

It may seem a long step for some Christians from the rejection of the deicide charge to an acknowledgment of the validity of Judaism. They would argue that the causes and forms of anti-Semitism can be renounced on moral grounds without going on to a theological position which touches the very roots of Christian self-understanding. Yet the possibility that Judaism is not only actual but valid must be considered even though such an admission might seem to undermine the traditional Christian definitions of Judaism. For Christians have never said that the message and mission of Israel retain a current validity, nor do they speak of Jews as God's people today. Christians think instead that the message and mission of Israel were cancelled or transferred to the church, leaving "God's ancient people" without redemptive experience or significance.

If the charge of the deicidal curse is false, as Christians have said it is, then there is no room for thinking that God has abandoned the Jewish people or cancelled his covenant with them. But if God has not abandoned Judaism, then it must be the case that Judaism has a valid base of its own in its convenantal relationship with God. In short, the very disavowal of the curse implies a recognition of the legitimacy of Judaism.

But many official Christian statements have already caused this traditional position to erode. For example, the LCUSA "Guidelines for Conversations between Lutherans and Jews" takes the stand that "on both sides, living communities of faith and worship are involved." According to the statement adopted by the 1974 General Convention of the American Lutheran Church, Judaism and Christianity "worship the same God .... We both call Abraham father. We both view ourselves as communities covenanted to God."

"Christianity and Judaism"

The declaration of the Second Vatican Council affirms the indissoluble tie between Israel and the church, and says that God has not withdrawn his presence from Jewish faith and worship. In accordance with Pauline teaching, God remains the Lord of his people and continues to endorse his promises in their midst. Many Catholic scholars find in this declaration an acknowledgment of the salvational status of Jewish religion. God continues to address his people in the worship of the synagogue.

The Christian tradition has not acknowledged Jewish services as the worship of the true God. After the displacement of Judaism by Christianity, Jewish religion fell into a state of blindness. Consequently the worship taking place in synagogues was not the adoration of the true God, but of false gods or demons. At the very least, it was empty and hollow because the God of the covenant was either no longer there, or was present as Creator and Judge but not as Redeemer. Thus recent Christian statements to the effect that Jews and Christians "worship the same God," and that Judaism is a "living community of faith and worship," do in fact challenge the traditional "theology of Israel" by suggesting that Jewish religion has a positive place in God's economy of salvation.

It is quite true that many passages in the New Testament seem to contradict the proposition that God continues to address his people in the worship of the synagogue. In the Gospels we read of the conflict between Jesus and the religious leaders of his nation. The faith of those who believe in him is contrasted with the unbelief of those who refused to accept his message. The rivalry between church and synagogue is apparent in the epistles and the freedom of the new covenant is compared with the bondage of the old. A focus on certain passages could lead to the conclusion that the Jews were hard-hearted unbelievers, excluded from God's mercy. But there are other passages that are much more positive. Paul affirms that Israel remains dear to God, that it remains a chosen people, that God's promises to her are irrevocable, and that the Jews possess spiritual advantages other men do not enjoy.

The New Testament's Two-Sidedness

It is clear that we must recognize a certain two-sidedness in New Testament references to the relation between Judaism and Christianity. Conflicting tendencies can be found in the gospels, especially in Luke, but they stand out in Paul's letters. Paul thought and wrote in antitheses. He was not much concerned about harmonizing apparently contradictory themes. He usually allows contrasts to stand side by side as pointers to a mysterious fullness of revelation which could not be scaled down to a simple synthesis. Thus Paul gives both positive and negative evaluations of the history and religion of the Jewish people and his readers are left to determine which note is the authentic one.

The Coexistence of Christianity and Judaism

There is a great difference between regarding alternatives as signs of self-contradiction and incoherence, and seeing them as contrasts or tensions which enrich a unity of thought that is greater than any particular theme. In order to deal with the two-sidedness of the New Testament teaching, it is important to start with the recognition that the New Testament does not contain a complete account of the relationship of the Jewish people to the church. The New Testament does not speak about the future of Judaism and Christianity as separate and independent religious groups. That situation developed after the New Testament documents had been written and it is the exegetes and theologians of later generations who have formulated a fixed posture of anti-Judaism. The New Testament presents us with mutual criticism within the Jewish community. At a later point in time these polemical remarks were taken not as statements of Jews against Jews but as judgments against the Jewish people from outside.

Thus the negative references to Jews in the New Testament should be regarded as words of prophetic criticism. In the tradition of the great prophets, they call the people to conversion. They criticize the official representatives of Judaism for their rejection of Jesus. But they do not denounce Jews as Jews, nor do they refer to all Jews living then or in the future, nor do they refer in any way to the whole question of Jews and Gentiles. They did indeed denounce those who sent Jesus to be killed, but both Peter and Paul are quite explicit in saying that the important Jews of Jerusalem were ignorant of the dimensions of their act. The deicide charge has no foundation in the New Testament. Nor can the idea that Israel has been rejected be found anywhere in the New Testament. Paul specifically denies such a notion. The harsh statements refer to selfishness, disloyalty, injustice, ignorance, and infidelity, but at no point do they pronounce final judgment on all Jews as a reprobate people and project that judgment into the distant future.

Since Paul was involved in the intramural polemics of his time, one finds in his writings depreciations of Judaism alongside a very positive outlook on Jewish religion. There can be no doubt that the fundamental theme in Paul's thought, consistent with his understanding of the primordial character of grace, is the positive aspect. This is made especially clear in Romans 9-11. Here Paul sets forth his "theology of Israel" with a degree of clarity and completeness not found elsewhere in the New Testament. All negative references to Jews and Judaism should be read in the light of these chapters. God's fidelity to his promises is the controlling thought in this treatise on Israel's role in the history of salvation. Paul states clearly that God's commitment to his people in the covenant of salvation can never be undone by any human decision. It stands forever. It is true that exegetes propose a variety of interpretations of Paul's sometimes puzzling words. But, at the very least, he is saying that God continues to address his people in the liturgy of the synagogue service. Judaism actually worships the true God. It is a living religion. Conversion to Christ is a conversion to the God of Judaism.

"Christianity and Judaism"

The synagogue is a place where God is present to his people in judgment and salvation.

If the New Testament provides no obstacles to an acknowledgment of the reality and legitimacy of Judaism, and if the already-accomplished facts of the rejection of the deicide charge and the expressed desire to engage in interfaith dialogue do in fact imply that sort of recognition, then it is possible to understand the Christian belief that the two faiths have been and are related in a unique way. One does not need to possess a definitive theology of the manner of God's presence in other religions in order to affirm that between Judaism and Christianity there is an altogether special relationship. These two religions belong to each other in an intimate organic way which classifies them together and apart from all other religions. We know that without Judaism there would be no Christianity. The Bible of the early Christians was the Jewish Bible. The New Testament writings became biblical by attachment to the Jewish Scriptures. The gospel of Jesus Christ presupposes the Torah and the Prophets. In both Testaments the same God of grace and justice is speaking. In both faiths the true God is present and active. Christianity does not enjoy this unique relationship with Buddhism, Hinduism, Confucianism, nor even with Islam. There is for the Christian, as for Jesus, no other God than the God of Abraham, Isaac, and Jacob.

Theological Options

How can this unique relationship best be understood? Several options are available within the sphere of Christian thought. The theory of rejection and substitution is unbiblical and inhumane and should be repudiated. At the other extreme is a universalism which sees no problem in recognizing the reality and legitimacy of Judaism or any other religion. This position has often been branded a heresy but it persists as a minority view in certain theologians and as a vague and unspoken hope in the hearts of most Christians. Somewhere between the extremes is a position which might be called "Disciplined Dialogue and Respectful Witness." It does not claim to have clearcut theological answers to the conundrums present in the traditional encounter between Judaism and Christianity. It understands that there are both Jews and Christians who believe that their particular revelation has a uniquely redemptive character and that it is normal to share one's most precious beliefs with others. But it holds that we ought to discipline ourselves in the dialogue so that conversation can at least begin and trust develop. As Jews and Christians reveal themselves to each other, both will witness to God's presence and cooperate in meeting human needs. Each will respect the right of the other to say "no."

A fourth option also falls between the extremes. It shows a greater interest in developing a theological rationale for Jewish-Christian relations than does the previous model. We might call it a "Theology of Mutual Recognition

The Coexistence of Christianity and Judaism

and Co-Existence.'' This position has affinities with the "two covenant" or "double covenant" theory associated, on the Jewish side, with Maimonides, Rosenzweig, Buber, Herberg, and Matt, and on the Christian side, with Niebuhr, Maritain, Stendahl, Flannery, Hruby, Rylaarsdam, and others.

This view traces back to Paul its impulse to make a place for both Judaism and Christianity in the divine economy. In Romans 11:25, Paul hints at a mysterious co-existence of the two covenants. He finds a positive quality in the negative response of Israel toward the Christianly-conceived message of salvation. This negative attitude is in fact a necessary aspect of the process of salvation as a whole. In reality, Israel did not stumble or fall (Romans 11:11). Its attitude was a necessity to bring the salvation which is in Jesus Christ to the Gentiles. By rejecting the Christian preaching of the gosepl, the Jews appear as "enemies," but this enmity is "necessary for your sakes" (11:28). Paul says the aloofness on Israel's part will last throughout the whole of Christian history, "until the full number of the Gentiles come in" (11:25). Israel therefore performs a permanent function in relation to the Christian community. What appears in one sense to be Israel's "trespass," turns out, in another respect, to be "riches for the world . . . and riches for the Gentiles" (11:12), even "the reconciliation of the world" (11:15). This means that Israel is not rejected or condemned. It is in full possession of all God's gifts (9:4,5), for "the gifts and the call of God are irrevocable" (11:29). When Israel has performed its function for the world and for the community of Christ, "all Israel will be saved" (11:26).

This Pauline view requires the abandonment of the traditional theory of rejection and substitution and gives a positive interpretation of the present existence of the Jewish people. To be able to fulfill their function for the Christian community, the Jewish people must preserve their identity and autonomy.[3] This function can take many forms and it is not easy to give it exact definition. But if fruitful encounter is to take place, Christians must be clear that actual Jewish existence is a necessity for Christianity. Christianity *cannot* desire a world without Jews and Judaism.

Both Jewish and Christian authors have recently given expression to the conviction that between Judaism and Christianity there is a necessary and lasting complementarity. Rabbi Seymour Siegel writes: "Catholics and Protestants have begun to work out an understanding of Judaism and Christianity which makes a place for both in the divine economy. This has been coupled with a heightened awareness of the Judaic character of Christianity and the danger of a Hellenized non-Hebraic form of Christian faith. This return to roots is a most promising development within the churches. Jews, too, building upon the bold suggestions of Franz Rosenzweig and Martin Buber, are beginning to realize that Christianity (and Islam) are not just other world religions but systems of spirituality which, being based on the Hebrew Bible, are bringing the word of God to the distant islands.''[4]

As he looks ahead to the next century, Father Edward Flannery foresees that "Christianity and Judaism, epiphanies of the one God, will be seen in balance; the first, Judaism, pointing to the work of the Father Creator, the goodness of His creation, and the spread of His kingdom on earth; while the latter, Christianity, will point to the work of the Christ, Son of the Father according to its faith, sanctifying the individual from within and preparing the present age for the age to come. The Spirit of God, conceived differently by both faiths, will be the unifying force, committing each to seek its own truth in love and work together throughout the great interim preceding the eschaton in a common task redeeming and sanctifying the earth and reflecting the divine light in the world."[5]

Dr. Krister Stendahl, also looking into the future, expects that "Christian theologians will become increasingly aware of the apostle Paul's vision of a coexistence of Judaism and Christianity, of Israel and the Church. For I believe that we can now see how Paul was the forerunner of Maimonides and Rosenzweig in their recognition of Christianity as a way of God to and for the Gentiles."[6]

Whether it be called the "double covenant," "two epiphanies of the one God," the "co-existence of Judaism and Christianity," or "two communities — one people," this point of view suggests a way of understanding how these faiths may "stand in a complementary relationship to each other in which each can acknowledge the validity of the covenant of the other, without qualifying its faithfulness to its own."[7] Serious consideration of such a proposal demands that three items be given a very high place on the Christian agenda. First, study must be given to a concept of "mission" which is consistent with the recognition of the reality of Judaism. Second, Christians need to become much more familiar with those elements of the normative content of Judaism which find identical counterparts in Christianity. Finally, it is important to introduce Christians to the broad outlines of Jewish worship and, in more detail, to the prayers and hymns which form part of the rich heritage of the Jewish tradition.

1)   *Seymour Siegel, "Jewish-Christian Dialogue – Prospects and Future," Face to Face, Vol. 1, Winter/Spring, 1976, pp. 13-14, Anti-Defamation League of B'nai B'rith, New York.*
2)   *Gerald S. Strober, Portrait of the Elder Brother: Jews and Judaism in Protestant Teaching Materials (New York: The American Jewish Committee, 1972), pp. 12-13.*
3)   *Kurt Hruby, "The Future of Christian-Jewish Dialogue," Christian and Jews, ed. Hans Kung and Walter Kasper (New York: The Seabury Press, 1974/5), p. 91.*
4)   *Seymour Siegel, op. cit., pp. 14-15*

5)   Edward Flannery, "The Next Century of Jewish-Christian Relations," *Face to Face*, Vol. 1, Winter/Spring, 1976, p. 4, Anti-Defamation League of B'nai B'rith, New York.
6)   Krister Stendahl, "Widening the Perspectives of Jewish-Christian Relations," *Ibid*, p. 18.
7)   J. Coert Rylaarsdam, "The Disavowal of the Curse *Dialog*, VI (*Summer, 1967*), 199.

XV

Towards A New Relationship Between Christians And Jews

BY DAVID CAIRNS

Dokumentation. A Publication of the Evangelische Pressedienst.
Frankfurt-am-Main, 29 September, 1980.

In recent years the appalling nature of the Holocaust of the Jews by Nazi fanaticism has awakened a world-wide feeling of horror which has given rise to a new movement particularly among Christians, and especially in Germany, though we in Britain are as yet little aware of it. The question has been asked in Germany why the Church (both Roman Catholic and Protestant) made so ineffectual and tardy a protest against this savage persecution; and further, whether it was not the doctrines and practice of Christian preachers and people down the ages that had been in some measure responsible for the diabolical outcome. There has been a growing conviction that Christian interpretation of Scripture requires thorough re-examination in relation to this issue, and not least our interpretation of the writings of St. Paul

It is not too much to say that there is at present a ferment of critical questioning in the German Church; and it is reflected in this typescript of over sixty pages, duplicated by the Evangelical Press Service in Frankfurt. The immediate cause of the publication was a meeting early in 1980 of the Provincial Synod of the Evangelical Church of the Rhineland, convened to consider a Study produced by a committee appointed by the Synod some four

Professor David Cairns resides at 29 Viewfield Gardens, Aberdeen, Scotland ABI 7XN. This essay is taken from the Scottish Journal of Theology, Vol. 34, 1981 pp. 357-367 and is reprinted with the permission of the publisher.

years earlier. On the 11th January the Synod passed a resolution 'Concerning Renewal of the Relationship between Christians and Jews' which strongly approved the committee's Study. *Dokumentation* contains:

(1) The Study itself, containing six theses, with explanatory material.

(2) Some excerpts from statements of the Synod President, Karl Immer, on the occasion of the Synod meeting.

(3) The Resolution of the Synod supporting the Study and suggesting lines of action for the Church.

(4) A four-page document highly critical of both the Study and the Resolution, produced by thirteen Professors of the Bonn University Theological Faculty, containing ten paragraphs, and entitled "Reflections on the Church Paper on Renewal of the Relations between Christians and Jews'—to which we refer hereafter as 'The Bonn Reflections'. It is to be noted that this paper has not the authority of the Bonn Faculty behind it, and some members of that Faculty would definitely repudiate it. It has however subsequently been signed by eleven members of the Theological Faculty of the University of Münster.

(5) Responses to the 'Reflections' of an extremely scathing character by Professors Klappert, Gollwitzer and Bethge, and a courteous criticism by a Jewish Professor, Pinhas Lapide.

The whole area covered in *Dokumentation* is a theological minefield, full of explosive issues both for Christian doctrine and for practical action. The material is rather intractable; the doctrinal substance of the Study presented to the Synod too full too summarise; and the arguments of the contestants are both involved and laden with frequent appeals to Scripture. The tone is sometimes petulant (as in the 'Reflections'), or reminds one of a schoolmistress's pencil rapping the knuckles of a backward pupil (as occasionally in Klappert's contribution). Nevertheless, the issues are of major importance.

The interests of clarity will be best served if we draw a broad contrast between the two outlooks represented concerning, first, the question of guilt and, second, the relation between the Old Covenant and the New. Under each heading we shall deal with (1) the Synodal Material; (2) the Bonn "Reflections"; and (3) the Professorial Rejoinders. As, however, the contributions of Gollwitzer and Bethge are too impressive to be divided up in this manner, we shall give them special notice in the later part of our summary.

A. The Question of Guilt

(1) The Synodal Material

So important is the Holocaust in the eyes of the Synod that the sense of guilt relating to it is recorded as the first of the four reasons given in its Resolution for the Church's entering into a new relationship with the Jewish people (p.1). The Resolution itself begins with a confession of shared responsibility and shared guilt of Churchmen in Germany for the Holocaust. Further, the President of the Synod made especial mention of this matter in his introduction to the discussion, referring to the tardy (and in his opinion completely inadequate) protests of the Evangelical Church when the Aryan paragraph was thrust by the Nazis upon the Church. He said, "The past years have brought us all, step by step, ever more explicit information about the incredible things that happened between 1939 and 1945.' And he added that the reaction in succeeding years had been terribly slow and inadequate. 'But perhaps the measure of our previous omissions, misunderstandings and half-truths had simply been too great to be grasped in a shorter period, or even brought to some extent under control.' (pp. 11-12)

In laying this emphasis upon the horror of the Holocaust, the President and Synod were only taking up the theme of the committee's Study, whose first section deals with the same theme at some length, citing the shock it had given to the faith of Jews, and quoting a number of moving expressions of Jewish faith trembling into despair as the disaster deepened. 'Never shall I forget the little faces whose bodies I saw being consumed in the whirling smoke under a speechless blue heaven. Never shall I forget those flames which destroyed my faith for ever. Never shall I forget the silence of that night, which for ever robbed me of the wish to live.' (pg. 3)

The Study goes on to warn against any attempt to find an easy answer or a facile theodicy to apply to these terrible events. Only a common search, it suggests, and the common prayer of Christians and Jews, will be able to find some answer to those frightful happenings of recent decades.

(2) The Bonn "Reflections"

When we turn from this material to the Bonn paper we shall not immediately register a difference; for the very first words state, "We commend without reserve the Synod of the Rhineland, and other Church circles before it, for the concern that marks the document, namely the wish, in consequence of historical guilt in relation to the Jews, to seek and to promote dialogue with the Jews, and to determine afresh the relation between Christians and Jews.' (p. 14)

Yet what the Professors have just given with one hand they proceed to take away with the other. On the point of guilt they comment in the seventh paragraph of their paper (p. 16) as follows: 'Confession of guilt, or of a share in guilt, in the murderous persecution of the Jews, and horror at what has happened, should not obscure our vision of theological truths and distinctions, as happens in the (Snyodical) document. Confession of guilt and/or share in guilt should not lead to a misinterpretation of the National Socialist ideology and its crimes as Christian, or as committed by Christians as such, or to be laid to their account. The National Socialist ideology was just as openly anti-Christian as anti-Jewish.

There is a suggestion on the part of the Bonn Professors that the desire for a new approach comes from admiration of the Jews (p. 16), that is, from sentimental motives—that the new movement is not a 'theology after Auschwitz', but a 'theology of Auschwitz'. So, in spite of their preamble, their paper indicates that they do not feel that they need, and that they really do not want, any substantive conversation with the Jews.

(3) Rejoinders in Defense of the Synod

In the Bonn paper's expression of consciousness of guilt, Bertold Klappert diagnoses 'a remarkable lack of consistency. While the Introduction "commends without reserve the purpose of seeking dialogue with the Jews, in the consciousness of historical guilt in relation to them," there follows in the seventh paragraph of the "Reflections" (p. 16) the weaker pair of concepts, "Guilt, or shared guilt," until at the end of the paragraph the reader is informed flatly and curtly that 'The Nazi ideology was as openly anti-Christian as it was anti-Jewish'." "So," he comments, "the Christian Church was free of guilt, and *is* consequently free of guilt. The transition is as easy as that." (p. 36)

B. The Relation Between the Old Covenant and the New

(1) The Synodal Material

"On this theme the Synod's Resolution states:
> In gratitude we confess the Scriptures (cf. Luke 24:32 and 45; I Cor. 15:3f), our Old Testament, as a common foundation for faith and action for Jews and Christians.
> We confess Jesus Christ, the Jew, who as the Messiah of the Jews is the Saviour of the world, and binds the people of the world with the people of God.
> We believe in the continuing election of the Jewish people as God's people, and acknowledge that through Christ the Church has been taken up into God's covenant with his people.
> We believe with the Jews that God's historical saving action is at one and the same time both just and loving. With the Jews we believe that justice and love are God's directives for our whole life. As Christians we see both established in God's action in Israel and in God's action in Jesus Christ.
> We believe that Jews and Christians each are witnesses in their different callings to God before the world and before each other, and therefore we are convinced that the Church cannot regard its witness to the Jewish people as being on the same footing with its mission to the Gentile world.
> We therefore declare: For centuries the word 'New' in the interpretation of the Bible was directed against the Jewish people; the New Covenant was understood as the contrary of the Old Covenant, the new people of God as the substitute for the old people of God. This disregard for the continuing election of Israel and its condemnation to annihilation (Ver-

urteilungzu Nichtexistenz) has ever and again characterised Christian theology, Church preaching, and Church action, and still does so today. By this action we have also incurred guilt for the physical condemnation of the Jewish people.

We wish therefore to regard in a new light the indissoluble connexion of the New Testament with the Old Testament, and to understand the relationship of 'Old' and 'New' in the light of the Promise: as the giving of the Promise, the fulfilment of the Promise, and the confirmation of the Promise. 'New' therefore does not mean the supplanting of the 'Old'. Therefore we deny that the people of Israel is rejected by God, or replaced by the Church.

In repentance we begin to discover what Jews and Christians confess in common. We both confess God as the Creator of heaven and earth. We both confess the common hope of a new heaven and a new earth, and the power of this Messianic hope for the witness and action of Christians and Jews for righteousness and peace in the earth.

The Synod of the Rhineland instructs the leaders of the Church to reappoint a Committee on 'Christians and Jews', and to ask the Jews for their cooperation in this Committee.

At this point a word of comment is needed on the statement about agreement of Christians and Jews that God is both just and loving, and, further, that God requires man to act both justly and lovingly. Misled, perhaps, by the attack of Paul on Jewish "work-righteousness", and not remembering that this belief in "work-righteousness" is itself a misunderstanding of the Old Testament revelation (as Paul himself testifies), Christians have tended to misinterpret the Old Testament as a Book of Law, and the New Testament as a Book of Grace in contrast with it. Renewed contact with Jewish life and thought has reinforced the realization that this is a caricature; both on the Jewish and on the Christian interpretation, God's grace is supreme, and righteousness is required of man, not as a way in which to satisfy God's demands, but as the right response to God's promises may be irrevocable, but it is not claimed that as a result anyone has a *claim* to enjoy their fulfilment.

(2) The Bonn "Reflections"

The Bonn Professors complain that the Synodal Resolution assumes the identity of the modern Jews with the Israel to whom the promises of God were made, and "fails" to distinguish between the Israel of the Old Testament; Israel as it is understood in the New Testament; Israel on the one hand with continuing prerogatives of salvation (Rom. 9:4), and on the other hand as Israel-after-the-flesh (I Cor. 10:18); the Jews as a New Testament description of those who do not believe in Christ; the Jews of post-New Testament times as the Jews of the Talmud; and the other very different forms of medieval and modern Judaism.

This confusing terminology, lacking in differentiation, brings with it a confusion of meaning; one can equally well regard as bearers of the Promise, or as the Chosen People, Old Testament Israel; Israel after the flesh in post-Christian times; the Jews who reject Christ; the Jews who obey the Torah; Jews in a legal sense; and Jews who have a Jewish mother.

Further, neither is the content of the Promise anywhere clearly expressed, although according to the unanimous witness of the New Testament all the promises are fulfilled in and through Christ, and Christ himself is this fulfilment (cf. Luke 4:21; II Cor. 1:20; 6:2).

No attention is paid to the fact that the specific Old Testament promises, the possession of the land, and historical existence as a nation, have lost their significance for Jesus and the New Testament witnesses to Christ, although the salvation bestowed in Christ retains an earthly dimension. It is characteristic of the thought of Jesus (and of the Baptist) in relation to the rule of God, that membership of the Jewish nation gives no claim to participation in the coming salvation. The Jew as such has no guarantee of salvation: "God is able of these stones to raise children unto Abraham." (Luke 3:8) Accordingly, for Christians, Old Testament promises concerning land and the gift of nationhood can no longer be regarded as blessings of salvation in view of the gift, already given, of freedom from the law, sin and death (Phil. 3:7f.). Granted that the Hebrew Bible is not for this reason to be in its entirety reckoned as "Old" in the sense of "invalid", yet it *is* the Old Testament because it can claim Christian validity only so far as it is confirmed and presupposed by the central event of the message about Christ. The Christian Church has never read or used the Old Testament in any other sense than this. It retains as the *Old* Testament its significance and its honour in Christian proclamation.

...The factual historical continuity between Abraham and the Jews is, according to Rom. 4:13; Gal. 3:7; and Rom 9:7f., without any theological significance.

It is indeed characteristic of Jesus that, with the exception of his word in relation to the Cup (Mk. 14:24), he develops his view of salvation without the conception of the Covenant ... Only Paul and the Letter to the Hebrews place the Old Covenant and the New side by side, and it is remarkable that they bring them into radical contrast (Gal. 3:15-17; 4:24; II Cor. 3:5, 14; Hbr. 8:7-13).

Essential utterances of the Apostle Paul, the very witness who, as a Jew converted to Christ, concerns himself most intensively with the problem dealt with in the paper, are completely ignored. The sentence used as a motto about the root which bears the Christian is torn out of its context in the argument, and used as a *Leitmotiv* which is now made to convey the opposite of Paul's obvious meaning, and of what he says in the next verse but one: "Well, because of unbelief they were broken off, and thou standest by faith. Be not highminded, but fear..." The eschatological mystery according to which "All Israel will be saved" (Rom. 11:25) establishes no special road to salvation.

While the Jewish people, as it developed in post-exilic times and then developed under the influence of Pharisaism ... has its firm hold of the Torah as the whole revelation of God, which is the exclusive mark of Judaism; according to the Christian view, Christ is the end of this Torah as a way of salvation. Torah-Judaism and faith in Christ are thus two incompatible things (Phil. 3:4-9).

(3) Rejoinders in Defence of the Synod

With the reference to the Bonn paper's claim that the Synod Resolution tears Paul's statment, "Thou bearest not the root, but the root bears thee," out of context, Klappert argues that the boot is on the other foot. It is the Bonn Professors who misinterpret the text. This passage in Romans lays emphasis elsewhere than on the fact that the Jews were cut off by reason of unbelief. It is addressed *to the Church:* it is the Church which is here warned of the dangers of self-complacency. Klappert continues, 'Finally, the question which concerned a Bonhoeffer in 1940, and which Eduard Schewizer asked his Bible Study at the Synod, is whether the warning to the Gentile Christians, 'Thou shalt be cut off,' has not become a reality since Auschwitz for the Christian Church, for a Church which, during the persecution and annihilation of Jews, did not stand as a sister by the side of the Synagogue, and by its failure betrayed Christ."

With regard to the statement that Christ is the fulfilment of all the promises, Klappert maintains that the Bonn paper takes this in too negative a sense. True, in Christ all promises find their fulfilment, but not necessarily in such a way that all other subordinate hopes are negated.

Further, in relation to the Bonn statement's claim that Paul and the Letter to the Hebrews place the Old Covenant and the New in radical anithesis to one another, Klappert replies that this simply ignores affirmations in both these sources on the question of Israel (p. 27). The Bonn "Reflections" further fail to distinguish between Israel's false claim to salvation, which Jesus and the prophets denounced, and the continuing valid promises of God to Israel. Bonn avers that Paul's statement, "All Israel will be saved," gives no basis for a special way to salvation. But the Synod never claimed that there was such a way!

Helmut Gollwitzer has also given an important contribution to the rejoinders to the "Reflections". Perhaps he speaks even more profoundly out of his experience in the Committee of Christians and Jews than does Klappert, who was also a member. What we now give is a digest and condensation of his comments rather than a literal translation. Speaking of the situation after Auschwitz, he says (p. 49):

"In this situation, in which we could not boast of our faith, we experienced anew the message of grace, not as a message which, as the possessors of grace, we had to proclaim to the Jews who did not possess it, but as a message that we had forfeited, and that we were now able to hear for the first

"Christianity and Judaism"

time, as a word of life for men whose pride had so long been nourished on 'fundamental Christian principles' (Bonn Statement, paragraph 8, p. 15), and who now deserved only to hear the stern words of Paul, 'Thou also shalt be cut off.' (Rom. 11:22) It was precisely this verse of Paul which turned its edge against us, and we were given to see the severity of God to us, to those who fell (Rom. 11:22), and to see the goodness of God in the case of the persecuted Jews, the steadfastness of him who has not forsaken his people, 'which he acknowledged of old as his own.' (Rom. 11:2)"

"Thus, as men to whom all boasting was forbidden, even Christian boasting, as men truly living by grace alone, we began, slowly, tentatively, to live with the Jews, to receive every friendly approach from them as a sign of God's forgiveness, not to 'admire them' (Bonn "Reflections", paragraph 8, p. 16)-what a fatuous idea! We began to listen to the Jews, to study their history and their thoughts about faith, to listen to their witness to their God and ours, and then at last with them to 'meditate upon the law of the Lord' (Ps 1:2), and also on the message of their brother Jesus of Nazareth and his Apostle from the Jewish people." (p. 50)

"We rejoiced with them that many of the survivors from Hitler's 'final solution' could return to the land of promise. Like the Jews, we are anxious about the State of Israel, and the right behaviour for it, a behaviour that answers to their mission, in relation to the Arabs. And we pray and act in order to promise a peaceful association between Jews and Arabs in Palestine. But we have also learnt to take seriously the Biblical promise concerning the land for the Jews, and no longer accept the traditional, and in our opinion exegetically untenable, attitude of the theologians that these promises concerning land and people have lost their significance (Bonn "Reflections", p. 4). (p. 51)

"Our Jewish partners in the conversation do not expect us to give up the 'Christian fundamental beliefs' or to keep silence about them. Only in the new dialogue, which begins by listening, and by being willing to learn from one another, is there a possibility of bearing such witness to these truths that we are willing to take one another seriously, and to 'provoke them to emulation' (Rom. 11:14)." (p. 51)

"Especially in this time when the pride of our confession of faith (Christian and Jewish) is so humiliated by our failure in discipleship, and when all who share such a confession are so challenged by the distresses of humanity, we can only do justice to our mission by acting together. We have learnt this in the Ecumenical Movement. How can we, Christians especially, refuse to share in such activity with the Jews?

The Bonn declaration sets the Jews exactly on a level with pagans. This is true of their relationship to grace. But on this ground the "Reflections" go on to state that 'a special relationship to God on the ground of race or descent is alien to the Christian Gospel.' The fallacy of such thinking lies in the false assumption, traditional among Christians, that election gives a special privilege in relation to salvation. But salvation is not the only fundamental

204

Towards a New Relationship

category of Biblical thought in the relationship between God and man. God's calling and election is an equally important category, and we have to think of the calling of the prophets, of Jesus, and of the Church. Only from this viewpoint can we truly appreciate the Jews' understanding of their calling, which always implies a special task and obligation, and gives no ground for self-complacency. (p. 53)

All this seems to have escaped the notice of the Bonn Professors. Their whole attitude is academic in the worst sense of the word. If we compare the two texts, it becomes evident that the Synodal paper issued from historical experiences and challenges. And on this basis it discovers the togetherness of Christians and Jews, and also calls previous tradition in question because of its disastrous outworkings, and strives for a new fellowship between the Church and Israel, the Church and the Synagogue, in order to prevent a recurrence of the terrible disasters of the past.

These considerations play no part in the Bonn declaration (when one discards its obligatory gesture about our historical guilt against the Jew). The preamble indeed says that the concern of the Synod is to be welcomed without reservation; but the whole of the rest of the document proceeds to frustrate this concern. Its authors open the New Testament in order to select from it what 'fundamental Christian truths' separate Christianity and Judaism.

In a single step they stride over two thousand years, using an exegetical method that does not let itself be limited by other interpretations, and that knows a *priori* the facts about Judaism and Christianity. Here, nothing new can happen; there is no possibility of movement; the Jews are thus and we are thus; and so it will remain until ultimately the Jews are converted. What fresh discoveries can be made on such a basis?

By contrast, how seriously the Synod envisaged its task! Its committee sat for four years with Jews as full members, and in so doing went through an historical experience to which the theses brought before the Synod are witness. Here too, the Scripture principle was taken seriously, but not by looking up the New Testament as if it were a compendious 'System of Dogmatics'. The way in which it pursued its task was that Jews and Christians, as living representatives of their faiths, startled into wakefulness by the appalling story of guilt and suffering, sought together for a way into the future, and looked for guidance from the fundamental texts of our combined and separate traditions. We inquired, "Do the New Testament texts give us help and suggestions for the overcoming of our so fundamental and calamitous schism, or at least for fruitful partnership between Christians and Jews?" That was 'theology after Auschwitz', and that is why the Synod's Resolution has evoked such a powerful response. Theology as it is being practiced in Bonn seems to have all this yet to experience. One can only hope that even out of Bonn there will yet come some good thing! (p. 59)

Eberhard Bethge also finds fault with the whole tone of the Bonn paper. What happens in its ten paragraphs is simply the laying down of the law as to who the Jews are, and what the right way to deal with them is. Faced by Bonn's pedantic differentiations on this point, Bethge asks what reaction we might expect from the Christians if Jews began to lay down the law to us as to who were Christians and who were not! The "Reflections" betray a lamentable failure to appreciate the actual situation. Here a guilty Church seeks to address its Jewish partner, and to request a renewal of relations with it, but first does its best to annihilate it by means of theological definitions. This is to make any renewal in the relationship impossible. The Synod's approach was quite different—it turned towards the relatives and survivors of those to whom for centuries the Church had done violence, using Christ and the New Testament as its excuse. The "Bonn approach" had to be avoided by the Synod at all costs.

The Bonn paper's exegesis must be disputed both as to its detail and as to its general tendency. It betrays a self-assurance that seems to forget that theologians both from the Rhineland and elsewhere have taken a contrary view. (Here Bethge cites an illustrious list of names, beginning with those of Karl Barth—of Bonn!—and Dietrich Bonhoeffer.) The assertion that the Nazis were just as opposed to Christianity as to the Jews is more than questionable; but even if it were true, how would this help the renewal of Jewish-Christian relations? The sole impression left by the "Reflections" is one of smug self-satisfaction at once and for all having set down in black and white the Christian faith over against that of the Jews. How, after the Holocaust, can the Church afford to behave thus? For Bethge personally, the Synod's action is a first step in appropriating the heritage of Dietrich Bonhoeffer. It is understandable that it can have confusing effects on Christian self-assurance, because it draws the consequences of Christian discipleship for today. But it is certainly not itself, as the "Reflections" aver, confused or unreflected. (p. 63)

Such are the main points raised and developed in this *Dokumentation*. It is surely important that today in countries beyond Germany there should be similar movements for renewal in the relationship between Christians and Jews. Threats of a recrudescence of anti-semitism in various quarters make the need for mutual understanding even more urgent. As far as Scotland is concerned, the Report of the Overseas Council to the General Assembly of the Church of Scotland in May, 1980, tells us that "In Glasgow and Edinburgh the regular meetings of Christians and Jews are well attended, and contribute to the mutual respect and goodwill which prevail between Christians and Jews in Scotland." It is to be hoped that the information contained in *Dokumentation* may be helpful in stimulating this activity.

Towards a New Relationship

Index

Index

Index

Index

Index

Index

Index

Index

Index

Index